The Development of Education in Botswana (1937–1987)

The Role of Teachers' Organisations

The Development of Education in Botswana

THE ROLE OF TEACHERS' ORGANISATIONS

T.P. Vanqa

Published by *LIGHTBOOKS*
a division of
LENTSWE LA LESEDI (PTY) LTD
in collaboration with the Botswana Teachers' Union
Tel 303994, Fax 314017, e-mail Lightbooks@Info.bw

First published 1998

Reprinted with new cover 1999

Copyright © T.P. Vanqa, 1998

This book may not be reproduced in whole or in part by any means without the permission of the copyright holder.

ISBN 99912-71-06-6

Typeset and designed by
LENTSWE LA LESEDI (PTY) LTD
Printed and bound by Printing and Publishing Botswana (Pty) Ltd

For Mandisi

Contents

Foreword .... *ix*
Acknowledgements .... *xi*
About the Author .... *xiii*
Abbreviations .... *xv*

INTRODUCTION 1

CHAPTER ONE. THE EARLY BEGINNINGS: THE LATE 1930s 5
    The Formation of the Association and Its Early Programme of Activities 11
    Future Programmes of the Association 15
    The Business of Conference 18
    Conclusion 25

CHAPTER TWO. THE YEARS OF CONSOLIDATION: 1941–1959 27
    The Future of the Association 31
    The Image of the BPATA 32
    Change of Attitude: The Turbulent 1960s 42
    Conclusion 52

**CHAPTER THREE. THE PROBLEMS AND SUCCESSES OF THE BPATA
(1954–1969)** 53
    BPATA and Its Successes 62
    The Provident Fund 66
    The Foundation of the Unified Teaching Service (UTS) 67

CHAPTER FOUR. THE HUTTON REPORT AND ITS AFTERMATH 77
    Introduction 77
    Conversion Tables 80
    The BTU and the Teaching of History 88
    The BTU and the Teaching of English 93
    The BTU Conferences at Mochudi (1968) and Lobatse TTC (1969) 100
    The BTU in the 1970s (And Beyond) 104
    The BPATA and Women's Issues 106

**CHAPTER FIVE. THE SEARCH FOR A PHILOSOPHY OF EDUCATION:
THE 1970s AND 1980s, DECADES OF CHANGE** 111
    The Common View of Education 111
    The New Executive: Its Link, Its Problems and the Years of Enlightenment 113
    A Call for Appropriate Education 116

Birth of Botswana's Philosophy of Education 117
Drake Selwe Becomes the President 119
The Coming of the Education Law 121
Contributors to Botswana's Philosophy of Education 128
Conclusion 138

Chapter Six. A New Direction Towards Education: Advice and Inspection 139

The Early Reports in the Protectorate 140
Later Reports and Their Significance 142
Dumbrell's Directorship 143
The Early Reports 145
The New Approach of Inspection 151
The Dismal Reports of the 1960s 153
The Teachers' Cases 160
New Directions in Inspecting and Advising 164

Chapter Seven. The BTU: Its Dilemma and the Way Forward 171

Selwe's Years of Toil 172
The National Commission on Education – 1977 175
The Task Forces and Their Contribution 179
The Quality of Teachers at Secondary School Level 192
The Stop-Order Payment of Subscriptions to BTU 194
The WCOTP Link and Its Significance 198
The Emergence of Other Teachers' Organisations in Botswana 203
BTU is 50 Years Old 208
Whither Goeth the Union ? 210

Author's Epilogue 211

References 213

Botswana Archives Sources 214
Botswana Teacher's Union Documents 215
Government of Botswana Publications 216

Appendix 218

Foreword

In this book Temba Vanqa outlines the history of educational development in Botswana between 1937 and 1987, and the role teacher organisations played in this development.

First seen as a bunch of agitators, teachers gradually projected a more and more positive image over the years, so that they and their union are now perceived as valuable partners with government in the development of education in Botswana.

The book gives us a clear picture of the teachers' struggle for better wages and conditions of service; the hardships, hopes and setbacks, their failures and disappointments. But the outcome is a positive one, and we are shown how their clarity of vision, persistence and determination paid off, helping to create an education system in which teachers and education authorities see each other as indispensable partners in the provision of more and better quality education for all in Botswana.

Teachers today serve on a number of committees in the Ministry of Education which deal with curricula, professional development of teachers and organisational issues. They are also represented on the University of Botswana Committee on Education. Their improved status and the respect they have earned have given them a well-deserved feeling of accomplishment, and the hope for an even better future.

Professor Vanqa's book is a most useful addition to the fund of knowledge in the field, and will help encourage informed decisions about educational priorities. It demonstrates in particular, how through determination and clarity of vision, teachers can bring about much needed changes in an educational system. But above all, it reveals the importance of a good working partnership between teachers and government for the benefit of the country as a whole.

We welcome this valuable record of Botswana's educational development.

Dr G.K.T. Chiepe PH, MBE, MP
Minister for Education

Acknowledgements

I wish to acknowledge the valuable assistance of colleagues in the Department of Educational Foundations at the University of Botswana who read and revised the manuscript at the early stages.

I also wish to acknowledge the guidance and encouragement given by Dr Jeff Ramsay of Legae Academy (Gaborone) and Dr P. Themba Mgadla of the History Department, University of Botswana.

Appreciation is also expressed to the staff of the National Archives, the artment of Information and Broadcasting, Gaborone ,and the staff of the Botswana Collection at the University of Botswana Library for their assistance and cooperation.

I am equally grateful to the Botswana Teachers' Union for generous funding of the project from its inception – *mazenethole mawethu'*.

Many thanks are also extended to Ms Lucy Gulubane and Ms Florence Nunoo for typing the manuscript.

Thanks ar e also due to the following for the provision of photographs: JB Gabaake (p58), JT Khama (p72), KG Kgoroba (p74), KM Masogo (p99), Dr QKJ Masire (p37), EN Kedikilwe (p17), CAR Motsepe (p165), LG Mothusi (p209) and P van Rensburg (p129), for photographs of themselves or their relatives. Thanks also to the Depatment of Information and Broadcasting, The National Archives and the Botswana Teachers Union for a range of photographs. Some of the owners of phographs are untraceable and thanks also goes to the owners of such photos.

Le ka moso bagaetsho.

About the Author

Temba Vanqa received his Primary and Secondary Education at the Lovedale Institution, and his higher education at Fort Hare University in the Eastern Cape, and the University of New England in Australia.

He started teaching at the Grahamstown Secondary School in the Albany District and later joined the Newell High School, Port Elizabeth in the Eastern Cape.

In 1963 he joined the Bechuanaland Protectorate Education Department where he served for thirteen years. In 1975 he was appointed lecturer in the School of Education of the University of Basotholand, Bechuanaland and Swaziland. His main responsibility during those years was the teaching of history curriculum to students who were training as teachers. As co-ordinator of the Primary Teacher Training Colleges from 1981–1984 he helped in their development.

At the University of Botswana he has served in different capacities, namely, Acting Registrar, Head of Educational Foundations and Dean of the Faculty of Education, and a member of Senate. These years at the University he found extremely rewarding.

Professor Vanqa has done some research in the area of Teacher Education, and with a colleague, Professor E.L.M. Bayona, they co-authored the *Resource Book for Teacher Education in Botswana* 1995. He has also contributed chapters in books on education. His main areas of research interest are in the history of education and teacher training in Botswana to which he has contributed considerably.

Abbreviations

AAC	African Advisory Committee
BCSA	Botswana Civil Servants Association
BEC	Botswana Extension College
BERA	Botswana Educational Research Association
BOFESETE	Botswana Federation of Secondary Teachers
BOPRITA	Botswana Primary Teachers' Association
BP	Bechuanaland Protectorate
BPATA	Bechuanaland Protectorate African Teachers' Association
BPTA	Bechuanaland Protectorate Teachers' Association
BTU	Botswana Teachers' Union
BTC	Botswana Training Centre
BULGSA	Botswana Unified Local Government Servants Association
CATA	Cape African Teachers' Association
COSC	Cambridge Overseas School Certificate
DC	District Commissioner
DEMS	Division of Extra-mural Services
DNFE	Department of Non-formal Education
EI	Education International
EO:	Education Officer
HCTFTA:	High Commission Territories Federal Teachers' Association
IAE	Institute of Adult Education
IFFTU	International Federation of Free Trade Unions
ILO	International Labour Organization
JEUT	Job Evaluation Unsatisfied Teachers
JC	Junior Certificate
LMS	London Missionary Society
NAC	Native Advisory Council
NCE	National Commission on Education
NCTE	National Council for Teacher Education
NDP	National Development Plan
NPHC	Native Primary Higher Certificate
NPLC	Native Primary Lower Certificate
ODA	Overseas Development Administration
PEIP	Primary Education Improvement Project
PESC	Pre-Entry Science Course
PTTC	Primary Teacher Training College
RC	Resident Commissioner
TSM	Teaching Service Management
TVC	Teachers' Vocational Course
UB	University of Botswana
UBLS	University of Botswana, Lesotho and Swaziland
UBS	University of Botswana and Swaziland
UNE	University of New England
UNESCO	United Nations Educational Scientific and Cultural Organization.
UTS	Unified Teaching Service
WCOTP	World Confederation of the Organization of the Teaching Profession

Introduction

It has been more than a half century since the Bechuanaland Protectorate African Teachers' Association (now the Botswana Teachers' Union) was founded. This is a short time for an organisation which has turned a loose body of teachers into a formidable organisation. From its inception, the Association was beset with innumerable problems ranging from the most archaic regulations reminiscent of the middle ages to a deep mistrust that eventually culminated in the formation of a strong and influential body.

For instance, there was no clear policy of acceptance of the role of and what the Association stood for. The idea of the Association was completely new and there were no regulations that controlled its operation; everything was done on an *ad hoc* basis. Teachers were treated so differently by their employers and were subjected to undue harrassment in case of transgressions.

In spite of these early problems, particularly its rejection as an irrelevant Association, it has done extremely well. Teachers of whatever persuasion have always been at the vanguard of national development. Yet throughout the world they have always been among the most vulnerable class of workers or professionals. They have, through the ages, been subjected to abuses and restrictions. The bad conditions of service that obtained at some places and lack of them elsewhere had their echoes in the Bechuanaland Protectorate as late as the close of the 1950s. In the Protectorate, lady teachers in particular were threatened in many ways. For instance, an unmarried lady teacher who lived with a man risked expulsion, and it was the expressed desire of some employers that married women confined only during the holidays. An unmarried teacher who fell pregnant earned herself an immediate two year suspension, sometimes followed by expulsion. Therefore, it can be seen that teachers have been sacrificed on the altar of defunct and moribund moralities and have been regarded as the standard bearers of virtue and goodness. Fortunately, some of the conditions described above no longer exist and their modification, and in some cases their complete scrapping, has to a large extent, been brought about by the growth of teacher organisations and militancy.

In this country, it was through the work of a handful of dedicated teachers that the Association made headway in the development of education. First, it was the support given by the Department of Education during the time of H.J.E. Dumbrell as Inspector of Education and later as the Director of Education in the Bechuanaland Protectorate (BP) that the Association grew in strength. Secondly, it was the unswerving determination of the early founders and their commitment to education that gained acceptance in the country.

Teachers ceased to be seen as a bundle of agitators always clamouring for improved salaries and better conditions of service.

For instance, from the 1930s up to the 1950s, if one takes into account the quality of teachers in the schools, it is gratifying to note that they were not only concerned about improving their teaching skills, but they were also vocal about the conditions of service and low salaries. It was this aspect of their operation that exposed them to unwarranted censure from some quarters. Those teachers were very dedicated if one recalls that during times of drought many teachers went without pay as happened in Serowe in 1918.

The 1960s and 1970s were years of reckoning and soul searching on the part of the Association. Never before was the teacher's organisation faced with so many challenges. The BP in the middle of the 1960s was on its way to independence and the Association was aware of the role it was expected to play in relation to the improvement of education and its relevance to the newly acquired political status of Botswana. All forms of discrimination were noticeable at every stage – separate schools for black and white children, discrimination in salaries between government and non-government teachers, poor accommodation, and no pension scheme of any description for them.

Before Independence, the Association saw its role clearly in terms of manpower development since secondary education had been neglected by the Colonial Administration. At Independence, it was those people who emerged from the secondary sector and further education who could replace the expatriates and man the fast growing social, economic, political and administrative services. From 1966 the BPATA was seen as a vital partner with government in nation building through education.

Coupled with this major responsibility of nation building from the early 1960s onwards, the teachers of this country cast their eyes beyond the borders of this land in order to join hands with other teachers' professional organisations in this region. Later in the 1970s they became fully-fledged members of the World Confederation of the Organisations of the Teaching Profession (WCOTP). Through these efforts, the BPATA then known as Botswana Teachers Union was beginning to make its mark on the international scene. At home, the BTU had made tremendous strides, for it had representation in all the Committees of the Ministry of Education, a fine commentary on the contribution of the Teachers' Union in the development of education. Now the question is, what has the BTU done?

It will be seen in the later chapters that the BTU has been in the vanguard of education in this country. From the earliest times, while negotiating for a fair deal in the treatment of teachers by asking for better conditions of service, the organisation never wavered in its commitment to make Botswana's education viable. At the early stages one must take into account the nature of the teaching profession and the status of the teachers in terms of their qualifications and the rather unaccommodating environment projected by the Colonial Administration. The BPATA, later BTU, has come to be accepted as an invaluable partner in nation building through education. The teachers were able to work with other teachers in the region (Lesotho and Swaziland) in the 1960s. At the beginning of the 1970s the BTU was even able to join the WCOTP, and deal with national teachers' organisations of teachers in Malawi, Sweden, USA, Zimbabwe and many other countries. The joining of hands with such organisations has widened the vision of the local teachers, and above all the BTU has put Botswana on the map of the world.

CHAPTER ONE

The Early Beginnings: The Late 1930s

The Bechuanaland Protectorate African Teachers' Association was launched in 1937 at the Bakgatla National School by A.M. Tsoebebe and a handful of teachers and some interested persons. However, there were already teachers' organisations in the neighbouring countries of South Africa, Lesotho, Swaziland, Zimbabwe and Zambia.

South Africa (SA) influenced the events in the BP since the main actors in the drama of the formation of teachers' organisations came from SA. Furthermore, some of the local teachers attended schools in SA, and could not have failed to appreciate the efforts of teachers in that country to improve the standard of education of their children and enhance their lot. The start of the teachers' organisation in the BP must be seen in the light of events in SA and the concern for change in this country. It was a felt need to put education in BP on a sound footing. For instance, the first African Teachers' Association in South Africa was formed in the Transkei as early as 1880. 'The Transkei Teachers' Association was not only the first professional Association, but was also the first organisation of any type to be successfully launched by Africans for the promotion and protection of their rights' (Peteni, 1979). Dr D.G.S. M'Timkulu, a prominent South African educationist and former principal of Adams College in Natal, is life president of the Natal African Teachers' Union and former president of the South Africa Teachers' Federation. In the 1970s and until recently Professor of Sociology and Director of Social Development Studies at the University of Waterloo, Ontario, Canada, he stated that 'one cannot but be impressed by the vision and foresight of these early pioneers' (Peteni, 1979) who led the way to the formation of other bodies such as the Cape African Teachers' Association (CATA) formed in 1920s and the African Teachers' Association. The formation of the latter body, planned by four teachers at a meeting scheduled to take place at Blythswood Institution in Nqamakwe near Butterworth, was postponed because the convener failed to attend. The first successful meeting took place late in 1880 at Zazulwane in the Butterworth district. Peteni (1979), the author of *Towards Tomorrow: The Story of the African Teachers' Association of South Africa* and former English Lecturer at the University of Fort Hare, reported that one of the items of business was a 'discussion of the easiest method of teaching long division'. Equally interesting is that the Cape Education Department granted this body official recognition.

The Bechuanaland Protectorate African Teachers' Association which was formed in 1937 has a history stretching back to 1931. It all started with a letter from H.J.E. Dumbrell, then an Inspector of Education and later Director of Education in the Bechuanaland Protectorate, to the Resident Commissioner on 9 September 1931. The letter was in response to correspondence Mr Dumbrell had received from Levi Moumakwa, a headteacher of the Ramotswa School. Moumakwa had informed Dumbrell that during the last Teachers' Vacation Course (TVC) held at Mochudi from the 3rd to 10th of August 1931, 'the idea of forming the Protectorate Teachers' Association was raised, discussed and accepted' (S252/2/1) and needed approval from the colonial administration.

Having been instructed by his fellow teachers, L.C. Moumakwa wrote: 'I hereby most respectfully request that our application for the recognition of the proposed Association meet with your careful consideration to proper Authority for his approval and further that His Honour, the Resident Commissioner be asked to consent to become the patron of the Association' (S252/2/1). He (Moumakwa) enclosed in the letter the list of office bearers and a draft copy of the constitution 'for your perusal and retention'. The office bearers were: Alexander Mosheshe, Chairman (Mochudi), Levi C. Moumakwa, Secretary (Ramotswa), Rev. Lewis, Treasurer (Kanye), and Tau Kgosidintsi, Recorder (Molepolole). Among the Committee Members were Andrew Kgasa (Kanye) and Francis Phiri (Mochudi). The Honorary Members were Charles Benson and Inspector Franz of Tiger Kloof and the Transvaal Education Department respectively (S252/2/1).

The name of the Association was to be the Bechuanaland Protectorate Teachers' Association (Note that 'African' was not there originally). The aims of the Association were to promote further education in the BP, by raising the standard of efficiency of the teachers through the improvement of school methods and school organisation. This was to be effected through continuous discussion and presentation of papers and lectures by prominent educationalists. Basic to these aims was the attempt to help the less qualified teachers by mounting vacation courses or workshops. Finally, the Association had to assure the administration that it was 'entirely non-political' (S252/2/1).

L C. Moumakwa

When the Inspector of Education, H.J.E. Dumbrell, made his comments to the Resident Commissioner (RC), he stated that he saw the desire to establish a teachers' association in the country as a perfectly natural growth and felt that it be allowed to develop under guidance. At the same time, he felt that before taking any action, it was important to find out whether there was a similar association in Basutoland and Swaziland. It will be remembered that the two territories fell under British protection, and there was also a feeling that they should be handled in the same manner. As far as their aims were concerned, the Inspector of Education was satisfied and saw its advantages. But, he later stated that one was always afraid that the main aim of such a body would be 'agitation for higher salaries'. Yet he felt that in the BP that would not be the dominant factor, as teachers were not solely dependent on salaries received from the Department of Education. He went on to say that he thought the Association should be for the Protectorate as a whole and that membership in the early stages should be confined to qualified teachers. The pioneers were advised to secure the names of interested teachers in the northern part of the Protectorate. Finally, he asked the RC to inform the teachers that the formation of the Association would receive his consideration.

It should be noted that while Dumbrell encouraged the formation of the teachers' association locally, he feared that if such a body worked closely with the powerful African Teachers' Association in South Africa it might be difficult to control. Dumbrell, therefore, told the RC clearly that, 'We must not allow them to link up with the strong Native Teachers' Association existing in the Union' (S252/2/1). One must remember that Dumbrell was an inspector of schools in Natal before he came to the BP. He therefore knew the hard line adopted by African teachers with regard to poor conditions of service and low salaries. Perhaps the idea was to curb the activities of teachers and thus think for them. Again, it may have been a ploy to ensure that teachers did not challenge the authority of Chiefs, most of whom danced to the music of the colonial government.

Further to his reply to Moumakwa, he stated that he had received his letter regarding a Protectorate Teachers' Association for Native Teachers. He stressed that the matter required careful consideration but was inclined to view the request sympathetically and had directed that 'the proposals be placed before the Board of Advice on Native Education' (S252/2/1).

On 1 March 1932 he wrote to Moumakwa again and informed him that the Board of Advice on Native Education 'approved in principle of the formation of a Native Teachers' Association ...and commended the initiative of teachers in bringing the matter forward' (S252/3/1), but he further warned that the matter would be put before the Native Advisory Council at its next meeting. In the meantime, no action was to be taken until the views of the Council had been made known to teachers.

The thirteenth meeting of the Native Advisory Council took place on 30 March 1932 and the RC introduced the question of the formation of a Teachers' Association. He reminded the members that the issue had been raised by some teachers the previous August. As a follow-up, they submitted their proposals to Dumbrell asking him if there were any objections. He emphasised that 'the object of the Association was the desire to aid the improvement of teachers and the improvement of school methods' (S252/2/1).

In keeping with the practice of the colonial administration when dealing with indigenous teachers, the Council was told that the Association was to 'be entirely non-political'. Of interest is that invariably all teachers who were in the field at that time remembered these magical words 'non-political'. The RC went on to say that the proposal had been placed before the Board of Advice on Native Education and had been warmly received. It was felt that it showed progressive thinking on the part of the teachers and had suggested that it would be a good idea to place it before the Native Advisory Council. The climate of thought was clearly favourable for the formation of a 'non-political' Teachers' Association.

It was unfortunate that this progressive step taken by the teachers met with a negative response from most members of the Native Advisory Council. The negative response was spearheaded by David Kgosidintsi who was opposed to the fact that some names among the office bearers were not members of the teaching force in the Protectorate. 'It is not clear how the Association can be called the Protectorate Association if it is conducted by members not of the Protectorate' (S252/2/1). He claimed that the organisation might cause trouble if it was not entirely in the hands of 'local' teachers. For him, the Board of Advice and the Native Advisory Council were able to handle education matters within the Protectorate. The Association's desire to help those who were not qualified educationally could effectively be assisted by the vacation courses. These sentiments were ultra-conservative and were in accord with the Colonial Administration. He finally declared that, 'to my mind the time is not yet ripe for the establishment of this association' (S252/2/1) because there were few teachers who were qualified in the Protectorate.

David Kgosidintsi's remarks were fully supported by Kgosi (Chief) Bathoen II of the Bangwaketse who stressed that the Protectorate had local committees in charge of schools, and a Board of Advice on Native Education, and the Inspector of Schools who visited different towns as the need arose educationally. He advised that the procedures be watched before allowing the coming of some subsidiary bodies. 'Personally I suggest that this association be left out ...and let us strengthen the vacation course' (S252/2/1). David Kgosidintsi's conclusion was damaging as he claimed that 'some of our teachers are not sufficiently advanced to become involved in associations by themselves' (S252/2/1). Kgosi Kgari Sechele of the Bakwena reiterated the points raised by the two previous speakers and was not in favour of the association because 'of these people whose names appear on paper, there is only one who is a Protectorate man' (S252/2/1). Furthermore, since that was a teachers' organisation, and the teachers themselves were considered not 'mature' enough, there would be no one 'to listen to their discussion'. It was strongly felt that the country's trust could not be put in the hands of outsiders who for convenience might leave the aborigines in the lurch. From the local teachers, loyalty to Dikgosi and government was demanded and they were expected to comply.

The contribution of Molefi Pilane, the Bakgatla Kgosi, was brief and uncompromising, '...no one in this meeting is in favour of this Association, and we shall all just get up and say that we do not want it' (S252/2/1). The only dissenting voice was that of Sebopioa Molema, a Morolong (himself somewhat of an outsider from Mafikeng) who stated that, 'my Chiefs are a little bit mistaken because they themselves are educated men' (S252/2/1). One appreciates Molema's far sightedness and clarity of thought on a matter that was frustrating. For him, the teachers' request was straight forward as they were not even seeking financial support from the Colonial Administration. He dismissed the Dikgosis' suspicion that the association would include men who came from outside the Protectorate. 'They forget that what we have got from the missionaries is from outside: it did not come from the Protectorate' (S252/2/1). He pointed out that even though these men came from elsewhere, the Dikgosi would do well to accept them since they came to improve the quality of life in the Protectorate. He stated that the very provinces where the Dikgosi were educated had teachers' associations. The people he concluded, 'should not be hindered in their efforts to help themselves' (S252/2/1). Councillor Motswakhumo, who was the last contributor, dismissed the idea of a teachers' association as frivolous and unnecessary. He merely endorsed the misgivings of his colleagues.

In the face of strong opposition from the Native Advisory Council (NAC) to the formation of the Teachers' Association, the matter was closed only to be revisited later, for the idea did not die. On 3 October 1932 Moumakwa wrote again to Dumbrell enquiring about the NAC's verdict. The Inspector replied by enclosing extracts from the Council's minutes. The Dikgosi were opposed to the formation of the Association for they had a deep mistrust of foreign teachers who might bear no allegiance to the local authority. The local teachers feared that their authority would be undermined, but above all Dikgosi were by and large, autocrats.

The teachers no doubt were frustrated by the Council's reply but were not prepared to let the NAC get away with it. Their letter to Dumbrell dated 5 February 1935 was a challenge which was the result of serious planning since 1932. It forcefully stated: 'We the undersigned Protectorate Head and Assistant Teachers ...have the honour hereby most respectfully to request you to consider the question of the advisability of allowing us to form the Teachers' Association in the Protectorate' (S252/2/1).

The signatories came from all corners of the country and were the finest selection of teachers who were committed to the advancement of education. From Serowe came T.P. Sebina and Tom T. Kgosi, who had loyal supporters in M. Mpotokwane from the Bokalaka area and K.G. Mosieman of Lake

Ngami. The stalwarts of the vacation courses included A.M. Tsoebebe from Mochudi, D.M. Mpotokwane of the Tati settlement, and L.C. Moumakwa from Ramotswa who spearheaded the teachers' efforts to form the Association. The South was represented by B.G. Seoposengwe of Molepolole, M.M. Mabote of Kanye and R.O. Mokoto of Barolong Farms, as well as I.G. Matenge of Gaborone. So great was the desire to form the Association that the teachers were joined by the school supervisors including Monyaki of Tati, H. Keaikitse stationed in the Kgalagadi and B.H. Mothusi from the Bakgatla and Batlokwa reserves (S252/2/1).

The contribution was not different from the first constitution drawn in 1931. It stated: 'The name of this association shall be Bechuanaland Protectorate African Teachers' Association'. Its objectives were brief and simple – it was to enable the Protectorate teachers to work for the good of the coming generation, to educate one another through discussions at such periodical meetings as will be called and finally to enlist the cooperative assistance and encouragement of the Chiefs and missionaries and of all interested in African education by participation in meetings (S252/2/1).

On 14 December, Dumbrell was informed by the Government Secretary that 'His Honour's permission is given ... and you may inform the bodies accordingly' (S252/2/1). The question to ask is what prompted the Government's change of heart. From the outset the Government, through Dumbrell's initiative, was keen to see the teachers organise themselves into an association in order to improve the country's education system. The keenness might also have been influenced by the need to allow teachers to let off steam in public forums. But the Dikgosi in the Native Advisory Council felt that the teachers would turn into a pressure group that would agitate for better salaries and become a problem.

The positive reaction from the RC must have been received with jubilation by Dumbrell for, on 16 December 1935, he wrote a letter to Moumakwa, headteacher of Ramotswa School and informed him that the RC had approved the formation of the Association after careful consideration to the request made by a number of teachers, who, at Serowe, on 5 February 1935, wrote and asked that they be allowed to form in the territory, an Association to be known as the Bechuanaland Protectorate African Teachers' Association (BPATA). The new association was to operate under strict control. Dumbrell's letter stated that the association was to limit its activities to those set out in its application and that the RC had noted with satisfaction that the Association 'will be entirely non-political.' He further stated that in giving permission for an association to be formed, it was assumed that the administration would be kept fully informed of 'all business done at meetings of the Association' and be supplied with the names of office bearers and with copies of all minutes taken at meetings. The administration's response illustrates how the Association from the start had its hands and feet tied.

Tsoebebe who served the Association as the Secretary submitted the list of officials elected at the general meeting held at Serowe on 5 February 1935. The Executive Committee consisted of M. Mpotokwane as President, the Vice-President was T.P. Sebina, and A.M. Tsoebebe and I.G. Matenge served as secretary and Vice Secretary respectively. L.C. Moumakwa who had been instrumental in the formation of the Association became the Treasurer. The other Committee Members were D. Fernly, M.M. Mabote, D. Mpotokwane (a younger brother to the association President), B.G. Seoposengoe, R.O. Mokoto and T.T. Kgosi (S252/2/1).

After the granting of permission to the teachers to form the Association, Moumakwa took it upon himself to communicate with the Head Teachers and their staff. He endorsed what Dumbrell had conveyed to him and stressed that the RC, in giving such permission to the Association, was expected to limit its activities to those set out in the Constitution, that is, it would be non-political. Whatever may be said in the midst of endless admonitions, the teachers had been victorious. Their efforts had been rewarded and it was incumbent upon them to 'endeavour to merit the confidence reposed...' (S252/2/1) upon them. At the same time, one has come to feel that a dark cloud hung over the Association for there was fear that whenever they raised questions on educational issues such as racial discrimination, in payment of fees, and the poor state of African primary schools, it would be interpreted as delving on political matters. This association was a common feature during the 1950s and 1960s.

The Formation of the Association and Its Early Programme of Activities

An interesting feature in the relationship between the Association and Dumbrell on one hand, and Dumbrell and the general public on the other, was the unshakeable faith the Association had in him. He in turn reciprocated the faith they had in him and it is common knowledge that he admired and trusted Moumakwa intensely. It has been learned in many interviews that this deep trust was a source of suspicion among other members that Moumakwa might divulge the secrets of the Association to the Administration. However, this suspicion has not been substantiated convincingly. Dumbrell was held in such high esteem that on many occasions he was asked to open the BPATA annual conferences. Also it was not uncommon for speakers at teachers' conferences to solicit his views on what they should say. Sometimes speakers sent their speeches to be 'vetted' by him and as usual he would spout his 'fatherly advice', which in most cases reiterated what was originally presented. I suspect that the practice was intended to ensure that speakers at the teachers conferences did not say things that might embarrass the administration. It is also interesting that the General Secretary (A.M. Tsoebebe) of BPATA on 4 September 1936, when submitting the draft

Constitution of the Association to Dumbrell, stated that he would welcome any suggestions or amendments before its presentation to the General Conference.' (S252/2/1). Dumbrell who was keen to see the Association's activities implemented, responded favourably. It is interesting to listen to some oral testimonies explaining Tsoebebe's submission of the draft Constitution to Dumbrell.

A.M. Tsoebebe

The main reason given for submitting the Constitution to the Director of Education was to ensure that nothing savoured of 'political aspirations', as the Association had been warned to steer off politics. Another reminder to this practice was that the Association's conference resolutions were submitted to the Director of Education for forward transmission to the Government. All this was intended to monitor the actions of the Association. It is rather striking at times that Dumbrell who was so progressive and understanding, would subject teachers to what was almost humiliation. We may surmise that despite his liberal utterances he feared any form of militancy from the teachers. He accommodated their aspirations as long as they danced to his tune. As alluded to previously, from the outset he had pointed out that BP teachers should not join hands with the Teachers' Union or Associations in South Africa. With regard to the Constitution, he directed his attention to the tenure of office bearers by stating that the Constitution should state how and when the officers and committees would be elected. This was to be done at each annual general meeting. On membership, he suggested that all teachers in the Territory who were actually in employment as teachers should be entitled to join the Association. The Treasurer was required to pay all money into a Post Office Savings Bank Account and withdrawals were to be made by means of two signatures – his (Tsoebebe's) and the President's. Proper account books were to be kept and receipts given for all monies received. He concluded by wishing the Association success in its endeavours and by stating, 'I can count on your loyalty and cooperation' (S252/2/1).

The granting of permission to teachers to form the Association gave the teachers the first taste of success and they were now determined to maintain the pressure. The first task, therefore, was to strive to find representation in decision making bodies. The first of these was the Board of Advice on Native Education and was taken up by the Director and communicated to the Government Secretary on 13 July 1938 and it read:

> Subject: Board of Advice on African Education: Request by Bechuanaland Protectorate African Teachers' Association.
> 1. This Teachers' Association, which is recognised by the Government asks for representation on the Board of Advice on African Education.
> 2. In Swaziland, where there is a Board of Advice similar to ours, African teachers have representation and I know of other instances in South Africa.
> 3. My recommendation is that the Teachers' Association be informed that at the next meeting of the Board their application will be put forward for the Board's sympathetic consideration.

Shortly after that, A.M. Tsoebebe who was the General Secretary was informed by the Director of Education that the Association's application for representation on the Board of Advice on African Education had been submitted to the RC through the Government Secretary. Their request was to be placed before the Board at its next meeting towards the end of 1938.

The President of the Association, M. Mpotokwane, was informed by letter dated 22 March 1939 by H.G. Clarke (the Secretary to the Board of Advice on African Education) that it had been agreed that the BPATA's request for representation on the Board of Advice had been granted. His Association was therefore invited to elect a representative whose name was to be submitted to Clarke. Levi Moumakwa, the man who had been involved in the formation of the BPATA from the start, was appointed representative to the Board of Advice on African Education. The RC was to be informed of Moumakwa's appointment (S252/2/1).

The years following the establishment of the BPATA to the first General Conference of the Association were marked by heightened enthusiasm for the organisation of meetings at the branch level. The preparations for the first General Conference were started on time by the General Secretary. He set the machinery in motion by writing to the Bangwaketse, Bamalete and Batlokwa school committees informing them that the BPATA intended to hold its General Conference at Serowe in June 1939. He had also been instructed by the President of the Association to make a special application to enable the teachers to attend the conference. He explained that the week spent at the conference would be compensated by opening early in July to ensure that the number of school days remained unaltered. A letter was also written by the General Secretary to the Director of Education to use his influence on the school committees mentioned above to grant permission to enable the teachers to attend the conference. Dumbrell who was conversant with school regulations suggested that the District Commissioner (DC) in Serowe be approached and be informed that 'Rule 25 of High Commissioner's

Notice 110 of 1938 indicated that school calendars came under the control of District Committees...' (S252/2/1).

As if the problems of the Association were not enough, the situation was complicated by the confusion of the telegram sent by the DC in Serowe to the Director of Education alleging that teachers were scheduled to meet in May instead of June 1939. A stormy reply came from Dumbrell who unequivocally stated that he had not received any intimation of teachers' meeting in May. He suggested that permission for teachers attendance be refused as it was 'undesirable to close schools in the middle of term' (S252/2/1). Nonetheless the dust of confusion soon settled and the teachers prepared themselves to meet at the first conference at Serowe.

The first conference of the BPATA must have been a dream come true when it took place at Serowe from 19 to 21 June 1939. It was a historic event indeed, for teachers in this country had never met in such large numbers for a single purpose – to improve the education of their country and defend their rights. From the account given by some retired teachers, the conference was well attended and was extremely colourful. The conference was addressed by a group of selected speakers like Kgosi Tshekedi Khama, who had earlier indicated how pleased he would be to welcome the teachers at Serowe, Captain G.E. Nettelton (DC Serowe), the Director of Education and P. Cardross-Grant (Honorary Secretary of the Bangwato School Committee)

Perhaps 50 years after that epoch making event, we cannot catch the mood of that day. In welcoming the conference delegates to Serowe, the DC urged the teachers to make the Association a forum for resolving their problems. He further urged teachers with a fatherly advice 'to make teaching your profession and not merely a means of earning money' (S252/2/1).

Kgosi Tshekedi Khama who then addressed the conference, cleared the air and took the teachers into confidence. First of all, he reminded the teachers of their past toils when they first initiated the idea of forming an Association in the early 1930s and how their request had been rejected by the Native Advisory Council.

In his deliberations, he referred to an address given by the late Senator Roberts when he addressed the first graduates of Fort Hare in 1923. He told those graduands that they were the first 'Bantu' students to have the honour of a degree from the University of South Africa bestowed on them. Yet, there would be many such occasions in the future, but, 'on the list of the graduates of this College your names will always be the first' (S252/2/1).

Tshekedi assured the delegates that they would not only have the honour of being singled out as the founders of the Association, 'but also as the members who attended its first General Conference, and by reason of this fact, your names will always be the first in the annals of the Association. He promised the teachers maximum cooperation in their endeavours to enhance education in the BP. Nonetheless in the traditional fashion, he warned the

Tshekedi Khama

teachers not to incur the displeasure of the authorities and the public and render the Association vulnerable.

He challenged the teachers to be forthright and not allow the organisation to decline into a pressure group. 'It will devolve upon you to prove your Association worthy of its establishment' (S252/2/1). In conclusion, he invited the teachers to 'ventilate what they consider to be their rights or privileges, but I maintain that the privileges of teachers, parents and children differ in no marked degree' (S252/2/1).

After two days of conference deliberations came the long awaited speech by Montlhwatsi 'Mpoti' Mpotokwane, the President, a man of great ability, a preacher, trader and administrator. From the outset he reminded conference that 'for eleven years we have been labouring to have a meeting of this description but all our efforts have been fruitless' (S252/2/1). He remembered how the Training Course at Serowe had been instrumental towards the coming of the Association. Nothing excited the President more than the resilience of the Organising Committee that had kept the Association alive through sacrifice and hard work. He expressed gratitude to the founders of the Association for their clear perception and efforts to bring together the teachers of the territory professionally. 'Today I am pleased in saying that what has been a bud is now a fragrant flower – a reality – and we are now looking forward with joyful hearts expecting a good fruit' (S252/2/1). It was indeed fitting, since in one of the training courses it was agreed that the first General Conference was be held in Serowe, which was the true birth place of the Association.

Future Programmes of the Association

From the outset it was clear that the road the Association was to tread was a difficult one. Every possible move that the teachers made was to be subjected to close scrutiny both by the BP Department of Education at the Imperial Reserve and the local Dikgosi who had been sceptical about the usefulness of such an Association. No doubt the teachers were aware of this general suspicion, nonetheless, Mpotokwane was equal to the task. He inspired the

Association with brilliant and poetic addresses. He believed that the spark lit in Serowe should swell into a consuming fire and only then would these words mean anything to the teachers: 'Behold I kindle a fire in you. The flame should not be quenched' (S252/2/1).

M. Mpotokwane (third from right)

While in the past the education system of the territory was in the hands of the missionaries, tribal administrations and the Department of Education, and without understanding their role for the excellent work done, he reminded his colleagues that they had a role to play. The teachers responsibility goes beyond the classroom and is essentially to bring up the child as a fully functioning person with all possible attributes. He reminded the conference of the words of Dr Frazer, who saw the African as the greatest asset of Africa. Mpotokwane's greatest contribution at that conference was to exhort his fellowmen to look beyond the borders of the Protectorate. This was extremely far sighted if one considers that the Association was still in its infancy and was hardly organised. Dikgosi and Dumbrell actually feared this move and it was only in the 1960s that the BPATA was able to join hands with teachers in Lesotho and Swaziland. At the same time, Mpotokwane was not going to plunge into such a venture without first earning local respect through unswerving and undoubted leadership. The communities where the teachers worked would give support unstintingly if teachers were genuine. In a characteristic admonition he concluded, 'truly the field is great and reapers are few' (S252/2/1). The President's address set the teachers thinking seriously about their profession and their commitment. They combined their dedication to service with a ruthless defence of their rights as later events were to show.

The first discord to occur at the conference was when the Draft Constitution was tabled for discussion. The rejection of the revised Draft Constitution came from the Southern Protectorate delegates who declined to identify themselves with it. The rejection of the Draft Constitution was a result of lack of consultation. It is possible that they suspected that President Mpotokwane and later, General Secretary Sekunyane influenced the thinking in the Association. Since they claimed not to be aware of the originators they demanded that a new constitution be drawn. Though their request was accepted and when they were asked to produce their draft and failed, the revised Draft Constitution was discussed and adopted with minor alterations. It should be noted that Tsoebebe as mentioned above had written a letter dated 4 September 1933 to the Director of Education and enclosed the Draft Constitution of the Association and suggested corrections where possible before its presentation to the General Conference. Again, as indicated, Dumbrell had made the amendments as shown above with regard to the election of the officers and the Committee – preferably at each annual general meeting – the membership of teachers in the BP and the responsibilities of the treasurer.

It is interesting to note that at the election, Dumbrell was elected as the Honorary President of the BPATA. On one hand, this was a curious move for it is unthinkable that a Director of Education could be given such honour in the 1950s or 1960s when the Association was busy consolidating its position. On the other hand, one appreciates the fact that the Association wanted to lean on Dumbrell as their spokesman or advisor when negotiating with the Department of Education. The Executive Committee was as follows: Dumbrell became the Honorary President, while M. Mpotokwane retained his position as President, with S.J. Mokhesi as Vice-President. A.C. Sikunyana and K.K. Baruti (both prominent in teaching supervision and serious campaigners for the teachers' rights) became General Secretary and Recording Secretary respectively. W.S. Letsapa was elected Treasurer while E.M. Rakgole and T. Tamocha were elected Chairman of Committees and Chaplain respectively. The Committee membership consisted of B.M. Mokitime – Ramotswa, M.M. Padi – Serowe, F.H. Tau – Morwa School at Pilane, M.S. Maunge – Bokalaka and Tati, and J. Gugushe was asked to represent Maun. The Gen-

A.C. Sekunyana

eral Purposes Committee consisted of M. Mpotokwane, A.C. Sekunyana, W. S. Letsapa, S.J. Mokhesi and M.M. Padi. In order to ensure that the Association's funds were used appropriately, Levi Moumakwa and A.M. Tsoebebe were elected auditors. K.K. Baruti served the Association in another capacity as its representative on the Western Language Setswana Orthography Committee (S252/2/1).

The Business of Conference

After the elections, the conference discussed some burning questions within the profession and the teachers tackled these with utmost composure and dignity. It was in those discussions that they came out forthrightly, a characteristic that the teachers maintained sometimes in the face of provocation. For instance, they stated that the staffing of schools be determined by the roll together with attendance. Flowing from this were matters connected with shortage of equipment, blackboards and chalk supply. These were no doubt matters that merited the attention of the Administration and the School Committees. However these shortfalls were explained, they were a serious omission if one considers the low qualification of teachers at the time, and should be given all the assistance possible. It is a wonder how they were expected to work effectively as they had been exhorted to by a number of speakers at the start of the conference including Kgosi Tshekedi Khama and Dumbrell. Looking back, one does feel that these were some of the obstacles that delayed the development of education in this country. Perhaps no one was to blame since the BP was dogged by a perennial shortage of funds up to the eve of her independence from Great Britain. In the light of these discrepancies the Select Committee consisting of, E. Rakgole, M.M. Padi, C. Zaza, T.T. Kgosi, S.J. Mokhesi and Dan Mpotokwane resolved that, 'In view of the suffering of education in the Protectorate through the understaffing of schools, this conference respectfully requests the respective School Committees to ameliorate the conditions' (S252/2/1).

It should be noted that even at this stage the teachers used moderate language. Furthermore, the conference touched another sensitive chord when they implored the School Committees to ensure that foreign teachers were allocated decent cottages. The term 'foreign' in this context meant any teacher domiciled in the BP who was employed in another village other than his home. The conference deplored the practice whereby teachers were required to look for accommodation in a strange village. To show how those teachers who met at Serowe were committed to the profession and had the welfare of the children they taught at heart, they expressed shock at the negligence in some schools where classrooms were so dilapidated that school books and stationery were often in danger of being damaged by rain. So frustrated were the teachers that they even suggested that if continual requests were ignored by the Headmen and School Committees, teachers should close down their schools. The teachers were naturally desperate, but they had a point, for in the light of the poor economy, it would have been sad to see what had been secured, destroyed so easily.

Before the close of the historic conference, Levi Moumakwa thanked the President and Tsoebebe for their hard work in building the Association and their effort to enable the teachers to meet at Serowe in 1939. Tsoebebe who had been the Organising Secretary, was particularly thanked for his unswerving devotion to the cause of teachers and his continued support even after he had left the service.

However hard the road for the BPATA was, the most gratifying thing was the general acceptance of the role it was to play in the improvement of education in the territory. To drive the point home and to make the administration realise the seriousness of the Association, Sikunyana immediately submitted all the relevant correspondence as had been agreed upon, to the Department of Education. The Resident Commissioner, who appreciated the efficient manner in which the Association handled their business, asked the Director of Education to inform the teachers that 'in his opinion the Association should fulfil a useful purpose'. In an effort to show his support for the Association, he assured them that the resolutions set out would be placed before the Board of Advice on African Education by the Association's elected member at its next meeting.

The first meaningful communication between the BPATA and the Government and its agencies was through a memorandum formulated by the General Purposes Committee at Mahalapye in March 1940. It raised a number of thorny questions.

First, they complained that post-dated cheques were a source of undue hardship for teachers unable to leave for holidays on time and unable to settle their accounts. The authorities were entreated to stop the practice of paying with such cheques in order to avoid unnecessary inconvenience. Though the practice was subsequently dropped it persisted for a considerable number of years. One can surmise that the practice was a mere repeat of earlier times when teachers were not paid their salaries regularly.

Secondly, the Association requested that the authorities grant one month's leave on full pay for teachers who had given five years of unbroken service. Furthermore, that teachers be granted three month's sick leave, also on full pay, provided a medical certificate was produced. On the first point the teachers' plea was legitimate, if one considers the fact that there was nothing like sabbatical leave or study leave as was the case with civil servants.

Thirdly, the teachers struck a sensitive chord when they raised the issue of teachers' quarters. This problem, as we know, is a universal one and has defied all forms of solution to this day. The memo stressed the plight of teachers who lived far from their schools and travelled to and fro in all types of weather. Sometimes their quarters were not fit for human occupation. Finally, the memo stated that 'it was hoped that in putting up teachers' quarters, married teachers be speedily considered' (S252/2/1).

The housing situation of teachers must have been extremely bad in the early 1940s for even in the 1960s it was horrible, nay even into the 1990s. So bad was the situation that it became the annual cry from conference to conference. It is true to say that there were many members of the public who saw eye to eye with the teachers in their predicament but decided to remain silent. The man who could not keep quiet in the face of the teachers' raw deal and the general state of education in the BP and particularly at Molepolole at that time, was Sankoloba Matlhabaphiri, a Mokwena from Molepolole and on top of that a headman who had lived for some time in Johannesburg. At the time he was a 'radical' activist in the movement to restore Sebele II. He was, in short, a firebrand who was quite familiar with communist literature and was not very friendly to Kgosi Kgari's administration, though he was later co-opted. Matlhabaphiri took the most unusual and perhaps unprecedented step of writing and sending a memorandum to the Office of the Government Secretary in Mafikeng on 4 April 1942. This was treading on dangerous ground and must have caused many a hiccup within government circles. In his memorandum he lamented the backwardness of education at Bakwena schools. He wrote:

> 'Out here there is no teacher who can stay more than two years – this being the cause children suffer educationally because, of the teachers being wandering. It appears that there is some great cause which makes the teachers run away. What can be the remedy for this? The outstanding reason for the teachers to leave Molepolole so surprisingly soon – lack of living quarters' (S252/2/1) (DC Mol.1/8).

He lamented the shortage of classrooms and accommodation which caused many children to be taught under trees exposed to the sun, cold, winds and rain.

He further depicted the sorry plight of the classrooms at some schools. He quoted an instance when in March 1942 as a result of rain the Junior School was flooded. He reported that the building was dilapidated and in disrepair. It is an interesting coincidence that what Matlhabaphiri observed about the schools and their state of disrepair was often quoted by the school inspectors later.

Matlhabaphiri was extremely daring for he copied the letter to the Director of Education who showed interest in the memorandum and assured him that his suggestions would 'not be left aside'. Matlhabaphiri's daring episode was not anything to amuse the establishment. In order to discipline him, Dumbrell was instructed to call him to a meeting with District Commissioner Mathews of Molepolole and Kgosi Kgari in order to reprimand him publicly. Matlhabaphiri must have been incensed by the rebuke he received and the meeting served no good purpose. In despair, Mathews reported to the Government Secretary, 'I consider that this matter should be left alone. If no notice is taken of this man he will soon become hurt and stop his nonsense' (S252/2/1) (DC Mol 1/8). Mathews must have been angered by Matlhabaphiri's insolence and in despair he even referred to him as a man of practically no standing in the tribe and was always a trouble maker.

The meeting seemed to have fuelled Matlhabaphiri's criticism of the *status quo* for he advocated that 'natives' be given the responsibility of chairman and secretary (DC was Chairman of the School Committee and the Secretary was invariably a Minister of Religion). He asked, 'Is there still no native in the School Committee who can either be Chairman or Secretary?' (S252/2/1). He advocated that vacancies should be open to eligible 'natives' as vice-chairman and assistant secretary. Further the 'natives' as he put it, were rapidly developing and it was time that the School Committee addressed this issue.

The other issue, which was debated at length, was a circular which came from the Department of Education warning the teachers to desist from the habit of 'sending school children on private errands'. The conference rejected the circular as baseless, vague and unclear. The teachers took the view that in essence the whole issue was based on isolated cases and the General Purpose Committee was asked to examine the circular more closely.

The question of salaries among teachers has always been an extremely sore point, for they were discriminated upon from the colonial days. Sometimes, some people's judgement of teachers has been erroneous in that their organisations were seen to dissipate their energies wrangling with their employers for better salaries. The point to remember is that teachers like any group of professionals should not be expected to sacrifice too much and so at the first conference, the issue of salaries was raised. First, they pleaded with the administration to pay teachers according to qualifications and experience. Secondly, that a payment of allowances to married teachers be considered. These were reasonable recommendations despite the fact that the BP economy was unable to support such scales. The teachers once more touched a sensitive chord for it would appear that 'from the reports of both Burns and Sargent that there was nothing in the way of a scale of salaries for teachers during the missionary regime, not even for those teachers who were employed in the schools of the same missionary body' (Thema, 1947). The reason for these discrepancies is not hard to find if we consider that each *morafe* (tribe) ran its own system.

In fact, the Bangwaketse School Committee was the first to face a concerted demand from the teachers in its schools for an increase in salaries. The teachers on 19 June 1919 put their case to the School Committee meeting. Two years later at a meeting of the same Committee held on 20 December 1920, the Teachers' Association (an association of the teachers in the Kanye area alone) asked for a fixed salary scale. The Teachers' Association's request which was referred to the Government 'was not successful for Government did not consider the time opportune to draw up salary scales' (Thema, 1947).

If anything showed the Association's commitment to the improvement of education in BP it was their devotion to the idea of vacation courses which helped to inform teachers of new methods of teaching and the handling of the curriculum. Since such vacation courses served a useful purpose, the Government was to be encouraged to continue to mount them and they were to be conducted at different places in the country and courses were to be graded to meet the needs of teachers.

Other issues of importance discussed at the first meeting of the General Purpose Committee covered a wide spectrum of the teachers' problems.

These were dominated by the Association's lean finances. For instance, it became mandatory for members to pay their subscriptions promptly to the Branch Associations. The teachers as early as these times came forward with the idea of the 'stop order' system to facilitate payment. Twenty years later, the Botswana Teachers Union made a similar suggestion without success. This was only achieved forty years later in the 1980s. Further, to lighten the correct keeping of financial records, the General Secretary was empowered to check the Association's books as the occasion demanded. But above all, half yearly returns were a requirement accompanied by the number of members enrolled and the financial position at the branch level indicated. Though the teachers were in bad shape financially, they were not prepared to beg for 'hand outs'. The General Purpose meeting held in Mahalapye on 23 May 1940 was asked to appeal to the teachers to raise funds through concerts and other forms of entertainment. One can appreciate why the coffers of the BPATA were so low if one considers that a teacher with NPL or PT1 earned between £44 and £50 per annum and one with an NPH scale earned between £72 and £84 per annum. An interesting feature of this scale was that it did not indicate the rate at which increments would be paid, probably because the Inspector of Education did not see the possibility of paying increments regularly out of the meagre votes for education. The principle of the Association branches helping the delegates to the General Conference and the financial plight of the Association was highlighted by the Association's Branch report in Molepolole in December 1964. It stated that, 'more than R19.00 (Nineteen Rand) was raised at a concert staged by the Kwena Branch of the BPATA this week in order to enable delegates from the branch to meet expenses of attending the Annual Conference in Serowe...' (BP Daily News, 1964).

One stringent regulation which agitated the minds of the Association and has continued ever since, was the suspension which led to the dismissal of pregnant and unmarried teachers. While the Association did not condone the situation it viewed the problem as a social one. It felt extremely uncomfortable about the suspension and the expulsion of such teachers when they were most needed by the children. Further, to deny them some remuneration when they needed it most was considered extremely harsh. In the name of morality, many a teacher suffered. So hard at times were the School Committees' regulations that they completely controlled the lives of teachers.

The minutes of the General Purposes Committee were forwarded to the Director of Education by the General Secretary on 3 April 1940. It then remained for the Association's representative (Levi Moumakwa) on the Board of Advice for African Education to present the teachers memorandum for discussion at its next meeting. No doubt the teachers had made a tremendous breakthrough by being accepted at the Board of Advice level.

The events following the submission of the memorandum to the Department of Education are interesting as they constantly display the absolute trust and faith of the General Secretary, A.C. Sekunyana in the Director of Education. He gently pushed Dumbrell into almost accepting the memorandum without question on behalf of the Administration. Through persuasive language he nudged him to ensure that 'all the articles therein be fulfilled to the letter' (S252/2/1). He might have been aware the type of responses Dumbrell would receive from the Board but did not want to preempt these on behalf of the Board of Advice on African Education. Nonetheless the General Secretary soon ran into trouble when he suggested that since the memorandum had been drawn during Levi Moumakwa's absence, and he had not participated in the discussion, he thought the President (M. Mpotokwane) who was a supervisor of schools should be invited. Dumbrell turned the request down on the grounds that it would be improper to invite the President of the BPATA to attend the meeting of the Board in addition to the teachers' own representative. The Association should have realised how awkward their request was and the most sensible thing to do was to brief Moumakwa before the said meeting.

The Association's first Executive Committee meeting responded admirably to innumerable problems. The first of these was to query the salaries of Head Teachers in African schools. The step they took was a legitimate one for it was naked discrimination for the Department of Education to extend the privilege of salary increases over and above the official scale to a few individual head teachers of African schools in the territory. Strangely they said nothing about the high salaries drawn by their counterparts in European schools. They further deprecated the fact that some assistant teachers drew higher salaries than their headmasters.

Nonetheless, if the practice was done without favour it was an admirable move and today this is what parallel progression is all about. The Director of Education was entreated to examine these anomalies and bring about appropriate adjustments in an equitable manner (S252/2/1).

The other issue which came thorough this discussion was the suspension of teachers. It is understandable that without the Conditions of Service or a Code of Ethics the teachers were at the mercy of school committees who, as has been pointed out earlier, were insensitive to the teachers' problems. The Executive Committee requested that the school authorities should first stipulate the period of suspension of the teacher concerned and that this be communicated to the teacher promptly. Secondly, that the period of suspension be commensurate with the offence. Another reasonable request that the Executive put to the school committees through the Department of Education related to the transfer of teachers. Whilst they appreciated the legitimacy of the practice they appealed to the employers to inform the teachers on time when transfers were contemplated. Also the school committees were urged to bear the expense of transportation of the teacher, his family and personal effects.

The two resolutions which characterised the associations commitment to the improvement of education in this country was the plea for the recognition of additional certificates which had a bearing on teaching and teaching subjects on one hand, and the teaching of indigenous languages on the other. On the first one, the Executive Committee expressed disappointment at the failure of the Department of Education to recognise relevant additional qualifications which had a bearing on their teaching. They rightly resolved that additional qualifications such as the possession of a Junior or Senior Certificate or full Industrial and Domestic Science Certificate in addition to experience be rewarded by a salary increment. With regard to the teaching of indigenous languages, the Association was progressive, for this is a subject of present day debate at high level fora like the Botswana Educational Research Association (BERA). From the outset, the Association was preoccupied with the improvement of Setswana. Batswana in general were exhorted to interest themselves 'in the purity and growth of the language' (S252/2/1).

The teachers' request for uniformity of the school calendar so that schools opened and took holidays at the same time for vacations was again prompted by the educational considerations. The whole idea was intended to enable the teachers in the employ of different District Tribal Schools to attend the Annual Subsidiary Courses of training for teachers at the same time. The vacation courses were too precious to be left to chance and haphazard arrangements.

Though the Association in the years subsequent to the first conference at Serowe seemed to have gained some form of acceptability, one cannot help feeling that they were at times considered bothersome. Some of the replies churned from the Imperial Reserve through the Department of Education were not well thought out and conveyed to the teachers convincingly. For instance, the Executive Committee raised the fact that hand work was compulsory in all African schools, despite the fact that teachers had no expertise in this respect, and it suggested the employment of part-time teachers with the skill and who should be paid adequately. Dumbrell's reply was evasive but he was prepared to bring the matter to the notice of Native Administrators. On the question of the Head Teachers' salaries the reply was that in general the principle of paying allowances to heads of school had been approved by the Board of Advice on African Education, but funds were the major constraint. If anything emerged clearly from these evasive tactics, it is the alarming measure of neglect by the Administration to provide education to meet the needs of Batswana later. This neglect has continued to be felt long after the attainment of independence by Botswana in 1966.

The idea of a uniform calendar, one thought, would have been most welcome since it suited the arrangement for vacation courses as well as solved administrative problems for the Department of Education. All schools would start and finish at the same time. When the Director of Education responded, he mentioned some problems but these were not outlined. As was customary with him, since he was anxious not to disappoint the teachers, he promised to put into effect the teachers' recommendation in 1942.

Further, it was rather strange that the teachers recommendation that additional qualifications should be rewarded by the Department of Education was rejected. Additional qualifications like the Junior and Senior Certificate were not only a commendable acquisition for the teacher in terms of academic improvement, but it had a bearing on professional training and instruction in class. At that stage, the teachers should have been encouraged to study, as sound teacher training depends on sound academic qualifications. Disappointingly, the Department stated categorically that the Junior and Senior Certificates were not professional qualifications. Again, Dumbrell promised that he would prepare for submission to the Government recommendations in respect of their being recognised by means of additions to the salary scales then in force.

No doubt Dumbrell was able to stem the tide and the wrath of the teachers for a while. It was clear that the clouds of protest were gathering on the horizon. When this financial constraint was thoroughly worn out, its place was taken by the constant financial commitment to the second world war by the United Kingdom, and no increased expenditure would be entertained while the war continued (S252/2/1). The letter no doubt ended on a gloomy note for the Association as this was the first attempt to make such far reaching suggestions. This trend was to continue beyond independence in 1966. The Association's resolutions which entailed the general improvement of the lives of the teachers always foundered on the rock of finances.

Conclusion

This chapter has examined the efforts and problems met by the local teachers to form a teachers' organisation in order to improve, among other things, the standard of education in Botswana (BP) and protect their interests. Their problems were complicated by the resistance of the local administration which felt that their authority might be undermined. But with the help of the enlightened administrators in Mafeking, including Dumbrell and sympathetic Dikgosi, the Association took off in 1939 with the first conference held in Serowe. From that conference the teachers gained self confidence and began to assert themselves by even demanding to be represented in some decision-making bodies, such as the Board of Advice for African Education.

Equally important at this stage was the constant exchange of views between the Administration and the Association. This trust may have laid the foundation for the Government to see teachers as partners in nation building.

CHAPTER TWO

The Years of Consolidation: 1941–1959

The first chapter dealt with how the teachers were faced with endless problems even after the establishment of BPATA. At the same time, the chapter discussed how they worked hard to form a firm base. If the 1930s were years of the making of the Association, the 1940s were for the consolidation of the work of the Association. Despite the slow start, the Association made a dramatic impact if one remembers that by the close of the 1950s, not only did the Association engage the Administration in meaningful dialogue, but were prepared to examine the teachers' salaries.

The forties, the first decade after the founding of the BPATA, showed the rapid growth of the Association both at branch (local) and national (mother body) levels. At these levels, the Association was becoming articulate on issues which affected the individual teachers as well as the Association as a whole. Clearly the earlier days of subservience on the part of the teachers were gone. Teachers were beginning to challenge what they saw as insidious inroads affecting the profession. Some local authorities were inclined to be harsh and unreasonable in their dealings with the teachers in their employment. Nonetheless, once the teachers realised the power in their hands, they resisted with all their might.

The year 1941 was another important landmark in the history of the BPATA. In that year the second General Conference of the Association was held at Mochudi. As usual, the occasion was preceded by a number of invitations to local dignitaries. Kgosi Mmusi K. Pilane, the District Commissioner, Chairman of the Bakgatla School Committee, the Inspector of Schools, H.J. Clarke and the Director of Education. This General Conference was as well attended as the first one held at Serowe two years before. The teachers came from all corners of the Protectorate, from Zwenshambe, Nkange, Tshesebe in the North, the Imperial Reserve (Mafikeng), and Kanye in the South. Others came from Serowe, Tonota, Modipane, Morwa and Mabalane in Central District. So great was the interest in this gathering that a certain J. Tlhagwane, a cattle post teacher attended. This was an interesting development since information about conferences hardly reached cattle posts. The idea of cattle post schools was introduced by Dumbrell to counteract the imbalance between the boys and girls at the local schools. The idea of cattle post schools was sound, as it was intended to spread education at the grassroots level. Unfortunately, the idea died because of lack of support and funds. Of interest, one of the promising politicians in the country, Matlapeng Ray Molomo, who was the Minister of

Education from 1989 to 1994, was the product of Tlhagale cattle post school.

In June 1941, at the Dutch Reformed Church, a short address of welcome was made by the DC, R.B.M. Sullivan. He expressed hope that the leaders would soon settle down to grapple with their domestic problems. In essence his message was that long after the conference was over teachers would be faced with the classroom teaching and many other problems associated with education. Kgosi Mmusi Pilane was unable to attend the opening ceremony but his speech was read by his uncle Kgosi Bogatsu Pilane. The message among other things read,

M.R. Molomo

'*Ke solofhela letla baana le nako e atlegileng... Me ke solofhela gore maikano le itlano ya lona jaja ge le budıgile ke go ruta le go kaela merafe ya balona kafa tshiamong le poıfong Modimo.*'

(translated as 'I hope you will have a good time. I further trust your aim and fervent consideration is to teach and guide your fellowmen in righteous ways and fear of God'.)

The Honorary Secretary of the School Committee also addressed the conference. Levi Moumakwa, the teachers' representative on the Board of Advice on African Education, thanked the speakers. For no apparent reason, he fell on his favourite subject, namely that the BPATA was a non-political body but that it was an organisation for the furtherance of education by working in cooperation with the Government, the Kgosi and missionaries. One is inclined to feel that some teachers in the course of their service to please the authorities had overstepped the limits at the expense of the organisation.

One of the problems raised by Moumakwa concerned teachers' quarters. Reports from various reserves differed remarkably. In Kanye, it was reported that the community there was taking an active part to help the teachers with decent cottages. The teachers were even assisted when transferred from one school to the other. In the Tati Concession, the position was different. No accommodation was arranged for teachers and no assistance was given in the case of transfers. The conference felt that the Tati Concessions' case had to be followed up in order to improve the lot of the teachers. Such determination on the part of the teachers was credible for it underpinned their preparedness to challenge their employers when they were unfairly treated. The trend has continued unabated. It was also reported that in the Bangwato Reserve, Kgosi Tshekedi Khama had written to all headman instructing them to put up teachers' quarters and at some places the task had been completed.

The first item on the agenda of the conference was a call for a thorough examination of the syllabus. This matter had previously been raised at the first conference of the Association at Serowe in 1939. In fact, Dumbrell, the Director of Education had agonised on the absence of an appropriate syllabus. In this respect, a Select Committee was elected with the sole purpose of examining the syllabuses that were borrowed from the neighbouring provinces like the Transvaal and the Cape in South Africa and Lesotho. It should be remembered that soon after Dumbrell's appointment in 1928 he 'prescribed the Cape Primary Syllabus as a temporary measure pending the drawing up of a code for the Protectorate' (Thema, 1947). The committee consisted of L.C. Moumakwa (Chairman), L.L. Pheko, J.T. Phooko, M.S. Maunge and Joshua Chelenyane. As a result of its efforts, a Primary School Course, prefaced with the statement that it had been drawn up 'with due consideration for the conditions and problems prevailing in the Territory' (S252/2/1).

Then came a couple of motions introduced by L.L. Pheko of the Serowe Branch of the BPATA.

1. That Government be persuaded to introduce salaries identical with those that obtained in the provinces of the Union of South Africa and that there be regular pay increments. After a long discussion, it was decided that the matter be left in the hands of the District Association and that it would make recommendations and comments before submitting the same to the General Secretary for transmission to the General Purposes Committee.
2. That the Teachers' Association should appoint a Select Language Committee to examine Setswana in order to rid it of foreign elements where Setswana equivalents were available. This was an interesting development for it indicated the teachers' pride and appreciation of their culture.
3. That the Government be requested to introduce in the territory a Good Service Allowance.

The teachers at this conference were again addressed by the Director of Education. He congratulated the Association for what it had accomplished in its five years of existence, particularly the valuable assistance given to the Department of Education. He congratulated the Association on the fact that it was not pre-occupied with grousing and parading of grievances. Appropriately, it was concerned with professional matters such as the revision of the syllabus in order to make it relevant. He exhorted the teachers to go on with their work in the knowledge that instructing children is a fairly easy task – 'a hard task is to educate the people to be better able to cope with the coming world' (S252/2/1). This address was typical of Dumbrell's genuine advice to and his dealings with teachers. He also dealt with a number of issues that concerned the teachers, such as the overcrowding at schools and the need to revise the primary school syllabus. He discouraged completely the idea of promotion for pupils particularly those who entered Standard 5 without producing promotion cards. The use of the promotion cards as a gateway to further education may have been a harsh measure. But their use is quite understandable in a situation where the curriculum for the local schools was wanting and to a large extent dependent on the heads of schools. At the same time, it can be argued that the promotion card system delayed progress and stifled the efforts of people who sought education for their children.

The President's address highlighted some very important landmarks achieved by the Association. First of these was the honour bestowed on two members of the Association by the Administration. The two gentlemen were Rev. Andrew Kgasa and Levi Moumakwa who were presented with the Kings medal, an award that must have been the envy of many during those days. It was in recognition of service rendered to the country. It is possible today to associate it with colonial domination but then it was an honour not to be missed. The second achievement made by the Association was the granting of a Five Year Bonus by the Administration to teachers who had rendered five years of continuous good service in the Protectorate. This was a good gesture on the part of the Administration at a time when the teachers were calling for the betterment of their conditions of service and salaries. It was, however, minimal and no substitute for the revision of the emoluments of teachers in particular.

From that point, the President dealt with the General Purpose Committee and the Executive Committee and commended them for the solid work which they were doing, particularly their effort to speak with one voice in the name of the Association. Despite the excellent record effected by the BPATA, there were two developments which disturbed the Association and were endorsed by the President. First was the steady flow of teachers from the Protectorate to the neighbouring countries. This was because opportunities for better salaries were greater there. The President lamented this loss since the BP had a small teaching cadre. Secondly, concern was expressed at the fact that many teachers were not members of the Association at a time when they were needed most to strengthen the ranks of the Association. The swelling of the ranks of the BPATA was extremely vital as we shall see later as this study unfolds. The Association was often accused of being not representative enough.

Despite some of these early setbacks, the conference heard of the steady headway made by the Association in that some of the members had been incorporated by the Administration in the revision of the Primary School Syllabus for African schools in the BP. This was a recognition by the Administration of the sound input that a body of professionals could make in the improvement of education in the Protectorate.

What then did the conference held at Mochudi achieve? One of its major successes was that it created a deep sense of belonging among teachers. The Association was a body to which they could turn when faced with professional and other problems. It was for this reason that for some years later it became the rallying point for most teachers. The other important outcome of the conference was that teachers realised the Administration's commitment to cooperate with them in the development of education in the BP. This confidence in the role that the teachers were playing as useful partners in the improvement of education was amply demonstrated by their appointment in some decision making bodies like the Board of Advice on African Education and the Primary School Syllabus Committee.

The Future of the Association

Mpotokwane, the President of the Association, emphasised the fact that the Association was still tender, but needed a solid foundation to brave the unknown. The success of the Association depended on one aspect. The development of a spirit of cooperation between the Association and the parents, the Department of Education and the Administration as a whole, as well as the confidence of the fellow workers – the teachers. He criticised the belief that parents were ignorant and apathetic. He also proposed several motions among which was one that called upon the Executive Committee to request the Government to consider financial assistance for teachers who were referred to hospitals outside the country for medical treatment. As would be expected, a Government that was constantly under economic pressure was not likely to accede to such a request and it was turned down. Another motion required the Branch Associations to nominate their own representatives to the Executive Committee of the BPATA. This was intended to obviate the acquisition of deadwood. The conference felt that individual members were better known to branch associations than the general membership. This last point, in addition to the discussions preceding it, was an indication of the Association's awareness of the rights and obligations of membership and individual members. This was a welcome move since it laid the pattern for the future. Clearly they wanted to impress upon the Administration that a request for financial assistance on the grounds of health was legitimate and no luxury. What could be considered a valuable move on the part of the Association was the attempt to mould the organisation into a strong body, and above all, to stress that unity is strength. The final activity of the conference which examined, discussed and revised the syllabus was a step in the right direction and for many years it became the responsibility of teachers through to the present day national subject panels.

The conference concluded its work by electing the following to the Executive Committee:

Honorary President:	H.J.E. Dumbrell, Esq., OBE, BA, D/E
President:	M. Mpotokwane (re-elected)
Vice–President:	T.T. Kgosi
General Secretary:	A.C. Sikunyane (re-elected in absentia)
Treasurer:	G.L. Motalaote
Chaplain:	T. Kirschbaum
Chairman of Committees:	J.T. Phooko
Representative on the Board of Advice on African Education:	L.C. Moumakwa (re-elected)
General Purposes Committee:	M. Mpotokwane
	A.C. Sikunyane
	G.L. Motalaote
	J.M. Gasebuse
	M.S.K. Pilane
Representative on the WSLO:	Joshua Chelenyane

(Source: S252/2/1)

The Image of the BPATA

The 1940s showed an all-round acceptance of the BPATA by the Administration. The Department of Education continued to report the activities of the Association in a brighter light. For instance, the Annual Report of the Department of Education in 1940 stated that in June of that year, a conference of the Bechuanaland Protectorate African Teachers' Association was held in Ramotswa. A consequence of this conference was that some 16 resolutions were forwarded to the Department, and this was followed by a deputation to explain and discuss them. The report commented that a very wide range of topics were covered and 'bore witness to the professional growth of the teachers concerned during the last few years' (Report of the Department of Education, 1940). In order that others at remote schools might keep in touch with such representatives, copies of the resolutions and of the official comments upon them were issued to all headteachers. The report continued,

> 'this organisation, which in theory covers the whole territory, is revising its constitution, and that it has developed a better technique in handling its business and should prove not only a valuable sounding board for the Protectorate, but an important agency by means of which the teachers can convey corporate opinion on matters of educational importance, wider than that of individual grievances' (Report of the Department of Education, 1946).

So impressed was the Administration by the Association's performance that in 1948 it was reported that when the BPATA held its annual conference at Mochudi under the Chairmanship of T.W. Moeti, Acting Headmaster of the Government Teacher Training College at Kanye, with T.W. Motlhagodi of the Junior Secondary School at Kgale as General Secretary, that representations of the conference were forwarded to the administration in resolution form. Among other topics were the need for an accepted terminology in Tswana Grammar, the primary school syllabus, examination procedures, allowances for unqualified married teachers and sick leave for teachers. It is clear from these resolutions that teachers in this country were committed to the improvement of education and also concerned with the plight of teachers generally. No administration worth the while could have missed the well meaning and serious approach of the teachers to improve the learning of the child in the classroom manned by a disciplined teaching force.

The resolutions, which were drafted with commendable restraint and which were constructive in character, were discussed later with a delegation selected for this purpose. The Education Department then issued a circular notifying all schools of their nature and of the comments upon them made during the discussion at Headquarters. The report continued, 'this is indicative of the value Government places upon corporate representation from African teachers whose collaboration in this way will continue to be encouraged' (S252/2/2). To this end, recognition had been accorded in the Department of Education Proclamation which gave ex-officio membership on the Standing Committee of the African Education to the approved nominee of the Association who then was on the staff of the Teacher Training Centre. It was then hoped that in spite of the widely scattered nature of the schools in the territory, the membership of the Association would grow and correspondingly influence its deliberations. It is important to note that although the Association seemed to have gained popularity with the Administration, the numerous resolutions passed unnoticed since the very Administration operated without any conditions of service. There was also the perennial claim of paucity of funds. Despite these handicaps the Association never wavered from its chosen course, that is, to help improve the standard of education in the Protectorate and ensure that the lot of teachers received attention.

Another striking feature of the forties was the conscious effort on the part of the Administration through the Department of Education on one hand, and the BPATA on the other, to consolidate the educational effort in the BP. The new Director of Education, H. Jowitt who replaced Dumbrell in 1945 came from Uganda. He was extremely critical of Dumbrell 'for being concerned with education as "social regeneration" importing "new hopes and outlooks" and for having replaced that secular missionary outlook by bureaucratic concern for numbers, finance and standards' (Crowder, 1984). Parsons (Crowder, 1984) put it well stating that the new Director started investigating buildings, chairs, blackboards and latrines. Jowitt wanted the establishment of a broader educational base for more Batswana children and would have nothing to do with the elitist type of the selected few.

In a letter to the DC in Kanye, the Chairman of the Bangwaketse School Committee, referring to the minutes of the Bangwaketse School Committee meeting held on 28 August 1946, stated that the new Director of Education had expressed his concern at large staff changes reported and which he believed adversely affected progress. To him, good progress was synonymous with low staff turn over. He nonetheless expressed the view that there was evidence of sound organisation to cope with the problem (Department of Education Annual Report, 1945).

He must have read closely past resolutions of the BPATA which had been submitted to the Department of Education. He first of all pointed out the need for full reports to be submitted regarding suspensions and dismissals of the DC as a Chairman of the Bangwaketse School Committee. He advised the Department of Education to take notice of their actions and cooperate in order that the re-appointment of such teachers elsewhere within the period of suspension would not have the Department's approval.

Another development hailed by Jowitt was the proposal that each school would in future be under the management of its own headteachers. His interest was not only confined to the problems facing educational organisation but was concerned with the well-being of the teachers generally. He did not hesitate to tackle some of the long standing problems that constantly affected the teachers such as the construction of teachers' quarters in the districts, the meagre salaries paid to teachers, and above all the poor buildings in which they taught as well as inadequate equipment.

The new Director of Education had hardly warmed his seat when he received resolutions passed by the BPATA at a conference held at Ramotswa in June 1946. The Association's resolutions covered a large range of topics largely concerned with the development of education in the BP. The first resolution was a proposal to discontinue the third class in School Leaving Certificate Examinations. The Association saw the practice as a hindrance to the admission of candidates holding a third class pass to secondary schools or teacher training. The Director of Education did not agree with the Association on this issue and contended that it was academically desirable that the students should be classified according to their results, a procedure found in most territories if not the world. He even went on to say that in some territories there was a fourth class pass which had been discontinued since it had little significance. He explained that in 1945 the minimum required for a pass was raised from 40% to 45% and in the year in question it had been raised to 50% which meant that a third class pass in 1946 examination would reflect a much higher standard than previously. It would then be indicated in the certificate that to secure a third class pass a student had to obtain from 50% to 59% (S252/2/2).

In consequence, the restriction which was primarily placed against the admission of candidates holding third class passes to secondary schools and teacher training would be removed. But as long as accommodation difficulties remained, it would be necessary for the headteachers of institutions to select the best material from those who applied. Nonetheless, this did not necessarily mean the exclusion of students with a third class certificate.

Contrary to the prevalent view that teachers were forever bargaining for higher salaries, the next issue raised by the teachers was the need to revise the Primary School Syllabus. Note should be taken that when Dumbrell came to the Protectorate, first as an Inspector of Education, and later the Director of Education, there was heavy reliance of this country on the Union of South Africa for the curriculum. However expedient this arrangement was, it was rather untenable since these syllabuses were not appropriate for the needs of the BP. While the teachers themselves were aware that the syllabuses in use were intended to suit teachers who had low qualifications, it was not a satisfactory arrangement. One of the reasons was the need to prepare their pupils for further education. The Director of Education accepted the arguments put forward by the teachers that no syllabus was good at all times, but any syllabus if wisely drafted had to be related to the capacity and competence of the teachers concerned. The need was recognised by the Department, and everything possible was done to address the issue. At the same time, he warned that one could not draft new regulations, new curricula, and new examination procedures in a short space of time. Finally, he assured the teachers that work was being done in connection with the revision of the syllabus in question.

In one of the resolutions, the Association raised a long standing problem which, throughout the years, had defied solution. The problem was that of large classes which were considered counterproductive. The Director of Education, instead of explaining the problem, simply accused the teachers of being responsible for large classes. He was extremely insensitive for he did not explain how they contributed to large classes. He claimed for instance, that it was the African parents who insisted that there be no limitations on enrolment. It would have been reasonable to point out that the whole problem was tied up with the lack of funds at the disposal of Tribal Treasuries. Perhaps what many people failed to detect was that Jowitt's policies, as Parsons put it, 'entailed dependence on neighbouring colonies at a time when ... those countries were beginning to squeeze out pupils from the BP' (Crowder, 1984). What was needed was a bold and far seeing policy which would substitute educational dependence on South Africa and Southern Rhodesia. 'But time and time again the BP authorities had reiterated the policy of educational dependence, building on perceived strengths abroad rather than remedying perceived weaknesses in local education provision' (Crowder, 1984). In the light of the above, he stated that the 'shift system' or 'stagger system', an arrangement by which one teacher taught two groups of the same class at different times in order to avoid a large class and was intended to solve the problem, was a mere 'papering over the cracks'. The possible solution lay in boosting the Tribal Treasuries and employing qualified teachers.

The other resolution referred to the need for the early publication of examination results and this received a favourable response from the Department of Education. The Association also advised the Department of Education to allow the teaching of Afrikaans in high classes such as Standard 5 which would enable non-Setswana speaking pupils to proceed to South Africa for higher education. On this subject, the Director of Education left the door open, and merely stated that information would be sought regarding the number of teachers in the BP who were capable of giving instruction in Afrikaans, since it was felt that the number of such pupils was not large. It is of interest to note that this issue once again emerged in the 1960s, and there was a strong feeling among the teachers that Afrikaans as a subject be excluded from the BP schools. Obviously, the political climate of compromise had changed since the 1940s.

One other remarkable feature of the resolutions was the Association's attempt to stake their claims boldly. For instance, the conference held at Ramotswa in 1946 resolved that the BPATA should be at the same level as the Native Advisory Council. It should be noted again that it was this same body that had rejected the formation of the Association in 1932 since it was considered irrelevant; but to request that their voice be heard from within was extremely ambitious. In a lighter vein, Sir Charles Rey, in his frightening spite referred to the Native Advisory Council in 1931 as my 'Native Parliament'. Here the fate of the education of Batswana was decided, including the children and teachers.

Sir Charles Rey was appointed Resident Commissioner of Bechuanaland Protectorate (Botswana) in September 1929 to understudy the retiring Resident Commissioner, R.M. Daniel. He actually assumed full responsibility in April 1930 and retired in 1937. At the time of his appointment he was described as 'someone who is enterprising, keen on development – a fresh and vigorous personality who will look at the situation with new eyes...' (Parsons and Crowder, 1988).

Regarding free medical treatment, the Director of Education was not sympathetic. He held that the matter had been dealt with by the Director of Medical Services in 1945, and his comments had been forwarded to the BPATA. He was surprised that the Association revived the issue, for the teachers together with members of the African community were indeed fortunate in being able to obtain medical treatment at such a small cost – a sum of two shillings and six pence (S252/2/2). On the question of sick leave, the Director of Education showed a sad lack of understanding, for he quoted the terms of the regulations controlling sick leave promulgated under the Resident Commissioner's Notice of 23 February 1940 which stated that in any one year, 'not more than two weeks' sick leave should be on full pay, and not more than two weeks on half pay, the remaining period if any, being without pay' (S252/

2/2). Nonetheless, the Department of Education was advised to recommend to the School Committees that three months' sick leave on full-pay should be provided if necessary. This item was to be brought to the notice of the RC to determine whether a more generous provision was desirable. The matter was turned down as there were no funds.

At this point, one needs to take a pause and examine the intricate and rather unusual relations that developed between some Tribal Administrations and the Branch Associations of the BPATA on one hand, and the Tribal Administration and the BPATA (central body) on the other. Sometimes there were hard feelings between the Bangwaketse Tribal Administration and the local Bangwaketse Teachers' Association. Yet in spite of the hard feelings, at times the Association continued to invite officials from the local Tribal Administration or the Department of Education to open their conferences. Such an invitation was extended in a letter dated 17 November 1947 to Kgosi Bathoen II the Paramount Chief of Bangwaketse, by Joshua Chelenyane: 'I kindly beg to inform you, Chief, that the Bangwaketse Teachers' Association ask that the Chief may come to the Association meeting...' (S252/2/1).

The issues that were discussed by the teachers at that meeting were many and varied, but the one that was most irritating and attended to closely was the burden of walking 'up the hill' to the Headquarters of the Tribal Administration to collect their salaries once a month. The letter which was intended to draw the attention of the authorities, was written to the Secretary of the Bangwaketse School Committee in Kanye (the Rev. John F. White) by Quett Masire (later Dr Masire, and at the time of writing His Excellency, the President of the Republic of Botswana) then the Secretary of the Bangwaketse Teachers' Association. The tone of the letter was moderate but firm. Having been instructed by the Kanye teachers, he stated that 'they humbly request the School Committee to devise means whereby their salaries will be sent to them at their various schools.' (DCK). The request was communicated to Kgosi Bathoen II by the Secretary of the School Committee.

Kgosi Bathoen's reply of 23 March 1952 was uncompromising. He categorically rejected the request that teachers not collect their salaries from the tribal offices since they often travelled long distances to the cattle posts and fields. He saw their visits to the Administration Offices as appropriate since they had to familiarise themselves with the

Sir Ketumile Masire

subtle cultural activities like any other Mongwaketse. The 'teachers' humble request' as he put it was thrown out. Obviously the Kgosi was incensed by the request since it implied preferential treatment of teachers as a class. Tradition simply demanded an appearance at the Kgotla as a sign of respect.

Obviously, the local teachers' branch was not prepared to take the rebuff lying down for they replied in a forthright manner and placed 'on record its dissatisfaction with the Administration in that time and again they have submitted their humble request to the Administration which has consistently dismissed them summarily' (DCK). The letter continued that the history of the relationship of the Association with the Administration was anything but cordial. It was a series of rejected requests. While the Association understood the awkward situations faced by the Administration in making certain decisions on teachers' requests, the one in question was a legitimate one and the Administration was obliged to concede. The teachers pointed out that they neither objected to walking to the Tribal Administration Office or attending kgotla meetings. The reference to these two points had no bearing on the Association's request. As responsible members of the tribe they questioned the wisdom of dismissing their requests as frivolous.

The continual feud between the Bangwaketse Branch of the BPATA on one hand, and the Tribal Administration under Kgosi Bathoen II on the other, must be seen in two ways. First, on the part of the teachers their stand must be seen as a trial of strength. They were irritated by what they considered petty demands imposed on them by the Administration. There seemed to be no attempt to treat teachers in a more becoming manner as a professional class. Seemingly, at the crack of the Administration's whip, they had to comply with irrational demands. Obviously they resented this cavalier treatment and curt replies. Their persistent resistance paid dividends later for they came to be treated decently and accorded their status. Secondly, the Administration was unreasonable and harsh. To them the teachers were mere cogs in the Tribal Administration and had to obey the commands of the Administration. The Administration was proved wrong as the BPATA gained strength at the national level and thereby supported the stand adopted by the local branches. The 1960s proved this beyond doubt, for the Government of the day realised the power that the teachers had and above all, they were seen as partners in national development.

Nonetheless, in the middle of this furious battle of words the Bangwaketse Teachers' Association drew up a list of requests to the Administration. These are outlined below.

1. They requested that latrines be erected at each school. (In the opinion of this author, a remarkably progressive stand. The prophets of health for all by the year two thousand would have been impressed).
2. That they should be represented in the School Committee by one of the teachers.

3. That it is a burden on teachers to sell school books.
4. That a Board of Examiners be appointed to examine Standard 4 and 5.
5. That understaffing at the local schools be corrected.
6. That school children and women teachers should not queue for water in the afternoon.
7. That the teachers' salaries be paid to them at their respective schools.

(Source: DCK)

The tone of the letter written by the Bangwaketse Teachers' Association to the Tribal Administration and the Administration, who showed little or no interest, are reminiscent of the letters that the Botswana Teachers' Union wrote to the Ministry of Education prior to the demonstration mounted by the teachers in 1972, when they had their annual conference in Gaborone. The present Government was then in power and some of the participants of the Bangwaketse Teachers' Association drama had by then changed position. One wonders what they thought of the teachers stand on that occasion. The truth is simply that the Government was shocked, for teachers had never behaved in that manner before.

The Ngwaketse Tribal Administration was swift to reply to the letter of 20 April 1952 from the local Association. A letter dated 9 May 1952 was addressed to the headteachers of Maisantwa and Western Schools in Kanye. The letter was written by the Deputy Chief who reminded the teachers concerned that some three days ago a meeting had been called by the Kgosi at the Maisantwa School to look into the complaints of the teachers.

The Deputy Chief's letter to the Association was caustic and was intended to strike fear in the members. Their actions were considered irresponsible. He challenged their claim about the unfairness of the Tribal Administration. Their assertions were dismissed as unfounded. Furthermore, to persist in that defiant mood could be interpreted as open defiance to the Kgosi's orders.

The events following the letter castigating the teachers on their seemingly bad behaviour concentrated on the discussion of points raised by the teachers in a letter written to Rev. White the Secretary of the Bangwaketse School Committee.

Regarding the issue of latrines, the explanation was that the sum of 200 pounds had been voted in the previous year (1951-52), but owing to a shortage of corrugated iron, the construction was stopped. With regard to representation on the School Committee, it stated that K.M. Kgopo, the Chairman of the Bangwaketse Teachers' Association had been on the Committee for a long time and in fact Kgopo endorsed it. Whatever the reasons, it was strange that the teachers seemed not to know their representative. But it was unreasonable to consider the teachers' reluctance to sell books trivial. It was unfair to ask them to do so since they did not have accounting skills, and more serious was the fact that they had no time to do such a laborious job.

The question of the Board of Examiners was a progressive step on the part of the teachers. They were aware of the need to make school results reliable and thereby ensure that teachers followed the syllabuses. The reply that the local teachers participated in the exercise was irrelevant since the very practice was unsatisfactory if one considers the low qualifications of the majority of teachers at that time. The constant question of understaffing was a sore point to the School Committee. Their actions and decisions were governed by the availability of funds, and there was also the question of obtaining teachers. The problem was even more complicated during the course of the year when teachers had either resigned, absconded or had been dismissed.

It is also true that the teachers made unjustifiable requests. For instance, when they asked that school children and women teachers should not queue for water, the School Committee rejected the idea. Equally true, their attitude left much to be desired and no employer would have been happy with their negligence of work. Where was the reason for teachers to crotchet and knit during school hours or even send children on private errands. Admittedly, this behaviour was unacceptable if these accusations were true. Perhaps this attitude on the part of teachers was the cause of constant friction between them and the School Committee. At the same time, we should not lose sight of the fact that the Committee tended to be high handed. Their approach simply infuriated the teachers.

In the wake of the storm, on 24 May 1952 a letter was addressed to all Kanye school teachers and K.M. Kgopo and Miss Kgopo signed on behalf of Kgosi Bathoen II. It sent B.K. Keaiketse instructing them 'to attend a meeting at the famous King George Memorial Hall that same day' (DCK). This was, to say the least, another example of insensitivity in the Kgosi's dealing with the teachers. The fairest thing would have been to tell the teachers what they were being summoned to the Memorial Hall for. This would have given them the time to prepare themselves for the meeting.

However dark the cloud on the home front, yet it was not without a silver lining at the national level. The relationship between the Executive Committee of the BPATA and Kgosi Bathoen II was extremely cordial. Obviously the Association saw merit in harnessing the services of Kgosi Kgolo, for the salvation of the Bangwaketse Branch was in his hands and he was wielding a lot of power. For instance, the Organiser South, P.N. Motsumi constantly appealed to the Paramount Kgosi Bathoen of the Bangwaketse to help the Association by arousing interest among the members of the Bangwaketse Teachers' Association which appeared to be on the verge of disintegration. This was a sensible strategy, for if the Kgosi was uncooperative, very little could be done to help the teachers develop themselves. Nothing must have delighted the Kgosi more than when the Organiser South, stated in a letter that 'I am convinced only by appealing to you, can the Bangwaketse Branch be revised to take the leading part in the Association as it has done in the past' (DCK). He saw the performance of the branch as a dismal failure and it had to be saved. Perhaps the organiser failed to appreciate the firm grip the Kgosi had on teachers and that the teachers were not only inexperienced but were not qualified to understand the essence of a teachers' organisation. They may have been indifferent as they saw no advantage in it. The organiser was concerned that a pioneering branch like Kanye was on the decline when younger associations were active. For this reason, the Kgosi was implored to encourage the said Branch to send delegates to the conference which was to take place at Kgale in June 1955. He saw it as the Kgosi's responsibility to 'do all you can to get the branch alive again' (DCK).

Kgosi Bathoen II was keen not to betray the trust that the BPATA had in him. He was, above all, concerned to see the teachers succeed in their function, since he had been instrumental in the coming of teacher education in the BP. Nonetheless, his cooperation was concomitant on their recognition of his unlimited control over the teachers in the Ngwaketse reserve. His reply to the organiser South underpinned his appreciation of the respect and esteem in which they held him. He had therefore, wasted no time in contacting the chairman and secretary of the Bangwaketse Teachers' Association and had been assured that 'they would send one delegate to Kgale to attend the conference' (DCK). It does appear that Kgosi Bathoen was unpredictable and the Association must have been pleasantly shocked when he expressed solidarity with the organiser by saying, 'I am interested in the Association and I will see what I can do to revive it' (DCK). To have won the Kgosi's support was a major breakthrough, for as will be seen later he gave his support wholeheartedly to the Association.

At this stage, the road to cordial relations between the Kgosi and the BPATA had been set. The General Secretary, T.W. Motlhagodi, made a tactical move by writing a letter to Kgosi Bathoen II in June 1956 to underscore the appreciation and respect accorded Mongwaketse as he referred to him. In asking the Kgosi to address the conference be wanted to secure his support and soften him, particularly by ending his letter humbly, *ka boikokobetso* (humbly). In his reply, the Kgosi was most accommodating and wrote back to the General Secretary in Setswana as the latter had done. *'Ke keletso eame e tona thata gore mo dilon tse di dirwan ke bagaetsho go tsamaela kwa*

T.W. Motlhagodi

pele ke nne ke tsene mo go tsonne', (translated as, 'It is my sincere hope that all that is done by people involves me fully') (DCK). The early founders of the Association would have listened to such utterances with disbelief, if one recalls that he was one of those members who had no faith in the local teachers and their ability to run an organisation.

Change of Attitude: The Turbulent 1960s

It should be clear by now that whatever controversies the teachers were involved in did not derive from selfish interests. Central to their queries were matters of educational concern, the interests of their pupils, and the desire to improve the standard of education in the BP. That is why from the outset they sought representation on such bodies as the School Committees and the African Advisory Council (AAC) in order to be involved in decision making and to influence current thinking.

The 1960s will go down in the history of the teachers' organisation in this country as a period further strengthening of the BPATA. Those years saw the emergence of a concerted objection on the part of the Association to those policies which were seen to either retard the advancement of education in the BP or to frustrate the teachers' efforts. To some who had received their education in South Africa, the writings of Dr C.T. Loram in the 1920s were still ringing clearly. The writings of Loram, who was an Inspector of Schools in Natal Province of South Africa, depicted in this region (Southern Africa) the feelings of those who thought that offering any form of education to the African was misguided, while others felt that schooling would only promote colonial policies. Such an attitude, as existed then, was fuelled by the able pen of Loram, who, incidentally was a member of the Phelps-Stokes Commission that examined and made recommendations on the state of education in Africa in the early 20s. He wrote:

> 'In his raw state – the native leads an arcadian existence. His simple wants, food, cattle and women are easily satisfied. He is more moral than his educated brother. His few savage virtues, courtesy, charity – shine in use, and above all he is no trouble to the white man (Loram, 1917).

It seemed then the height of folly to send him to school for:

> 'As soon as he goes to school, he puts on unhealthy European clothes – his thin veneer of European civilisation makes him wish to consort with low class white men, from whom he learns many vices, he refuses to be subservient to the European and becomes the swaggering, impudent and universally detested school kaffir' (Loram, 1917).

Loram's utterances were even echoed in the BP. Sir Charles Rey, the Resident Commissioner in this country, had this to say on the occasion of the death of Kgosi Gaborone in 1931.

'...he was a wonderfully picturesque figure. 110 years old, and a splendid type of dignified courteous chief of old times before they were spoilt by European custom and clothes and education and all that rot' (Parsons and Crowder, 1988).

As late as 1975, the words of C.T. Loram were echoed by Monica Wilson and Leonard Thompson when they discussed the growth of towns and the rise of industries in South Africa. The claim was that the existing labour scarcity might indeed have been expected since it was not likely that a savage people, who before the advent of Europeans lived their own lives, in which industrial employment had no place, should at once acquire the needs and habits of industrial communities and come out voluntarily to meet the labour demands. 'The only pressing needs of a savage are those of food and sex, and the condition of life in Africa are such that these are as a rule easily supplied' (Wilson and Thompson, 1970). The views expressed by Loram and Wilson and Thomson are difficult to accept coming from scholars of their calibre. Yet there is nothing new in their utterances about the Africans and education. It is simply the failure to explain an intricate situation and resort to stereotypical racial innuendos. It is an attempt to see the African in a dim light.

Yet we must not lose sight of the fact that in the midst of these crude labels, there were voices of sanity who realised the African's thirst for education and did not hesitate to make their views known.

> 'Surely we who affect to prize education so highly have no right to deny it to the Native. Should we not, rather, encourage this laudable ambition by every means in our power' (Loram. 1917).

The coming to power of the Nationalist Government in South Africa in 1948 had cast a menacing shadow on the education of the Africans in that country. Perhaps to many of the latter day Nationalists, the views of Dr Loram held sway and now it was time to implement these dreams. By 1949, a Commission to look at African education had been set up under the Chairmanship of Dr W.W. Eislen. Its terms of reference were clear, and were intended to exclude African education from the education stream of other races in that country. Nothing could have been more diabolical and mischievous than separating people who belonged together on an educational plane. But more grave, it was most inhuman to deny a people the right to acquire the education they needed so urgently for their own development. The 'Bantu', as Africans were called, had to be prepared through education for a particular station in society, since they were different from other races and cultures, and in many other ways. Dr H.F. Verwoerd, the architect of Bantu education must have rocked South African parliament with his eloquence in an attempt to show that the 'Bantu' deserved a different treatment. It is fair at this point to say that Loram was a captive of the racial prejudice of his time. The Nationalists who came to power in 1948 were trapped in their political ideology of discrimination on the basis of colour. It was the policy of apartheid that brought them to power. Contrary to what the BPATA stated when they wrote to the Director of Education, H. Gardiner, and the Chairman of the African Advisory Council, Kgosi Bathoen II, they wanted to see a type of education in the BP that would make an African child an equal to the European child. The Eiselen Commission recommended that educational practice, 'must recognise that it has to deal with a "Bantu child", that is a child trained and conditioned in "Bantu" language and imbued with values, interests and behaviour pattern learned at the knee of a "Bantu mother"' (Horrell, 1964).

Dr Verwoerd, then the Minister of Native Affairs, took these utterances of the Eiselen Commission and used them in parliament to support the Nationalists' policy of apartheid when he said, 'Native education should be controlled in such a way that it should be in accord with the policy of the State ... Good racial relations cannot exist when the education is given under the control of people who create wrong expectations on the part of the native himself' (Horrell, 1964). Education, to him, was to train and teach the *Bantu* in accordance with their opportunities in life and according to the sphere in which they live. According to him the role of education was to produce a subservient and colourless African. This was the evolution of the 'Green Pastures' theory wherein the blacks would never graze. The same sentiments were expressed in 1959 by another Minister of Bantu Education, W.A. Mares, and yet another exponent of segregation. He said that the 'Bantu must be so educated that they do not want to become imitators of the whites, but that they will want to remain essentially Bantu' (Horrell, 1964).

The changes that were taking place in that country were bound to affect the standard of education in the BP, since many young Batswana attended school in that country. Botswana had suffered many years of neglect educationally and the BP Administration counted on South Africa accommodation for Batswana students in their schools. After all, this was the most logical thing since the BP and her sister territories of Basutoland and Swaziland would be incorporated into South Africa. Bantu education was rejected by the African populace and other racial groups in that country but with teachers' organisations spearheading the resistance, the BPATA in this country was swift to make its objections known.

It was the rejection of Bantu education by the National Government that stung the BPATA most. On that occasion in 1960, the General Secretary of BPATA, J.I.B. Sekgwa, wrote a letter to the Director of Education, J. Gardiner, copied it to the Chiefs and the Divisional Commissioners in the North and South. He notified the Director of Education of the BPATA's representatives, namely; P. Matoane, R.S. Molomo and T.W. Motlhagodi, who were to sit in the Committee that was to draw up the BP Primary School Syllabus. In addition to this, the General Secretary conveyed the Associations' concern about the type of education that the BP should offer – a non-discriminatory type of education fit for all the citizens of this land, where there would neither be black, white or yellow children. The Association had as their major point equity at its very best. Some members of the Association had experienced the humiliating and crippling effects of discrimination in education from neighbouring countries. To introduce those sickly policies in the BP which, as we know by the beginning of the 1960s, had its eyes set on independence and thereby self determination. The Association unequivocally expressed its dislike for Bantu Education in the Union of South Africa.

Rev. J.I.B. Sekgwa

The Director of Education, in reply to the General Secretary's letter, informed him that while the membership of the Syllabus Committee had not been fixed, the BPATA would be invited to send two members representing primary and secondary education. The General Secretary was also informed that a number of subject subcommittees were likely to be appointed on which teachers would be requested to serve.

The Director of Education further confirmed that the aim of education was to equalise standards in the schools in the Territory. He pointed out that in African secondary schools, the syllabuses were identical with those of European schools elsewhere. However, his view that complete identity in all primary schools was undesirable since the Standard 6 results were entrance to secondary education. For instance, he singled out vernacular teaching and the teaching of English as a second language. Nevertheless he promised to convey to the Committee the Association's views.

It should be noted that since the 1960s were the years when the Association was seeking to establish itself as an organisation and gain respect, this move manifested itself in the strengthening of relations between the Association and local Tribal Administration by taking advantage of the favourable climate of reason. One of these instances was when the Association, through the General Secretary, and after the General Conference of the BPATA held at the Teacher Training College in Lobatse, agreed to put before the Chairman of the African Advisory Council their requests.

The requests were far reaching and showed serious thinking on the part of the teachers. For instance, they suggested that arrangements be made with tribal administrations to establish social centres in the big centres of the BP. Furthermore, where tribal administrations owned trucks, school children attending sports and music competitions be conveyed in these trucks without pay, and in the event of the tribe not being in possession of such trucks, to pay transport costs incurred on such a trip. It is interesting to note that thirty years later these sentiments were expressed in the North East District by the District Council Secretary. Finally, that arrangements be made for teachers' representation on all school committees, as was the practice in other parts of the BP.

The Chairman's reply (Kgosi Bathoen II) was encouraging, but not helpful. He acknowledged the legitimacy of the requests made by the Association for discussion in the African Advisory Council. His reaction was that the items seemed to be purely of a local concern and should correctly and rightly be referred to the tribal administrations and school committees respectively. He pointed out that such matters did not affect the central government and it would be improper to include them for discussion in the Council. Kgosi Bathoen's reply did underline his deep knowledge of central administration procedures and he did not want to embarrass the teachers and himself. However, what emerged clearly was that Kgosi Bathoen of the 1960s was a different man from that of the 1930s when the attempt to form the Association was sounded. At the same time, the teachers must have been happy with their performance for they were being treated with respect by a high ranking officer in the Office of the African Advisory Council.

Interestingly, the respect accorded the BPATA was even extended to the Bangwaketse Teachers' Association by the *Kgosi e kgolo ya Bangwaketse*. The existent relations between Kgosi Bathoen II and the BPATA was fascinating in that he was deluged with invitations to deliver addresses at the conferences of the Association and local branches. At times he almost acted like the official of the Association for the General Secretary of the BPATA, J.I.B. Sekgwa. He took advantage of this cooperation by communicating through him the information for the Bangwaketse Branch. A clear example was that of the letter whereby the General Secretary informed the Kgosi of the conference which was to be held at Kanye in June 1961. It is possible that the swift action to inform the teachers was prompted by the honour given him to address the same conference after the official opening by the Resident Commissioner. His reply was prompt and stated that *'Go boitumelo go utlwa fha Motlotlegi a tlaabo a le teng'* (It is heartening to know that the Resident Commissioner will be present) (DCK). The Ngwaketse School Headteachers were rounded up by the late K.R. Bome, a loyal friend of Kgosi Bathoen, for he wanted them to realise the role the Tribal Administration was prepared to play within the BPATA. Such action was bound to boost the image of the Tribal Administration. The letter of invitation to the conference from *Kgosi e Kgolo* underscored the warm relationship between him and the Association in general.

The conference held at Kanye in 1961 must have raised the expectations of the teachers, for in November of that year a Select Committee on Examination Leave of the BPATA Ngwaketse Branch submitted a letter to the

Secretary of the School Committee regarding examination leave. The teachers questioned the difficulty involved lately in securing examination leave since in the past there was no such problem. Obviously, the teachers saw such a stringent measure as an attempt to interfere with their academic progress. In fact, such action was high handed on the part of the School Committee at a time when the academic qualifications of the majority of teachers were very low. What prompted the teachers to adopt a hard line was the letter of 9 November 1961, which challenged them to account for the lost time of the pupils during the time of teachers' examinations.

Delegation at the Kanye conference, 1961

Obviously, the teachers did not pull their punches on seeing this letter. First, they interpreted it to mean that no examination leave would be granted. Secondly, they felt that it was intended to discourage teachers from improving their qualifications. Thirdly, the tone of the letter was callous and indifferent to the needs and interests of the teachers. Further, the Select Committee stated in their submission that the attitude was in conflict with the generally accepted policy of the country, which purported to foster happy and friendly relations among all sections of the people: employers and employees, rich and poor. The Association was naturally perturbed at the trend of events because we are of the opinion that examination leave should be a right which every progressive teacher should enjoy. Looking back, one feels that teachers should have been encouraged to further their studies, particularly in a country where for some reason difficult to explain, teaching as a profession was looked down upon. To create healthy and acceptable conditions would have encouraged younger Batswana to join the profession since it held hope for them. In the minutes of the Bangwaketse School Committee held in Kanye on 27 February 1962, and in the Director of Education's Circular Memorandum (E362/1) of 16 December 1961 it was resolved that the teachers should apply for leave in good time so that satisfactory arrangements could be made. It was stressed that, this is a privilege not a right as some teachers think, and that each case was to be considered on its merit. No doubt, the teachers were triumphant.

However congenial the relations were between Kgosi Bathoen II and the BPATA, the Ngwaketse Teachers' Association had from time to time been reminded who the Kgosi was. They had to know their proper place, for the letter of the Select Commission must have annoyed the Kgosi, particularly the assertion that there was some external influence which was calculated to keep low, the already 'low standard of qualification of teachers'. The teachers then were summoned to the famous King George V Memorial Hall and the signatories of the letter were asked to read their letter and explain its intention. Whatever may be said about the merits of the gathering, it was unfair to hold the signatories responsible for a letter which was written on behalf of the local branch of the BPATA. The signatories including, S.M. Gabatshwane, P.M. Matoane, K.P. Mosiieman and W. Mzondeki, were perfectly correct in refusing to read or explain the letter without the mandate from the teachers.

The Kgosi unleashed some hard words and abhorred the fact that the teachers had adopted an attitude which he considered defiant, discourteous and inconsiderate, and above all 'a challenge to his authority by people who are supposed to be educated with some sense of responsibility'. It is quite clear from the tone of his address that he had sensed in the teachers an ulterior motive.

He lashed out and produced some documents showing some misdemeanours and acts of commission and omission by the teachers. It is sometimes difficult to understand why the Kgosi resorted to these intimidatory tactics when dealing with the teachers. Possibly he wanted to make them aware that they were his subjects in spite of their professional qualifications. They were, in his eyes, essentially tribesmen. His actions were to some extent fuelled by the petty and frivolous reporting by some headteachers who should have disciplined their staff in a manner befitting professionals. For instance, was the issue of late coming by staff a matter to be reported to the Kgosi, who had an array of responsibilities to attend to? The scathing report on a teacher who left the school without permission to sit for examinations was a serious and unacceptable behaviour that needed attention. The Kgosi, a typical hard liner warned the teachers 'to hold their mouths' and not to lay themselves open to unnecessary criticism and rebuke.

Despite the setbacks experienced by the BPATA, steady headway was made. One of the far reaching recommendations made by the Association early in the 1960s was the need to establish a Unified Teaching Service. The teachers were aware of the disabilities they were subjected to as a result of the absence of such a structure within the Department of Education. The idea emanated from the general dissatisfaction about the state of affairs in primary schools which led to doubts about the efficacy of the present system of control. This prompted an inquiry during the first meeting of the African Council in May 1961 as to the advisability of switching to a system of central control. For, since 1931, the non-professional control of primary schools had rested largely with Tribal School Committees.

The suggestion that responsibility for administration of primary education should be taken away from Tribal School Committees and handed over to the Education Department was turned down on the grounds that 'no advantage would be gained by changing to a system of central control and that in fact it might be a retrogressive step ... and that local interest in education might be destroyed by depriving Tribal Administration of their most important responsibility' (DCK). Without any hesitation, this was a very strong point for it sought to involve the community in the education of their children. This trend was maintained to the mid 1960s when Botswana gained its independence, and even after 1966 communities worked hand in hand with the Ministry of Local Government and Lands to participate in the management of primary schools. That philosophy of self-help has been extended to the present Community Junior Secondary Schools which have mushroomed in this country in the past few years. Whatever the shortcomings of this ideal, it has helped Batswana to understand the workings of an education system.

The need for improving the efficacy of the working of the present system was fully accepted, however, it was felt that the introduction of the Rusbridger Report would be one way of achieving this. The establishment of a United Teaching Service implied that all teachers would be members of a common service from which they would be posted to government and non-government schools. Salaries and conditions of service would be related to qualifications and would be uniform throughout the territory. Both teachers and employers would have clearly defined rights and obligations. 'Establishment of such service would correct many of the anomalies which now cause discontent and which have arisen because conditions of service with local authorities differ from district to district'. It was felt that this would enable the Department of Education to exercise much closer control over all staffing matters.

The coming of the Rusbridger Commission which led to the revision of the teachers' salaries was a remarkable event since the major handicap of the BPATA had been a financial one. Rusbridger came from the United Kingdom at the insistence of Sir Rex Surridge to examine the plight of African teachers. So, in 1959, for the first time, allowances and conditions of service for the civil servants, as a result of Sir Rex Surridge's recommendation were reviewed. It must be noted that the teachers were left out even when Fitzgerald, the first ever Commissioner reviewed the salaries and conditions of service of the civil service in the BP from 1947 to 1948. Surridge urged that 'a full investigation to cover all teachers in the territories ... should be undertaken by an educationist with at least one financially minded member to assist him'. The High Commissioner accepted the recommendation and the Rusbridger Commission, comprising G.H. Rusbridger the educationist, and H. Weber the finance specialist, was appointed.

The appointment of the Commission was a milestone in the history of BPATA. The many teachers who were affected by the Rusbridger Report (Rusbridger and Weber, 1959) remember it with great respect. In the press statements of 1960 and 1961, it was hailed as 'one of the most important events of the present time in the BP'. The significance of the event was that it provided the inducements which enabled the government to attract the qualified teachers so urgently needed if the schools were to give their best. Furthermore, in framing their recommendations, the Commission had particular regard to two main points. First, that competition for the services of people with a good standard of education, especially at the post matriculation level was very keen in the territory and with increasing political and economic development was likely to be intensified. Secondly, that the existing disparity between the salaries paid to teachers in government service with educational standards and those paid to teachers in tribal and other non-government assisted or maintained schools had to be reviewed (BNB 803).

The commission stressed that any additional funds for education should be devoted to ensuring that all teachers regardless of their employing agency, be met in full or in part from public funds which were placed on common basic scales appropriate to their qualifications. Also, that special regard should be given to the need to attract and retain more qualified teachers. As was expected of the Commission, it also addressed the plight of the unqualified teachers and recommended: 'that better salaries than those in force must be offered ... on the other hand it is hoped younger and more promising untrained teachers will proceed for training after a comparatively short time in service' (BNB 803).

To crown its noble work, the Commission recommended increments for higher qualifications and appropriate experience, and certain special allowances to teachers in responsible positions. These and related recommendations were met with approval by the teachers at different levels. The relief brought by the Rusbridger Commission urged the Association on to more vigorous action. The teachers never looked back and embarked on the road to negotiation to improve their lot.

It was in these circumstances that the Association had raised the issue. Sometimes the Association acted rather rashly in order to drive home their impatience in a situation where the Administration seemed unconcerned. Fortunately, the new Director of Education, C.J. Hunter, saw eye to eye with the BPATA in their endeavour to extract from Government decent conditions of service. For instance, in his memorandum to the member of Tribal Affairs and Social Services commenting on the Association's letter, undated and received on 3 July 1962, he cautioned that in spite of the intemperate language and at times slightly hysterical tone, he confirmed that some of the grievances and problems referred to were real and by no means imaginary. Hunter simply understood the plight of the teachers and they must in turn have cried for a thousand Hunters. So concerned was Hunter to ameliorate the suffering of teachers that be intimated that a Unified Teaching Service had been introduced in Swaziland and thought it was time the BP followed suit.

Despite these assurances and deep concern by the Director of Education, the Association was not prepared to let grass grow under its feet. They condemned the discrimination existing in the teaching profession in the BP as illustrated by differences in salaries and allowances of teachers in government and non-government schools. It is fair to mention that some of the grievances raised then, such as study leave, the establishment, management and control of pension or provident funds continued long after Botswana gained her independence in 1966.

One must understand why the Association at that stage was not prepared to pull its punches, for in all intents and purposes, the honeymoon was over. It set its mind on the establishment of the Unified Teaching Service which had been recommended by Rusbridger and Weber as the only way out of the impasse. It rejected outright the view that the introduction of the service was impracticable, since it had been implemented successfully in other territories. The Association in its characteristic stance, gave the Government three months in which to come up with something reasonable. In a thinly veiled threat, the Association warned that, 'it would be displeased to have to think of some other form of action'. The latest challenge to Government was issued by E.R. Maritshane, the General Secretary, supported by the President of the Association, R.I. Setshwane. To solicit support outside the BPATA, a copy of the communication was copied to Mr Seretse Khama, later Sir Seretse Khama and the first President of the Republic of Botswana. The teachers' tactics worked, for the Director for the first time, conceded the possibility of establishing a Unified Teaching Service. But the Association would have fought more viciously if it had known that it would take more than thirty years for such a structure to come into existence.

If anything, this chapter has shown that numerous problems faced the Association at the beginning, but it is fair to say that there was always the light at the end of the tunnel. With the passage of time they won the support of individuals within Government, particularly the Department of Education and successive Directors of Education, from Dumbrell to Hunter. The period immediately after Hunter, when Smith and Dr Gaositwe Chiepe came to power, can be said to be a period of enlightenment. Dr Chiepe, many will remember, had joined the Department of Education after completing her BSc. degree at Fort Hare in South Africa. She worked first as a lecturer at the

Kanye Teacher Training College. Later, she was appointed to the rank of Education Officer and worked at the Imperial Reserve in Mafeking. After that, she was elevated to the rank of Deputy Director of Education, and she finally became the Director of Education before A.W. Kgarebe took over from her. It is therefore, not surprising that she came to understand the plight of teachers in this country, because she had been immersed in the culture of education of her land of birth. At the time of writing, she is Minister of Education. She obviously comes at a time when the education system has grown tremendously and the problems thus generated continue to agitate the minds of many.

These two Directors of Education supported the Association to the hilt. Many of the grievances that had become perennial issues at teachers' conferences like sick leave, maternity leave, lack of promotion, undue suspension and dismissal of teachers, and management and control of provident funds, received attention. The Association's grievances ceased to be considered frivolous. The member for Tribal Affairs and Social Services, Kgosi Bathoen II had undergone a tremendous transformation and was supportive to the teachers. The Association above all had projected a different image from that commonly anticipated, namely, its quest for high salaries. The Association, while it guarded jealously any form of interference in their legitimate rights, nonetheless demonstrated their commitment to improvement of the standard of education locally 'by raising the standard of efficiency of teachers through the improvement of school methods and school organisation' (S252/2/1). This was demonstrated by their desire to monitor syllabuses at the primary level, and efforts to gain membership in the decision making bodies, such as the School Committees and the Board of Advice on African Education.

Conclusion

The years 1941 to 1959 were indeed years of consolidation, in that BPATA's existence had become a *fait accompli*. The role that Dumbrell played, and the support he gave the President of BPATA, Mpotokwane, bore fruit, for the Association had received a measure of recognition and that was demonstrated by their participation in some decision making structures.

CHAPTER THREE

The Problems and Successes of the BPATA (1954–1969)

This chapter will deal with the triumphs and trials of the BPATA during the 1960s. These were years of hope and fulfilment for the Association in many respects. The 1950s from which it had emerged were hard and uneventful. The aspirations of the Association had not been met except for the salary review which followed the Rusbridger-Weber Commission in 1959–60. These were years of hope in that the Association was growing in stature and there was the realisation on the part of Government that teachers were the Administration's ally on educational matters. The emergence of political parties (BIP in 1954, BPP in 1960, BDP in 1962 and the BNF in 1965) during the formative years in this country made many focus their attention on the standard of education. The other factor which raised the Association's hopes was the political development from within the Territory and the possibility of self government culminating in the full independence of the BP. The outlook of the Association was influenced by those changes and the teachers became even more militant for they hoped that some of the teachers who were preparing to join politics would be sympathetic to their cause.

With these developments and impending changes in view, the teachers set out to organise themselves in order to make a meaningful contribution particularly in the unfolding of the education system in the country as a whole. There was an endless clamour from various quarters to examine the curricular offerings. Many seemed to think that it was a matter of throwing out the British system of education and bringing in a brand new kind of education with a Botswana flavour. The other matter that was taken up seriously by the Association was the desire to join hands with the other teacher organisations beyond the borders of the BP. Such a desire resulted in the formation of the High Commission Territories Federal Teachers' Association (HCTFTA) with Basutoland and Swaziland. Their participation in that important organisation was revealed in a letter dated 22 December 1960 and written by the newly elected General Secretary, T.W. Motlhagodi to the High Commission Territories Office in Pretoria, South Africa. It informed the High Commissioner that at a Conference of representatives of Basutoland, Bechuanaland and Swaziland Teachers' Association held at Maseru (the capital of Lesotho) in December 1960, it had been decided that the Association should form a Federation. The letter contained a list of resolutions passed by the HCTFTA at the same conference. The office bearers were a colourful selection of personalities from the three territories. They were the President General, G.P. Ramorebodi from Basutoland, Deputy President General, E.R. Maphalala from Swaziland, Secretary General, T.W. Motlhagodi from Bechuanaland and Assistant Secretary General, P.M. Matoane from Bechuanaland, Treasurer, E.S. Mohapi, from Basutoland and Editor and Press Secretary, R.S. Molomo from Bechuanaland (S252/3).

In order to give the newly formed Federation publicity, copies of the letter to the High Commissioner were sent to the Resident Commissioners, Paramount Chiefs and Directors of Education in the three territories.

The aims and objectives of the HCTFTA, whose motto was *not by favour but by merit,* were broad, varied and far reaching, and underpinned their desire to promote a sound education system for the nationals of their countries. Their aims and objectives among other things sought to develop unity, mutual understanding and cooperation among the teachers of the three territories; to promote the professional welfare of teachers within the territories; to promote further education in the High Commission Territories through discussions, reading of papers and lectures; to cooperate with and affiliate with world bodies concerned with education such as UNESCO, the World Confederation of the Organisation of the Teaching Profession (WCOTP); and to establish a legal defence fund for the protection and promotion of the rights of teachers in the High Commission Territories (S252/3). The teachers' efforts were admirable for it showed their keenness to set their sights beyond their own narrow confines and join hands with teachers throughout the world. They must have been aware of the shrinking world and the political changes that were taking place in other parts of Africa – changes which were bound to influence the thinking in Southern African and particularly in the three High Commission Territories.

The teachers' communication to the High Commission with regard to the formation of the HCTFTA was not welcome if judged by the utterances from the Imperial Reserve in Mafikeng. The reason was not far to seek, for whenever teachers wished to improve their lot their activities attracted a lot of suspicion. The officer at the Department of Education in Mafikeng denied any knowledge of the formation of the HCTFTA at a meeting held at Maseru. The Resident Commissioner in Mafikeng expressed his discomfort with the formation of the Association in his letter to the High Commissioner when he stated that there was 'no reason why the Association should be treated as a negotiating body in territorial matters superseding the Bechuanaland Protectorate Teachers' Association' (S252/3). The BPATA was therefore expected to continue to submit for consideration by Government any matters which in the opinion of the local Association required attention. While he saw the importance in the formation of the Territorial Association, the encouragement of the BP Association had to take priority over the recognition of an inter-territorial association. What seemed to disturb the bureaucrats at the Imperial

Reserve was the fact that they had learned subsequently that the initial aim of the delegates was to promote joint action in order to expedite the implementation of the Rusbridger Commission proposals. The significance of the Rusbridger Commission lay in that the teachers were left out, even when Fitzgerald, who came before Sir Rex Surridge, reviewed the salaries and conditions of service. The Commission, therefore, must be seen as a 'healing of old wounds exercise'. The recommendation indeed hit the nail on the head. The teachers felt that the Administration shared their concerns. The Rusbridger Commission resulted from a recommendation made by Sir Rex, who at the beginning of 1959 completed a review of the whole range of salaries, allowances and conditions of service in the civil service in the Territories of Basutoland, the BP and Swaziland. Sir Rex had stated that the Directors of Education had been experiencing 'considerable difficulty in recruiting qualified teaching personnel at the present salaries...' (BNB 803).

Therefore he had suggested that a full investigation, to cover all the teachers in the territories should be undertaken to review their salaries in the light of the Government salaries revision. Rusbridger was made aware that the disparity between the salaries paid to teachers in Government Service and those employed in non-Government assisted or maintained schools was the basic cause of the serious discontent among non-Government teachers in Basutoland and particularly in Bechuanaland. Although there were very few Government teachers employed, the non-Government teachers were aware of the 'higher salaries which are payable to Government employees of similar educational standards' (BNB 803). The significance of the Rusbridger report was that not only did he advocate parity between non-Government and Government teachers, he strongly recommended equal pay for men and women. At the same time he pointed out that the question of equal pay could not be considered in isolation, for, 'If and when the principle of equal pay is accepted for the public service ... the position of women teachers will need consideration' (BNB 803). Significantly it was the first commission to attempt to eliminate discrimination on the basis of colour, for one of its recommendations stated that, 'irrespective of race, basic salary scales for various grades of teachers should be related to qualifications' (BNB 803). The teachers had taken a commendable stand and though this was recognised by the Department of Education, the same Department expressed the view that while the quality of the Swazi and Basuto office bearers was unknown, the Batswana were considered mediocre at best. That was an attempt in fact to discourage the local teachers' association to work with foreign teachers as this might threaten the authority of the Department of Education. Nonetheless, the High Commissioner would have found it difficult to refuse to recognise the body. However, he could confine their activities and resolutions to general matters affecting the three territories strictly to subjects of an educational nature. The teachers had to be reminded that while there was no objection to international exchanges of views particularly in professional matters it had to be understood that the international association 'had no power to negotiate with the BP Government'. The BPATA was categorically advised to put matters to the Government and take stock of its position and organise itself effectively rather than dissipate its energies in inter-territorial activities. Obviously the BP Government did not wish to see the association influenced by foreign teachers' organisations. The association was to be 'non-political' as Dumbrell had put it.

It was against this background threat and admonition that the Association geared itself to make the government pay heed to their grievances. We are aware at this stage, if we refer to the findings of the Rusbridger Commission referred to earlier, that the Associations grievances were genuine and not imaginary. For instance, the Association was disturbed by the disparity between salaries and conditions of service for teachers in non-Government schools. 'The scales of salaries for non-Government teachers had for many years been less than the scales for Government teachers or for persons with similar qualifications in the Civil Service...' (BNB 803). Though there had been some increases since 1947, they had not kept pace with the improvements in the Civil Service scales.

Cost of living allowances had been granted in Basutoland and Swaziland to aid teachers and had been revised from time to time. The rates were 12% for married teachers and 6% for single teachers in Basutoland and 10% for married teachers and 5% for single teachers in Swaziland (BNB 803). In addition to this, double increments were introduced in Swaziland in 1956 in order to close the gap between the Mission and Government salaries. In Bechuanaland, only small increases in salaries in Tribal Schools were awarded in 1952. The disparities were real and problematic for the teachers in this country. The disparities were bound to lower morale among teachers and they decided to fight against what they saw as a naked mismarriage of justice from that time to the close of the 1970s. The other cause of discontent for teachers in Bechuanaland was the absence of the Unified Teaching Service which they believed could cure some of the ills encountered by the Association. As we shall see later, the Association's insistence persuaded the Administration to think seriously about it and to finally implement it.

Furthermore, the teachers objected to being denied benefits as tribal employees. These benefits, such as proper housing, pensions, generous leave conditions, better promotion prospects and protection against unfair dismissals were enjoyed by teachers in government schools. All these anomalies would be removed through the establishment of the Unified Teaching Service which had been recommended by Rusbridger. It was in the light of these anomalies and mounting tension that the Association in 1961 invited the Resident Commissioner to open their conference. The invitation provided the opportunity for the Department of Education to tell the teachers of their displeasure at the formation of the suspicious High Commission Territories Federal Teachers' Association. The teachers were to be told that it was futile to think that they could work with teachers' organisations in Swaziland and Basutoland since the territories had little in common. This was a strange thought, since the three territories had worked closely together on different issues and levels, including education, as the Directors of these territories consulted extensively.

The 1961 Conference held at Kanye came at a time when there was a lot of suspicion between the Administration and teachers. There were innumerable anomalies and recommendations made to ease the lot of the teachers that had been ignored. This attitude incensed the teachers in the extreme. The Kanye Conference was followed by a meeting of the teachers' representatives and officials from the Department of Education in 1962 in Mafikeng. Again, the Association reiterated what they considered discriminatory practices by the Administration at the Imperial Reserve. The Department of Education repudiated the charges of deliberate delay in order to perpetuate the existent anomalies. The teachers had genuine grievances, but one must appreciate the invidious position in which the Department of Education found itself. For instance, for the salaries of teachers they were dependent on British Government aid. The Department of Education appreciated the anomalies which patently existed. But no one could deny that other problems were within the reach of the Department of Education, such as the establishment of the Unified Teaching Service and the treatment of unmarried lady teachers who fell pregnant.

However, the Mafikeng meeting produced positive results in that the recommendation made in the Rusbridger Report that a delegation consisting of the Director of Education and the representatives of the school proprietors and the Teachers' Association visit one or more of the countries where a unified service had been established. The Association must have been delighted with their success and were prepared to press on with their demands. The Department of Education, while unable to meet the teachers' requests, was nonetheless aware of the growing militancy that was building up among its members. There was, no doubt, a realisation in the Department of Education that the 'anomalies now so clearly apparent and frequently referred to by teachers, had to be addressed even if they did not press for a general level of salaries for all teachers as high as those now paid to government servants' (S252/2/2). This would ensure that funds available were shared out in a more equitable manner.

The establishment of a Unified Teaching Service was the most urgent matter which was to receive attention. The administration revealed that arrangements had been made to visit Lusaka in Zambia to study the service on the spot. The Director of Education recommended the formation of a committee to consider the regulations for a Unified Teaching Service. Its members were: the Director of Education, two representatives of the Teachers' Association and two representatives of the Tribal School Committee. In recognition of the teachers demands, and insistence on their grievances being addressed, it was decided to send the following to the Department of Education in Mafikeng: P.M. Matoane (President), R. Setshwane (Vice–President), M.K. Segokgo (General Secretary) and J.B. Gabaake and W. Mzondeki (S252/2/2).

P.M. Matoane (standing)

The high powered delegation must have been seen as a threat to the Director of Education who might have felt that he would not be able to handle it. It is not surprising that he resorted to some derisive tactics to discredit some members of the delegation by stating that 'Messrs Matoane and Mzondeki are not local teachers' (S252/2/2). Matoane was labelled an ex-Johannesburger, while the other three teachers were described as Protectorate Batswana. Mzondeki was labelled a Xhosa who had come across from the Republic of South Africa. They were described as having come 'with obvious chips on their shoulders and in my opinion both are somewhat dubious characters' (S252/2/2). As if to cover his nefarious tracks he revealed that 'in fairness to them however, I must say that their chips were much less evident at the meeting in my office than they normally are' (S252/2/2). Again, as if to push the thin edge of the wedge, he described the three local teachers as reasonable and responsible men. The General Secretary, M.K. Segokgo, whose credentials were sound with the newly emergent local political party, and likely to play an important part later was singled out as 'an extremely good teacher.' (In fact he later became a prominent member of the Botswana Democratic Party and even became the Minister of Mineral Resources and Water Affairs).

In fact, it is interesting to note that the affairs of the Association came under heavy attack as they were said to be managed in a most unbusinesslike manner and 'in spite of protestations to the contrary I doubt if it is yet fully representative' (S252/2/2).

It is therefore in this climate of mistrust from the Department of Education that we must consider the efforts of the Association for equity and a fair deal. So poisoned was the atmosphere that even those officers

J.B. Gabaake

M.K. Segokgo

who appreciated the grievances of the teachers tended to turn a blind eye for fear perhaps of being seen to associate with teachers and urge them to make endless demands. Some of these officers had been teachers themselves and they were aware of the disadvantages that teachers were subjected to. So, when the meeting took place on 13 October 1962 between the Resident Commissioner in his office in Mafikeng in the presence of the Government Secretary, the Director of Education and the Acting Member of the Tribal Affairs and Social Services, the teachers were not prepared to pull their punches. The Association's representatives considered it unfair for the Administration to seemingly perpetuate the disparity between the salaries and allowances of teachers in Government and non-Government schools, particularly when the Rusbridger Commission had recommended that all teachers, regardless of the employing agency, whose salaries were met in full or in part from public funds, should be placed on common basic scales appropriate to their qualifications.

The Commissioner was conscious that after examining the position in each territory it was vital 'that there ... be an assured supply of teachers with qualifications at post matriculation level' (BNB 803). It is, therefore, not surprising that the Association in the BP was so incensed by the differences of salary, not only between the Government and non-Government teachers within the country, but to realise how their country lagged behind the other two territories under the control of the British Administration. Obviously, the teachers could not help comparing their plight with teachers in the sister territories. Their discomfort was quite legitimate. In Bechuanaland the disparities were a sensitive issue among non-Government teachers for although there were very few Government teachers employed, the non-Government teachers were aware of the 'higher salaries which are payable to Government employees of similar educational standards' (BNB 803).

Rusbridger went further in tackling the endemic problem of discrimination based on colour when he recommended that irrespective of race, basic scales for various grades of teachers should be related to qualification. There were to be common basic scales throughout the territories and such scales were to provide salaries comparable with those available to persons with similar qualifications in service other than teaching in order to attract more qualified personnel and to retain many of the better qualified teachers already in the profession. He recommended the recognition of additional qualifications acquired by teachers which were considered likely to improve their value as teachers (BNB 803). This last point was a crucial point, for from the inception of teacher training institutions in the BP in the 1930s, teachers were discouraged from improving themselves academically as it would make them concentrate on such studies to the detriment of their teaching requirements. Although attitudes were to change later, there was a lot of resistance if one considers the problems teachers experienced when they applied for leave in order to sit Junior or Senior Certificate examinations. The most far reaching recommendation made by Rusbridger was the acceptance of equal pay for men and women as a result of the representations made to the Commission. At the same time, the Commission pointed out that the question of equal pay could not be considered in isolation for teachers. 'If and when the principle of equal pay is accepted for the public service ... the position of women teachers will need consideration' (BNB 803).

Faced with this barrage of anomalies, one must appreciate the fact that the Association was agitated to the limit. The Ramage Commission came again to look at the salaries of Civil Servants which were low in comparison with the situation in other territories. There was, therefore, need to match the salaries with the cost of living. The recommendation and the implementation of the Ramage Report (Ramage, 1961) had in fact resulted in the anomalous position of teachers in the Government schools who were civil servants, being granted salaries far in excess of those paid to their counterparts in non-Government schools who held similar qualifications. When the Resident Commissioner's Office was challenged on this matter, which was the cause of a deep seated grievance, the reply, and the usual stereotypic answer to the plight of the teachers was that for various reasons it had been decided that teachers in Government schools, as civil servants would be eligible for Ramage salary awards. This was one of those arbitrary decisions which the Association found extremely hard to accept. Could any one blame them for insisting on those issues which to all intents and purposes were unattainable. With clear hindsight, it is fair to say that the Rusbridger Commission recommendations were extremely farsighted, for the suggestions were finally adopted though not without skilful bargaining. The financial situation had improved, along with political enlightenment after Botswana attained her independence in 1966. Such utterances have become part and parcel of later National Development Plans spearheaded by President Seretse Khama and the Government of the day, bent on social justice for all: 'we will continue to be alert against all forms of racial discrimination and will work to preserve a stable and democratic environment...' (National Development Plan, (NDP) 1968–73). Similar sentiments were expressed by Peter Mmusi, the Minister of Finance and Development Planning almost 10 years later. 'Social justice, economic independence and sustained development remain unchanged...' (NDP, 1979–85). Such statements helped to kindle the flame in many a teachers' heart. When, after a protracted discussion the RC told the teachers' representatives that in considering any review of the teachers' salaries it would be necessary to take into account the other many varied development needs of the territory and to 'assess priorities within the limit of funds available' (S252/2/2). The teachers did not feel that the door was closed to further negotiations, but this meant that they would have to wait. Those who taught in non-Government schools know so well that the agony they bore was almost unbearable at times. In the true sense of the word, only the tough survived.

Without doubt, the Association's firm stand on the defence of its members did bear fruit, for the first half of the 1960s saw the development of a meaningful dialogue between the BPATA and the Administration. But things moved very slowly for the teachers and they were losing their patience. At the same time, the new Government brought by the B.Ps self rule was hard put by the British Government's slow response to the varied challenges. The teachers' impatience with Government, though couched in moderate language, was reflected in the General Secretary letter to the director of education in 1964. The Executive Committee, under pressure from the unrelenting membership, demanded the improvement of teachers' salaries and for the first time singled out the plight of the primary school teachers, and the introduction of the Unified Teaching Service which many teachers believed would solve the problems of, for example, provision of housing and medical benefits. The communication concluded in despair as teachers were 'disappointed ... with every representation our delegation made – mere promises none of which is ever carried out' (S252/2/2). Such indifference tended to drive many teachers to despair and frustration. The teachers were incensed by what they considered naked discrimination on the treatment of non-government teachers who were equally involved in the development of the nation.

However mild the General Secretary's letter, it indicated the Association's indignation and frustration. The letter did not pass unnoticed, for a circular was issued by the Secretariat announcing the review of the emoluments by T.M. Skinner. The memorandum No. H.287/8, No. E of 1964 announced that a 'review of teachers salaries will be undertaken following the review of the Public Service salaries' (S252/2/2). It would appear that Skinner stuck to the terms and conditions of his appointment and the teachers who were not in government service were not included. The Association felt this separation from their counterparts very keenly. As if to add insult to injury, the review of the salaries of tribal employees as well was pushed into the distant future. The Department of Education through the Secretariat informed the General Secretary, Mr Segokgo, that a UNESCO Educational Planning Mission was to undertake an examination of the education plans for the territory in June 1964. However, one sees that the Association's effort was making a significant impact and the government was aware of the role the Association could play in shaping the future of the BP's (hence Botswana's) education system. The year 1964 was significant in that the BP attained self-government which was preceded by the movement of offices and personnel from Mafikeng to Gaborone, the new capital of Botswana. The teachers were watching these developments with excitement as they felt an African government would tend to listen sympathetically to their problems. But as many will remember, things were not to be easy even for the new government, for at Independence in 1966, it was faced with numerous problems, particularly economic ones. Even with economic assistance from Britain, their programme was just as extensive. To establish a fully-fledged government with diverse programmes was a monumental task. The only consolation, in-spite of the prolonged agony, was that the Association was given recognition by government as its major partner in the development of education. As later events were to show, the Association (later called the Botswana Teachers' Union) remained true to that ideal.

BPATA and Its Successes

In spite of the numerous problems that faced the Association during the 1960s, it continued to make progress. Perhaps one of the most fortunate things to happen to the Association was the election of P.M. Matoane as the President of the Association. He came from South Africa as a *bona fide* citizen where the role of teachers' organisations was recognised. After the passing of the Bantu Education Act in 1955, the teachers had become even more vocal and uncompromising. So Matoane came to Botswana from a fighting environment to uphold the principles of democracy in a land dominated by apartheid and its repressive laws. He was a forceful, frank, fearless and articulate leader who wished to see the Association fulfil its role as the mouthpiece of all the teachers in the country and he believed that it could do so if given its rightful place by the Department of Education and the Government alike. He solicited their support and sympathy to the utmost but never hesitated to defend the interests of the Association when he felt they were threatened. He spared no effort to challenge what he considered discriminatory and unjust in any guise. To a large extent, through his fearlessness, he often burnt his fingers, and his utterances were becoming unacceptable and a source of irritation to the establishment. Perhaps as a non-citizen he was considered a little dangerous, and therefore, his stay in the country was intolerable. This attitude brought an unexpected end to his sojourn in the country. Without doubt Matoane was a skilful leader who moulded the Association into a fighting unit. In one confidential report he was described by the Office of the Director of Education as a 'capable leader and that the Association had made marvellous progress under his leadership' (S252/2/2). This had, no doubt, earned the Association's respect from all quarters. Matoane's organisational skill had made the Association a respectable body. But as we have seen before, others had an entirely different view of him. They saw him as a rebel rouser who was forever spoiling for war.

It is now time to mention some of the successes of the BPATA, however humble. The first of these was the invitation to the Association in 1961 to elect two members to the Syllabus Committee. This was no insignificant move and a realisation by the Department of Education that the Association could no longer be ignored. Its expertise had to be harnessed for the progress of education in the country. The new members were the two stalwarts of the Association, T.W. Motlhagodi and J.I.B. Sekgwa. Such duty and honour had not been bestowed on the Association before and the gesture must be seen as the breakthrough of all time. This was a recognition of what the Association stood for – the betterment of education. The services of the Association were again called upon by the nomination of a member to the Board of Management and the Disciplinary Committee. The composition of the Committee was interesting in that it had an officer from the Law Office who was to pay heed to the legal aspects of cases brought to the attention of the Disciplinary Committee. This officer was Chairman and three members were nominated by the BPATA and the Secretary of the Teaching Service (S252/2/2). Looked at closely, the Committee was a challenge to the teachers to exercise their administrative skills on educational matters through regular meetings. Consistent with this requirement was the aim to put the onus for maintaining and improving professional standards squarely on the shoulders of the teachers themselves. In essence, the teachers through the BTU were to be accountable for what happened to the education of Batswana children.

The creation of meaningful dialogue between the Department of Education and the Association was further strengthened by the nomination of two representatives of the BPATA. These were P.N. Motsumi and R. Setshwane to serve on the Setswana Orthography Committee. It is significant to note that teachers themselves had taken the initiative in order to counteract the introduction of Setswana literature from South Africa into the BP after Bantu Education had been legalised. The Bantu Education legislation was meant to separate Africans in that country from the mainstream of education in order to prepare them for an inferior status in that society. (The policy of apartheid was the basis for the creation of an education system that would prepare the black child for life in a subordinate society). The matter had been raised when the Association held discussions with the Director of Education in 1963. The item on Orthography appeared on the comments submitted by Assistant General Secretary of the Association, J.B. Gabaake, following the discussions referred to above. The aim was to provide for Tswana authors in the Protectorate the widest possible market for their publications and to ensure that '...orthography used by printers is acceptable on both sides of the border' – that is South Africa and BP (Kutlwano, 1964). The teachers had stated clearly that 'no cooperation or collaboration be sought with the Bantu

Education Department in the framing of our dialect, notwithstanding that we have no publishing houses' (S252/2/2). The new wave of protecting the purity of Setswana was understandable since independence was still two years away in 1964 and many realised the important role Setswana would play after 1966.

Despite the successes registered by the Association, and the fact that the Department of Education was keen to cooperate, many issues were still unresolved. These included the problematic ones like low salaries and salary differentiations between Government and non-government teachers. The thorny question of housing for teachers which, as we know to date, had been hard to resolve as funds had been unavailable. The question of slow and sometimes lack of opportunities for promotion to the inspectorate had also been slow. Sometimes the insensitivity of the Department of Education was disappointing. The Director of Education constantly reminded teachers that applications from non-graduates for appointments as inspectors of schools 'would be considered only if no suitably qualified and experienced graduates were available, but that ambitious non-graduates would doubtless wish to prepare themselves for appointment by studying privately for degrees' (S252/2/2).

One of the questions that lent itself to lengthy debate was that of bursaries and scholarships for European children who enjoyed the privilege to the exclusion of the majority of African children. The teachers believed the practice was discriminatory and demanded that it be discontinued. Indeed, the preferential treatment of European children was unfair but one should bear in mind that the BP was part of the South African political and economic configuration. The discrimination that was applied with impunity in South Africa operated here without question sometimes. For instance, the estimated expenditure during 1963–64 on bursaries for European children was R6700 for primary education and R10 000 for secondary education. Obviously the granting of bursaries outside the Protectorate implied that facilities within the country were either inadequate or unsuitable. It was accepted that the standards in many, if not in most of the Tswana medium primary schools, were so low as to be unacceptable. It was also true that the English speaking children in such schools would be at a disadvantage because of their inability to follow instruction in Tswana. Although the standard in European schools was generally satisfactory, considerable extension of facilities would be required to provide bursaries for all attending schools outside the territory. That would have been a more expensive undertaking than the continuation of the present policy. The wisest course to follow would have been a progressive reduction in the number of bursaries awarded accompanied by improvement of facilities within the Protectorate. The teachers were rightly angered by what they considered the denial of opportunities to Batswana children by the Government. Their protests at such practices were strengthened and supported by the newly formed parties, particularly after the

Protectorate had attained self-government. The idea of democracy, social justice and equity were uppermost in the minds of many. 'My government will be alert against all forms of racial discrimination and will work to preserve a stable and democratic environment' (Transitional Plan for Social and Economic Development, 1966). The system of bursaries was extremely discriminatory. Not only European children received bursaries, but coloured children were also awarded bursaries. For instance, during the 1963–64 financial year R3639 was spent on coloured children who attended school at Kabwe in (Northern Rhodesia) Zambia. Naturally, the teachers were concerned about the lack of equity and fair play. They were not of the view that it was necessary to give priority to the award of scholarships for courses of training which would prepare students for entry to the Public Service, especially in the professional and administrative grades (S252/2/2). Though the preferential treatment that obtained before independence continued after 1966 it became clear that the post colonial Government would not sustain a practice that was unjust and morally indefensible. It had to be discontinued in the face of persistent opposition from the teachers and other quarters.

One of the problems that infuriated the Association was the 'dual session' introduced in the primary schools to cope with the large numbers of young children when classroom accommodation was inadequate. The 'dual session' was an arrangement whereby large classes were divided into two groups and their daily attendance staggered in order to accommodate each group comfortably. In this way, the teacher taught classes of a manageable size. The two disadvantages of the programme were that teachers were overstretched because they taught for longer hours and the pupils' time in the classroom was shortened. As if to give a blessing to this arrangement the Director of Education, in his communication to the education officers, confirmed that in fact 'the dual sessions were already in operation at certain schools and that senior supervisors and supervisors were encouraged to continue the programmes at schools in their areas' (S252/2/2). In spite of all these arrangements the problem of staff, accommodation and equipment varied at each school and, therefore, it was not possible to lay down hard and fast rules about the organisation of dual sessions. It is quite clear that no one believed that the dual sessions arrangement was the answer to the problem, and it was 'regarded as a temporary measure and was not extended beyond the standard two level' (S252/2/2). The Association once again showed their commitment to education when they turned their attention to the Standard 6 examinations. For a long time there had been inconsistencies and different measures adopted in the administration of the same examination. The thrust of the argument was the introduction of some uniformity. As a selection examination, the teachers felt that there was a need to regularise the level of those exposed to the examination by eliminating inequalities emanating from differences in facilities at different schools. The teachers' concern was legitimate in that the success of the country's education system depended on a fair distribution of resources matched with qualified teachers. One is happy to say that through the systematic application of equality, uniformity has been achieved. It is fair to mention that uniformity has been criticised in some quarters as being unrealistic in the light of a huge country like Botswana with different physical regions and wide cultural differences.

The Provident Fund

The Association keenly felt the differentiation between the teachers in Government and non-Government schools, but even more, their exclusion from the non-contributory pension fund. The plea for the introduction of the Provident Fund to cover all teachers in non-Government schools was quite legitimate. It took sometime for the Administration to get into full negotiations on the matter and finally its installation brought relief among the teachers though they were required to pay a percentage of their salary. This was a remarkable achievement, for the first time when the teacher left his job he was entitled to something, albeit small. The only snag that diminished the importance of the Provident Fund was that it excluded the unqualified teachers who had toiled for many years and manned most of the country's schools under the most trying conditions. What was also unacceptable to the Association were the conditions connected with the termination of service. For instance, if a teacher retired at 55 years, the amount standing to his credit in the fund on the closure of the account relating to such a teacher 'shall be paid out of the fund to the depositer'. But where a depositer ceased to be a teacher without the approval of the Director of Education or if his service were terminated as a result of misconduct, such a teacher was entitled only to the amount of the deposits made by him. The employer's contribution including interest would not be paid to the depositer but would be refunded to the employer. It was these discretionary powers of the Director of Education that became the source of irritation for the Association. The teachers detested the fact that they were handled differently from other groups of Government employees. It is again fair to say that after many years of campaigning during the Presidency of Drake Selwe from 1975 to 1986 and many years before, that teachers had become beneficiaries of the non-contributory pension fund. This came after many years of negotiations and sacrifices.

The Foundation of the Unified Teaching Service (UTS)

The present Unified Teaching Service is another good example of the resilience and commitment of the teachers' organisation to strive for the betterment of the education system and the improvement of the terms and conditions of service for the teachers. The UTS was vital to the Association, for it was felt that it could regularise some of the practices which were considered arbitrary. UTS made the teachers aware that not only had they the rights, but they were expected to meet their responsibilities as professionals. It was J.B. Gabaake, the new General Secretary in 1964, who took up the matter of the teaching service with the Director of Education. Though the Association was not happy with the Department of Education's slow reaction at the meeting of the BPATA Executive Committee at Mochudi, the Deputy Director of Education (Mr Dixon) informed the teachers that the Teaching Service Bill would be introduced at the Legislative Council meeting to be held in November 1964. But because of the confidentiality of the draft legislation he did not divulge details of the Bill. In spite of the promise to expedite matters the Association's representatives expressed their disappointment. There was definitely a misguided approach to the teachers' queries, in that within the Department of Education there were individuals who were critical of the teachers' simultaneous handling of their professional and political matters. Nonetheless, there was no way the Association could separate education from political considerations in the light of political changes taking place in the region and the whole of Africa. Such harsh criticisms that teachers were 'intoxicated with their eloquence' (S252/2/2) served no good purpose.

To show the gravity of the teachers' concerns which could no longer be ignored, even the Resident Commissioner attended the meeting at Lobatse of the Executive Committee of the BPATA consisting of P.M. Matoane (President), J.B. Gabaake (General Secretary), M.L.A. Kgasa and E.S. Masisi (Members). Also attending the meeting were two government officers, namely J.A. Allison, and C.J. Hunter (Director of Education) (S252/2/2). While the old concerns were raised, the discussions concentrated on fundamental and crucial issues in keeping with political maturity on the part of the teachers. They were concerned with the image of the profession in the light of the discrepancies within the Administration. For instance, they objected to the offensive nature of the illustrations and the content of Afrikaans books used in English Medium schools inside Botswana. The teachers were consciously guarding against the infiltration of apartheid policy in the country – a policy deliberately tied up with Bantu Education to prepare the black child for a subservient position in society. The differential provision of facilities in the same schools for the teaching of Afrikaans, considered a non-official and foreign language, was considered unreasonable. The apparent freedom from inspection of the English Medium schools was another cause of bitter dispute. In other words the teachers in the English medium schools were not to be subjected to the detested 'police' tactics of the inspectors of education. The teachers detested the apparent absence of laws governing the European Schools and questioned the free education they enjoyed and the wealth of equipment they had while Batswana enjoyed no privileges. The fact that the Ramage Commission (intended for the civil servants) recommended that the salary scales of civil servants be introduced at Moeng College and Government Teacher Training Colleges, irritated the teachers.

It is now quite apparent that more than ever, the Resident Commissioner, like many other prominent persons in Government, was conscious of the numerous dehumanising violations within the education system. His reply at the Lobatse meeting pointed out his concerns. For instance, he revealed that the Government had accepted the 1960 Rusbridger-Weber Report, including the recommendation of a Unified Teaching Service, as a measure toward uniform conditions of service. What must have relieved the teachers' representatives was the mention that a new review of teachers' salaries was imminent. That was the famous Hutton Commission of 1965, and a word on that Commission is now appropriate. The appointment of the Hutton Commission was a landmark in the history of the teachers' struggle for parity with their counterparts in the Civil Service and the improvement of their conditions of service. The most significant thing about the Commission was that it was the 'first salary review charged with consideration of salaries of all teachers...' (Hutton, 1965). Previously, as was indicated above, the salaries of the European teachers and later those African teachers who were appointed to posts in what were called Government schools were considered separately. The Commission's concern, therefore, was the ultimate unification of the teaching service and removal of anomalies which were a constant source of discontent. Another far reaching recommendation to come from the Hutton Report was equal pay for men and women at the insistence of the BPATA instead of 4/5 of those of men that had been recommended by Rusbridger and 5/6 in the case of the Ramage scales. The parity of scales for men and women that we witness today was the pinnacle of triumph for teachers and it was Hutton who helped establish the principle of non-differentiation of salaries by sex. Hutton recommended that the ratio of 5/6 be raised to unity on 1 April 1967. To show the arrogance of Government, when E.K. Okoh became Commissioner in 1970 not all the recommendations of the Hutton Report had been implemented. No doubt the feminists should find comfort in the fact that the teachers had been on their side for some time.

Equally, the Commission grappled with the problems attendant on the working of the Provident Fund which was considered by teachers as a continuing disparity between the two categories of teachers. The Pension Scheme was a viable proposition as it offered a 'valuable protection to a teacher and his family against temptation — to spend immediately considerably more of the lump sum than is wise' (Hutton, 1965). So farseeing was Hutton that he did not confine his recommendations to matters of emoluments and conditions of service, for he had in mind provision to support the future pattern of education and its development. For instance, he advised on the Joint Committee which would include representatives of teachers and representatives of employers, including the voluntary agencies as well as the Ministry of Local Government Authorities. It was felt that such a committee in the face of educational expansion would render unnecessary *ad hoc* decisions and would present the opportunity for an exercise in negotiation. Through such representations, teachers' views would be heard at higher levels in Government circles.

It was recognised that the Education Law was obsolete and that there was need for a new one when the Legislative Council began its life. Since 1938, responsibility for primary education had remained in the hands of tribal administrations which were somehow inadequate. In 1962, a Select Committee of the Legislative Council had been set up and by mid-1964 it had submitted to the Executive Council a new draft Education Bill (S252/2/2). The fact that the section of the Bill dealing with the teaching service had been presented separately and that it was not possible to present a new Education Bill before the elections was unacceptable. It seemed that the earliest such a bill could be presented would be after the introduction of the new Constitution in June 1965. As if to assuage the concerns and the misgivings of the Association, the former General Secretary, Mr Segokgo, who had by 1965 become the Parliamentary Secretary in the Ministry of Labour and Social Services, pleaded with the teachers to appreciate the problems of education facing the Ministry. He promised that the teachers' comments on the first draft of the Bill would be given consideration when the final document was drafted for submission to the Assembly in 1966. This was in keeping with the discussion held by Her Majesty's Commissioner, Sir Peter Fawcus, with the Executive Committee of the BPATA on the need for a new Education Law for the territory. The RC openly told the Association that the financial situation was a real problem and the matter which was now his would later become the Cabinet's responsibility. The message was that he approached the problem by considering how much one should allocate in a poor country to social services and how much one should allocate to economic development to allow the country to develop its own resources. He concluded that he

> 'did not think it was typical of Batswana to think that expatriates approach education purely from the personal interest motive ... While all education was important, government felt that priority should be given to expenditure on secondary education which was vital to the country's independence. Only secondary education could provide replacements. It would not do to bring standards down by lowering everything to poverty level. We must preserve high standards where we have them and seek to bring schools of lower standard up to better standards' (S252/2/2).

Another development at this time which brought the Association to grips with the Ministry of Education after the meeting with the RC, was the invitation to the teachers of membership on the Syllabus Committee. The Bechuanaland Government had long felt the need for a revision of the syllabus because the one in existence had been in use since 1962. The need for revision was caused partly by the steady increase in knowledge which called for constant syllabus revision and also because the primary course had changed from eight to a seven year course. The success of these changes depended on the full participation of teachers. The Association was further encouraged by the Director of Education, C.J. Hunter who supported their insistence on the teaching of civic education at both primary and secondary levels in the light of the impending constitutional changes. The only mistake that Hunter made was to think that an officer in the Department of Education would send ready made materials on civic education to the schools. In fact, what the teachers wanted was participation in the formulation of concepts and the philosophy of the civics syllabus to render it relevant. They also hoped to upgrade teachers with low qualifications. The Association asked the Department of Education to mount in-service training. It is interesting to note that the teacher's initiative brought about far reaching changes in this country's education system. It was during the In-service Project of the 1980s under the leadership of Bram Swallow that the qualifications of many teachers in this country were improved. But one of the most important targets of the in-service project was the child, and thus to work towards individual diagnosis of individual problems so that eventually children would grow in their adaptability, resources and self-reliance' (NDP, 1973–75). The project was indeed a progressive step intended to remove the drudgery and the stalemate often associated with our primary and secondary school education.

When in 1965 the Botswana Teachers Union became the official name of the teachers organisation, a move was made which was intended to make the teachers' association bargain with the Government like a trade union, and it involved itself with educational matters more intensely than ever before. Among its major achievements was the formation of subject associations, which at the beginning concentrated on mathematics, science, social studies and music. Teachers were concerned with the short supply of qualified teachers, particularly in mathematics and science. Such efforts were preceded by those of Ms. Elizabeth Williams (a primary education expert) who had been in the country to conduct workshops for primary school teachers of mathematics and science. In spite of the shortage of equipment in our schools, which she lamented, she encouraged teachers to 'improve their knowledge especially in science subjects...' (Kutlwano, 1964). Later the subject associations became known as subject panels, which covered a large range of subject areas. The panels monitored new syllabuses, teaching materials, examinations and texts. Every subject was viewed from the point of view of its relevance to the local situation. In this respect, the teachers played an important role in shaping the education system in this country. This was evidenced by the submission of the subject panels to the National Commission on Education (NCE) in 1976 which produced *Education for Kagisano* in 1977.

Through the vigilance of the teachers for instance, when the National Council for Teacher Education (NCTE) was revitalised, the BTU membership was invited. Its participation had been remarkable and had helped to sensitise the public of the problems within our education system as they affected the teacher in the classroom from day to day. One good result of the coming of the Subject Panels and the participation of teachers in the NCTE. was that it brought an end to the practice of importing ready-made packages of syllabuses which sometimes had no relevance to our local situation. Teachers had become the key to matters relating to education and the education of Batswana.

At this stage, mention must be made of the two teacher conferences held in Botswana which highlighted the challenge for the Union to put their shoulder to the wheel and help organise our education. The first of these conferences held at Mochudi in December 1968 was addressed by Kgosi Linchwe of the Bakgatla. He entreated and implored the teachers to help in what he called the 'decolonialisation of education' and relate it to the needs and problems of the developing country. While the teachers had a legitimate right to concern themselves with salaries and conditions of service, he stated. it was incumbent upon them also to look at the reorientation of our educational policy and restore our cultural values (Kgosi Linchwe's address will be dealt with in detail later). The same sentiment was echoed by Matlapeng R. Molomo, Deputy Establishment Secretary who pointed out that 'many of our good customs have been swept away together with what the Church has condemned as pagan' (Kutlwano, 1969).

Kgosi Linchwe

There seemed to be doubt if the subjects being taught at primary schools were relevant to our situation. It will be remembered that the close of the 1960s showed heightened concern for the primary school leavers. At that time, for 80% of those school children, primary education was the only formal education they would receive, but the education they received did not prepare them for life. The thought provoking discussions that followed that memorable conference demanded that the teachers rededicate themselves to the betterment of education in Botswana. The other important address delivered at the conference came from President Sir Seretse Khama. He acknowledge the role they continued to play in nation building through endless sacrifice. A great deal of emphasis was laid on the mutual understanding and cooperation that existed between the Union and the Department of Education. (President Khama's address will be discussed in Chapter 4).

Sir Seretse Khama

The second address to the BTU was the epoch making address delivered by the late President Sir Seretse Khama at the conference at Lobatse in 1969. On that occasion the teachers were praised for not simply discussing 'pay and conditions of service' but for considering how as teachers we could contribute to the development of Botswana. This was a clear acknowledgement of the role the teachers had played and were to play later, and a recognition of the Union as a partner in the difficult task of nation building. A great deal of emphasis was laid on the mutual understanding and cooperation that existed between the Union and the Department of Education. For the first time, the President volunteered his awareness of the enthusiasm and sacrifice showed by the teachers in Botswana in attending courses organised by the Department at the national, regional and local levels.

The President saw education as inextricable from the country's philosophy of social harmony which derives from the four national principles of democracy, development, unity and self-reliance. These were to serve as a guide in shaping the teachers' approach to teaching. The teachers, as he put it, had a singular opportunity to put those principles into practice. 'You have a unique and challenging nation-building role'. For success in this monumental effort, they had to work with parents who were interested in the development of education of their children. For him, development meant change 'not in our own way of life, but in the attitudes and values, the ways of thinking which underlie that way of life' (Khama, 1969). It was important to move forward and plan an education system which, from primary school to university, would reflect Botswana's social and economic aspirations and which would be related to Botswana's development needs. It was vital that the education Batswana children received should enable them to help Botswana achieve an economic revolution. This meant that our education system must not only be expanded but reformed. In this respect he said:

'We are beginning to move away from the academic curriculum designed in the colonial period to supply a handful of teachers and clerks. Industrial expansion demands that the schools introduce more practical subjects in the curriculum' (Khama, 1969).

There was, therefore, a need to develop in the future leaders not only a spirit of community service but an awareness of life. The Development Studies subject taught at Swaneng and Shashe Schools and the introduction of agriculture and home economics at Kgale, were considered the innovations that would bring about the desired innovations in the curriculum. The Swaneng Hill School founded by Patrick van Rensburg was a clear illustration and challenge to teachers to call a halt to an education system that did not relate to the aspirations and needs of Batswana, an education that was elitist. Typical of Khama's sensitivity to the plight of the teachers he stated:

'For too long you have been shouldered with the burden of providing the education base for our development, and the rewards have not been great. Secondary school teachers in particular have required great devotion to stay at their posts and the exodus to better paid jobs in the civil service has been heavy' (Khama, 1969).

It was significant that at that conference the Union was reminded of the White Paper which the Government had started to prepare, following the receipt of the Report of the Salaries Commissioner, Okoh, whose terms of reference, among others, was to have 'regard to the need to relate the salaries and conditions of service of the Teaching Service to those of the Civil Service'. Naturally, the notion of equity was greeted with happiness by the teaching fraternity. From that point the teachers never looked back for the recognition of partnership in nation building through the curriculum. Curriculum reform was grasped with intensity. The Union put forward proposals for the subjects to be taught in primary schools among which were woodworking, domestic science and animal husbandry. The subjects that were taught at secondary level also came under scrutiny. In particular were science and mathematics which had a short supply of qualified teachers and yet were considered important in the light of their importance to technological advancement. Botswana was not to be left out of the stream of advancement in that field. Also to be examined was the history syllabus both at Junior and Senior Certificate levels. History at the junior level was dominated by the South African version of history whose starting point was the arrival of Jan van Riebeeck, while at the senior certificate level, the curriculum ignored Africa completely. Jan van Riebeeck was the first commander of the Cape Provision Station under the Dutch East India Company, which sent exploratory voyages to find a sea route to India for trade in spices. Above all, the van Rensburg-Swaneng-Shashe experience captured the spirit of the time, especially its philosophy of making the young empathise with their communities and appreciate the economic and social plight of their fellow men.

Developments during the 1960s naturally spilled into the early 1970s and were full of promise. The teachers carried the mission of its predecessor, the BPATA, which sought to join hands with other teachers' organisations in Southern Africa, by becoming members of the World Confederation of the Organisation of the Teaching Profession W.C.O.T.P. (This organisation is now called Education International). The BTU was accepted as a member in 1972 at the WCOTP Conference held in London. The Union on that occasion emerged on the international scene and took its rightful place among the other teachers' organisations in the world. The BTU was honoured on that occasion, for the BTU President, K.G. Kgoroba, was called to address the conference on behalf of the new members. Raymond Smyke, who was then the Assistant General Secretary of the WCOTP for Africa, deserves special mention because it was through his untiring efforts and encouragement that teachers secured membership in that organisation. No doubt we place great value on this membership if one considers the role the BTU has played in international educational fora.

K G Kgoroba

Undoubtedly the 1960s will in future years be seen as the years of transformation from the mild and cautious BPATA/BTU to a robust, determined and confident organisation. It became a dauntless and challenging body that spoke with one voice when the rights of teachers were violated or flouted. There were a number of reasons that injected this new approach into the Association. One of the reasons was that the BPATA and later the BTU had toiled for many years without success. The 1960s had ushered in a new era in which the BP was poised for complete independence from Britain in which some prominent teachers were earmarked for ministerial jobs. It should also be mentioned that the BPATA ventured beyond its borders and the formation of the HCTFTA, and the BTU's exploits must have opened their eyes and widened their vision. People came to realise the Association stood for values other than sheer bargaining for better salaries and related matters. All the concerns that related to education and development were of paramount importance to the teachers as a body of professionals. Basic, therefore, to their contribution to nation building was their gaining of the Government's confidence in their ability to fulfil their role as teachers and the acquisition of influential positions within Government structures.

In this respect, the teachers had many hurdles to overcome but they did make remarkable achievements. At first there was a tendency on the part of both the local and central administration to dismiss the Association's issues as trivial and of no consequence. For instance, it took the Government a long time to address squarely the question of inequalities in terms of salaries between the civil service and teaching service. From the Surridge Commission in 1959 to the Hutton Commission in 1965, two commissions including that of Ramage and Skinner had ignored the teachers in spite of their fervent appeals. Only Rusbridger attempted to address the plight of the teachers meaningfully. However, it was the Okoh Report of the 1970s (Okoh, 1970) that went along way to settle the teachers' predicament. Of interest too is that parity of salaries between male and female teachers was achieved in the 1970s after a long struggle.

The absence of a Unified Teaching Service was another source of discontent among the teachers in the country. They believed its introduction would help to protect them against arbitrary decisions taken by the Administration that invariably disadvantaged them as professionals. All in all the teaching service would restrain the government from treating teachers in a cavalier manner. It was after endless encounters and negotiations that the Unified Teaching Service came into operation. The implication of the formation of the UTS was that all the teachers in the country came under the control of one employer who had the right to deploy teachers according to the needs of the country. Every teacher could be called upon to serve in any part of the country. This was a great and resounding victory for the Association.

Another issue that raged for many years was the Association's clamour for a non-contributory pension fund which had been denied them for many years, and its clamour to end disparities between the Government and non-government teachers. As if to appease the non-government teachers, a Provident Fund was introduced to give them a marginal sense of security. At least for the first time when teachers left the job they were entitled to a token reward. While the fund met a long awaited need, the Association felt that it discriminated against teachers as a whole since they made a contribution towards the fund while the civil servants enjoyed a non-contributory pension fund. It was again through the gallant stand of the teachers that they finally secured their rights to a non-contribution fund in the 1980s. That had been a long road indeed.

Other issues that marked some great successes of the Association/Union related to the participation of teachers in moulding the education system through the administrative structures. One of these was the National Council for Teacher Education, and as the title implies it is concerned with teacher training programmes, including teaching practice throughout the country. The teachers' representatives have played a significant role in directing and shaping the path of the Council through their invaluable advice as practitioners. Other committees of note were the Ministerial Consultative Committee, the Orthography Committee and many committees that were formed within the Association itself, such as the Music, Science and Editorial Committees and so on. It is clear, therefore, that while the 1960s presented the Association with numerous trials they also brought many triumphs for the BPATA/BTU.

Chapter Four

The Hutton Report and Its Aftermath

Chapter 3 has shown that when the Resident Commissioner met the Association's Executive Committee in Lobatse in 1965, he generally appreciated the numerous concerns of the teachers. One of the announcements that was made was the setting up of a Commission to review the teachers' salaries and conditions of service. The announcement had been brought about by the Association's cry for the betterment of the teachers' salaries and the need to bring them to parity with those of the civil servants. In despair the teachers claimed, 'We are disappointed to say with every representation our delegation makes, mere promises none of which is ever carried out' (S252/2/2). The situation as the General Secretary Segokgo put it, was gradually driving many teachers to despair and frustration.

Introduction

The Hutton Commission, unlike previous Commissions was not only the first to study the salary structure of teachers in the employment of Government, but also those engaged by other bodies. Secondly, since the BP (Botswana) was preparing for self rule, he was to examine the structure and the composition of a Unified Teaching Service whose absence was a sore point for teachers. He was expected to make a recommendation as to whether or not all teachers should be included in the Unified Teaching Service. No commissioner before had had such far reaching terms of reference. As will be seen later, while earlier commissioners did not pronounce on equal pay in definitive terms, Hutton did so unequivocally. But unfortunately, his recommendation was not implemented.

Other very crucial topics tackled by Hutton related to the Provident Fund, which had been in existence since the 1950s and was phased out in the 1980s, and the Joint Reference Committee. The effect of these changes on the teachers' organisation was tremendous, in that the teachers ceased to see themselves bargaining for the improvement of salaries and conditions of service, but were now more concerned with rendering service in order to improve education in this country. Their invitation to join Government bodies like the National Council for Teacher Education enabled them to contribute to the development of education meaningfully. This period saw the growth of subject panels, which helped teachers to make an input to the improvement of education. Teachers became even more critical of the curricula they offered. This progress to a large extent can be attributed to the change of attitude by the Administration towards the teaching profession. The Union was consulted on matters that related to education and it was Hutton and his predecessors who had started this way of thinking. Education was seen as the tool for development, and teachers were considered vital partners in that development.

The interview with the then Minister of Finance, Mr B.C. Thema (later Dr Thema), must have helped to reduce tension and relieve the suffering of the teachers from whom so much was expected with the imminent independence of the BP. Mr Thema himself, having served as a teacher, principal and administrator both in South Africa and the BP, was extremely sensitive to the plight of the teachers. Apart from that, he was humane and held the profession in high esteem, and never countenanced anything that tarnished the image of the profession he loved so much.

The appointment of the Hutton Commission in 1965 was another milestone in the history of the BPATA. Its importance lay in that it was the first salary review 'charged with consideration of the salaries of all teachers, provided these are subject to Government aid, directly or indirectly...' (Hutton, 1965). It will be recalled that previously, the salaries of European teachers, and, later those of African teachers who had been appointed to posts in Government Schools had been included in the reviews of salaries payable within the Public Service. For instance, before 1959 the salaries of teachers who were not in Government Service had been separately determined by the Administration for each territory, so that not only were there marked disparities between the salaries of those in Government Service and those who were not, but there were differences, though less marked, between the various scales in the three territories.

In 1959, Messrs G.H. Rusbridger and H. Weber submitted a report which laid down scales for all teachers in aided posts but excluding those in Government Service, as the scales of the latter had been revised by Sir Rex Surridge in the same year. Sir Rex's appointment by the Secretary of State for Commonwealth Relations in 1958 was the first of the significant commissions that Bechuanaland had before her independence in 1966. It was followed later by a number of commissions that changed the face of salary scales in this country. Its terms of reference were 'to review, in the light of all relevant considerations, including the neighbouring territories (Basutoland, Bechuanaland and Swaziland), the whole range of salaries, allowances and conditions of service of the civil service, excluding casual and daily paid staff...' (Hutton, 1965). It should be noted that the teaching service in its entirety was not considered. He was, among other things, required to pay particular attention to the structure of the service and the grading of posts in relation to responsibilities, the recruitment and retention of suitable staff at all levels, the question of incorporating all or parts of the then cost of living allowances with basic salaries, the introduction of basic salaries and salary scales, and the method of conversion to any new scales which might be introduced (Hutton, 1965).

It is important to note that the request for an independent commission to review salaries and conditions of service was raised in 1956 and 1957 in the UK at the Whitley Council meetings (Surridge, 1958). The arguments in support of this were that the 1954 local (BP) revision had not been entirely satisfactory and did not deal with conditions of service to any extent. Furthermore, the staffing of positions was unsatisfactory, due to the inability to recruit officers of the right calibre and due to the rapid turn over of staff due to resignations, transfers and premature retirement of some officers. What was problematic was the failure to keep salaries in line with the rising cost of living. In short, the salaries paid in the BP were out of touch with the economic reality compared to those paid in the neighbouring territories.

Of interest is the fact that the Surridge Commission touched on the sensitive issue of equal pay for women, a question that had raged for many years. Although it had been the practice to pay women on a salary scale approximately 4/5 of that applicable to their male counterparts, representations were made by the staff associations for equal payment for men and women. Though the principle was acceptable, it was felt that 'it will be a few years before it is fully implemented ... conditions in the territories are very different from those in the UK (Surridge, 1958). It was felt that the acceptance of the principle would not only affect Government officers, 'but would also have wide repercussions in other fields where large numbers of women are employed, e.g., in the teaching profession' (Surridge, 1958).

The problems raised by Sir Rex Surridge were reviewed in 1961 by Sir Richard Ramage after the Surridge Report was accepted and effect was given to its salary and certain related matters effective from August 1958. The Ramage Commission and the subsequent report was intended to consider the difficulties and the remaining anomalies arising from the Surridge Report as adopted and reviewed by the Public Service in Basutoland, the Bechuanaland Protectorate and Swaziland (Ramage, 1961). In effect, the review was not a revision of salaries as such in normal terms. Among some concerns, while taking into consideration differences in income tax, cost of living, climate, amenities, 'fringe' benefits and so on, the point was simply that the salaries in the territories for professional and administrative staff were 'out of pattern'. Since the areas affected by this bleak situation included what were referred to as the major difficulties and anomalies such as the inadequacy of certain scales which caused serious difficulties in recruiting and failure to hold staff when recruited. It was imperative to address it squarely. Also the lack of attraction to the service by well educated candidates had to receive consideration.

Like Surridge, Ramage raised the inequality of salaries between men and women. While he favoured the abolition of the differentiation, he accepted the fact that it was not appropriate for such a step, 'but a move towards the abolition of the differential '...where applicable' (Ramage, 1964). He recommended that where applicable, the rate for women should be 5/6 that of male officers instead of 4/5. But women officers appointed to post on Scale 4/P were to receive the same pay as corresponding male officers. Strangely, the only exception would be graduate teachers, treated as Civil Servants, to whom the 5/6 scale was to apply.

What was striking at that stage was that 'the pattern had become more confused because certain groups of the staff of the Education Department had been included in the Rusbridger review and were also included in the Ramage review' (Hutton, 1965).

Conversion Tables

Scale II (a)						Scale II (b)					
Proposed		Rusbridger 1959 IV (a)		Ramage 1961		Proposed		Rusbridger 1959 IV (b)		Ramage 1961	
M	F	M	F	M	F	M	F	M	F	M	F
360	300	216	168	216	–	372	310	228	180	–	–
372	310	228	180	–	180	384	320	240	192	240	–
384	320	240	192	240	–	396	330	252	204	–	200
396	330	252	204	–	200	408	340	264	216	264	220
408	340	264	216	264	220	420	350	276	228	–	–
420	350	276	228	–	–	432	360	288	240	288	240
432	360	288	240	288	240	444	370	300	252	324	270
444	370	300	–	324	270	456	380	312	–	348	290

(Source: Hutton, 1965).

When an uncertificated teacher becomes subsequently qualified for the payment of either of the scales in Group II (a) or II (b), the point of entry shall be, in each case, the minimum of the scales (Hutton, 1965). Therefore, the Hutton revision was intended to cover the salaries of all teachers working in the schools or training colleges. No doubt the review was the first and most important step towards the ultimate unification of the teaching service and towards the disappearance of this serious source of discontent within the teaching profession. It is fair to point out that parity was finally achieved through tactful negotiations in later years between the Botswana Government and the teachers.

The Hutton Commission which covered the three High Commission Territories of Basutoland, Bechuanaland and Swaziland had equally fascinating terms of reference. First and most significant, it was to review and make recommendations on the current emoluments of teachers in Basutoland,

Bechuanaland and Swaziland whose salaries were met wholly or in part from public funds as recommended by the review of the Public Service undertaken by T.M. Skinner. It was also to examine all other relevant considerations including the financial, economic and constitutional circumstances of each territory. It was also to consider and advise on the structure and composition of the Unified Teaching Service which it was proposed to introduce in Bechuanaland, and to consider whether all teachers in Government should be included in the Unified Teaching Service of that territory.

In May 1964, T.M. Skinner was appointed 'to review the current emoluments (excluding the inducement allowance paid to designated officers) of pensionable, established and contract staff in the Public Service of the High Commission Territories' (Skinner, 1964). In addition, Skinner was required to advise the British Government through the Secretary for Technical Cooperation on the inducement allowance payable to officers designated under the Overseas Service Aid Scheme. Of interest are the terms of reference which included all categories of civil servants, and excluded the teaching profession. On this last category of workers it was announced that 'arrangements are in hand for their terms and conditions to be reviewed separately' (Skinner, 1964). Skinner allowed for an increase between June 1961 and June 1964. Hutton took into account a percentage increase of nine percent for teachers on the Rusbridger Scale and five percent on the Ramage Scale. He appreciated the fact that the passage of time had 'moved so many of the Rusbridger scales out of line' (Hutton, 1964).

The question of equal pay for men and women was once more raised by Hutton. It had been raised earlier by Sir Rex Surridge, but rationalised in the sense that it had been the practice to pay women on a scale approximately 4/5 that applicable to their male counterparts. The easiest way out of it was that since not many posts were involved, as most of women's posts had been created for them, such as matrons, nursing sisters and lady clerks; although the principle was acceptable, it was felt that 'it will be a few years before it is fully implemented...' (Surridge, 1958). In a casual manner, it concluded that the acceptance of the principle would not only affect Government officers 'but would also have wide repercussions on other fields where large numbers of women are employed ... in the teaching profession' (Surridge, 1958).

So it was that Hutton was implored by the Association to bring the salaries of women, then payable at the rate of 4/5 of those of men according to Rusbridger's salary scale and 5/6 in the case of Ramage's scales, to parity. Hutton obviously saw eye to eye with the teachers, particularly since Skinner's Report on the Government Service had recommended the adoption of equal pay. The idea had been accepted in principle, but not for immediate implementation. However, he felt that to adopt the principle in full would be so costly a process as to limit severely the extent to which the report could deal with other fundamental problems that were urgent in terms of educational needs. Nonetheless, the teachers had made their mark and he conceded that women teachers would share in all other benefits and that there was a possibility to achieve equal pay by two steps. Hutton recommended raising the Ramage ratio from 5/6 to unity effective from April 1967. The recommendation indeed raised hopes within the BTU, but when Commissioner E.K. Okoh came in 1970, the recommendation had still not been implemented. It was these acts of omission that wore the patience of the teachers thin.

The issue of poor accommodation for teachers drew a barrage of criticism. Despite the fact that the Rusbridger Commission had urged the building of more and better premises at reasonable rentals, nothing was done. In fairness, some tribal administrations, were not of the view that the rentals could not be afforded by teachers. In some districts, no rentals were charged for accommodation provided by the tribal authorities or missions, apparently because of the low standard of the premises. Though on the face of it the problem could be resolved easily, events have shown how intricate the problem was. From the outset, the task of providing decent accommodation was difficult to achieve, if one considers the economic situation at the time, particularly in the tribal administrations. Teachers were generally poorly paid and it is inconceivable that their employers could build the type of housing the teachers called for. The problem was not confined to the teaching profession for even the Government was unable to meet the needs of the Civil Service. Nonetheless, the greatest dilemma lay in this differentiation between the treatment of Civil Servants and teachers. Whatever efforts had been made up to now, the provision had never been adequate, for as the education process developed with the training of teachers to meet the expansion, school housing remained inadequate. The cry for housing for teachers still echoes at the present time, particularly in the rural and remote areas.

An equally important issue raised with Commissioner Hutton was that of the Provident Fund. The fund had been instituted because of the teachers' financial insecurity when they retired or left the service. But at this stage, concern was expressed on the defective operation of the existing one. As mentioned before, there was the inevitable dissatisfaction which was brought about by a comparison with the position of the permanent teachers in Government Service who enjoyed a non-contributory pension scheme, while the non-Government teachers had no pension scheme. Instead, they contributed five per cent of salary to the Provident Fund with the Government contributing a further five per cent. On the issue of the Provident Fund, Hutton's response was fair though unacceptable to the Association, for they had borne the brunt for too long as Sir Seretse Khama had alluded to when he addressed the BTU Conference at Lobatse in 1969. Hutton's view was that the Provident Fund had only been in operation since July 1961, and therefore, it did 'not seem that time has yet arrived when the scheme could be converted to a pension scheme' (Hutton, 1964). He himself was concerned that apart from the continuing disparity between the two categories of teachers, which was one of the causes of grievances, that 'there is much to be said for the ultimate substitution of a pension scheme, which must not necessarily be a non-contributory scheme' (Hutton, 1964). However plausible Hutton's rationale was, the Association was firm in its demands, as it was aware of the advantage deriving from the Pension Scheme in that it offered valuable protection to the employee and his family against the temptation to spend considerably more of the lump sum than is wise. The essence of the Commissioner's report was that there should be 'a re-examining of the possibility after the present scheme has been in operation for a longer period with bigger working balances available' (Hutton, 1964). Happily, the 1980s witnessed the introduction of a non-contributory pension scheme for teachers. Nothing could have been more gratifying than that.

One of the far reaching recommendations the Hutton Report enunciated was the establishment of the Joint Reference Committee. That had been necessitated by the changing political and educational scenario as the BP was preparing for self-rule in that year. There was need to devise a means to predict either the pace or pattern of educational development. For instance, after the introduction of the Rusbridger scales in 1959, new circumstances and needs had arisen which had not been foreseen. In order to contain these contingencies, *ad hoc* adjustments were made. But changes which were bound to arise in the future had to be addressed, and such changes included fields within the education system that had never been thought out, such as special education for handicapped pupils, or secondary education with a practical or vocational bias, or further education of various kinds. For instance, 'in-service training programmes should create the need for the transfer of previously uncertificated teachers to scales appropriate to the stage they have reached' (Hutton, 1964). These fields at the moment had been introduced into our education system to address our social as well as economic problems. Education with a practical bias owes its origins to the Brigade Movement which was associated with the schools founded by Patrick van Rensburg at Swaneng Hill, Madiba and Shashe. The Brigades were intended to provide schooling with a bias towards production. It was a departure from the traditional approach of mere certificates. It should be borne in mind that such a dispensation had not been thought of. Our Vocational Training Centres are living evidence of that type of education. Through the Ministry of Education, a Centre for Special Education has been established. The University of Botswana offers a programme in Special Education and this has had an impact on our system of education. Coupled with such concerns, has been the incorporation of the in-service training programmes for teachers to enable the uncertificated teachers to enter local institutions involved with pre-service and even proceed to institutions abroad.

A need, therefore, was felt to 'establish a procedure for resolving such difficulties and for enabling scales to be interpreted to meet new needs' (Hutton, 1964). This move, therefore, led to the establishment of the Joint Reference Committee which included representatives of teachers and representatives of the employers, voluntary organisations and the National Government or Local Government Authorities. Such an arrangement was meant to eliminate the need for *ad hoc* decisions. Such a structure was intended to provide an opportunity for an exercise in negotiation. The truth was that the body of experience gained by the proposed Joint Reference Committee would be of value when the wider negotiating machinery was established.

The long awaited announcement of the date of implementation was greeted with jubilation by the Association in this country. The extract from the Secretary of State Telex No. 109 of 31 March 1966 stated: 'The Secretary of State has accepted the revised salary scales for men and women teachers as set out in paragraphs 29 to 45 of the Report of the Teachers' Salaries Commissioner, Mr R.S. Hutton, which should have effect from 1 April 1966 (Hutton, 1964).

There were at this stage definite signs that many realised the role the teachers were expected to play as our education system unfolded. The process of negotiation was in place and the teachers were prepared to take the challenge. For instance, when the Syllabus Committee was appointed by the Government, two places were filled from the Association. This was a fine gesture indeed. Obviously, at this time, there was a demand for syllabus revision, because the one in existence had been in use since 1962. The need for revision was caused partly by the changes that were taking place prior to the BP's attainment of independence. Setswana, among other things, was to become an official language and if it was to stand the rigor of communication in the world of commerce and international communication, it had to be upgraded. In addition to this, the primary course had changed from eight to a seven year course and that called for a large adjustment. The success of these changes depended on the full participation of teachers through the encouragement of the Association. There were obviously encouraging signs of commitment to revise the syllabus, for as early as 1964, specialists in different subject areas had been invited to advise on the innovations envisaged. One of these was Mrs E.M. Williams a mathematics and science specialist who had been sent by the British Department of Technical Cooperation to help in the process of syllabus revision. She proposed radical changes in teaching, from the old lecture method to the modern pupil activity method. This required full involvement of pupils through participation and learning to find out things for themselves. This marked a departure from the 'jug and mug' approach where the teacher simply tells the children and they in turn simply received everything without question. As teachers, we know how problematic this change must have been for those who were immersed in the telling method. The teachers obviously needed time and patience to acquire the new skills. They were required to attend courses in both the instruction and practice of the new methods under the guidance of experienced teachers. The Lobatse Teacher Training College hosted these courses and helped to improve the performance of teachers in science and mathematics. It was logical that the first teachers' centre be attached to the same teachers' college.

From this stage, the BTU became involved with education on a scale unknown before and seemed to sense the expectations of Batswana. Among the major engagements of the Union was the formation of the subject associations, and its members became the forerunners of the subject panels. The subject associations, like the subject panels, were later manned by specialists who were expected to give guidance to other teachers, particularly the less qualified. At first, the subject associations concentrated on mathematics, science, social studies and music. The subject panels of the early 1970s which spread to the secondary schools were to a large extent inspired by the initiatives of the Teachers' Union. At this stage the subject panels included almost all the subjects. The effort paid dividends, for teachers of varied academic strengths were assisted in various ways and the spin off was that teachers were familiarised with principles governing the curriculum, curriculum development and more effective methods of teaching.

The mid 1960s saw tremendous changes, and as the volume of Standard 7 leavers increased, there were many who were unable to secure places in the few secondary schools in the BP. The rapid growth in the school enrolments was the realisation by many parents of the importance of education, and many saw it as a ladder to success for their children. The situation was a challenge and it agitated the minds of many a man of vision. Patrick van Rensburg, at Swaneng Hill School, during those days tells of his agony when he had 'to turn away young people looking for a place in the school' (van Rensburg, 1974). 'Those years saw every headmaster besieged by imploring children and parents, some tearful and many bringing every influence and pressure at their disposal to bear personally on those of us responsible for admission' (van Rensburg, 1974). The Association was extremely moved by what they saw as tantamount to turning away from schools the children and future leaders of this land. They saw the challenge for what it was, and therefore requested teachers at various levels throughout the country to organise evening classes, the predecessors of the present day study groups, to help those who were unable to gain admission to secondary schools. At the General Conference of the Association held at Serowe in December 1965, the President of the Union appealed to the membership to do so in the name of advancement, development and brotherly love (BTU Conference, 1965). The humble effort made by the teachers brought them closer to examining new teaching materials, examinations and textbooks. Matched with this participation an attempt was made to view every subject on the basis of its relevance to the local situation. In this respect, the teachers played a significant role in shaping the education system in this country. The Union's contribution was evidenced by the submission of the subject panels to the NCE (1976) which produced the Report on *Education for Kagisano* in 1977.

The teachers' commitment to educational development and support for all structures that were educationally based, demonstrated itself in the invitation of the Union to join the National Council for Teacher Education (NCTE) when it was revitalised. One of the major functions of the NCTE is to monitor programmes relating to teacher training. That role has been maintained consistently and has paid dividends, if one considers the expansion of teacher education in this country and the improvement of the quality of graduates from the local institutions. Through the workshops and seminars, the Ministry of Education, in conjunction with the NCTE, has upgraded a considerable number of teachers. In addition to that, the participation of the Union has helped to highlight some of the problems within our education system as a group of professionals involved in the day to day activities in the classroom. One good result of the coming of the subject panels and the participation of teachers in the NCTE was that it brought an end to the importation of ready made packages of our syllabuses from elsewhere. The coming of the NCTE helped to broaden our educational horizons, for teachers were no longer only thinking of traditional subjects like, history, geography, English, Setswana, mathematics and science. New possibilities were sought and this brought to the fore a new subject called development studies. It was first introduced at Swaneng Hill School, founded by Patrick van Rensburg and a handful of teachers at Serowe. Development studies was intended to prepare our youth for the post-independence era, for it was a combination of disciplines ranging from economics, sociology, politics, accounting and so on. The key concept tied up with the philosophy of Swaneng Hill School was that the youth should empathise with their less privileged fellow men and cooperate with them. Above all, the main principle underlying the schools founded by van Rensburg was that education must not be used as a ladder to success. In the teaching of science, Swaneng Hill School had a great input in the use of local materials to give their pupils a new orientation and to make as practical as possible their instruction. There was, as indicated earlier, an attempt to use reading materials appropriate to local conditions as well.

From that point, the scientists came forward with the idea of integrated science at the secondary level. The idea of integration came not only from within but also from below. The approach, as enunciated at the time, was a subject of criticism. One should recall that as independence drew nearer people of all persuasions were suspicious of anything that savoured of a low quality or standard. The integrated version of science was considered a 'watered down version' of science. It combined the three elements of science, namely biology, chemistry and physics as opposed to pure biology and the physical sciences taught separately. The problem with integrated science was that the combination of subjects presented a difficulty in identifying those who had done biology or physical science during their training. Nonetheless, the arrangement resulted in two alternatives, introductory science syllabuses A and B. The arrangement, therefore, accommodated all the teachers of science, even those who were not trained in all the science disciplines. The outcome of what appeared to be a real dilemma was to encourage the teachers of science in Botswana, Lesotho and Swaziland to come together and write books of science for local use.

The activities that the teachers were engaged in within the Subject Panels must be seen against the background of the current thinking about education as a tool for development. While the BP enjoyed the support of other countries and the generous assistance from donor agencies, it was a constant reminder to improve the education system from within, in order to cope with political as well as economic changes. So, like the social scientists, the natural scientists were concerned with the emphasis on broader issues in the teaching of science. The ideal was to discourage the fragmentation of science simply to make pupils pass their examinations without the subject having a bearing on their lives. From that stage, need was expressed to expose the learners to scientific knowledge and to lead them to a clear understanding of that knowledge. Further, it was imperative to develop an awareness of the interrelationship between the different branches of science and the relationship of science to other subjects within the curriculum. Among these, there was a need to develop an objectivity in observation and help pupils acquire scientific skills and experimental techniques. To realise these objectives, discovery methods were encouraged in order for pupils to participate in practical work. The compartmentalisation of teaching was to be lessened and the teaching of science was to be by way of an interrelated subject.

However noble and realistic these objectives were, they had to be matched with action. So the first problem that militated against the programme was the lack of preparedness of most of the teachers to teach introductory integrated science, since a large number of them had been trained in one science subject at the degree level and would not be able to employ an integrated approach effectively. To help these teachers, workshops were mounted, and worksheets were compiled with the assistance of the teachers themselves. Also, detailed teacher's guides helped to put the practising teachers in good stead. Though the programme has experienced a number of setbacks, it is nonetheless, making decent headway in what is considered a sound approach to the teaching of science.

The BTU and the Teaching of History

One of the areas of study which had concerned the BTU was the teaching of history. It was the feeling of teachers that history was loaded with foreign concepts and had nothing to do with the local situation. This thought was further strengthened by the establishment of the Botswana History Association in 1976. The major task of the Association under its first Chairperson, L.H. Grant, who taught at Molefi Secondary School was to organise workshops to sensitise teachers to the new techniques of teaching and writing history materials. It was the BTU that helped to organise workshops and invited eminent historians to speak. Such a workshop was held at Gaborone Secondary School in 1972 and drew historians like Professors Pachai from Malawi, Stanlake Samkange of Zimbabwe, and Omer-Cooper from University of Zambia. Professor Blake, who was the Pro-Vice Chancellor of the University of Botswana, Lesotho and Swaziland was invited by the Historical Association to talk to local teachers on the new approach to the teaching of history. He stressed 'research as the basis of sound history writing and teaching (Blake and Haliburton, 1972). The teachers of history through their own research efforts on new materials became even more dissatisfied with the current Junior Certificate history textbooks and a particular one written some 60 years ago by de Villiers *et al.*, (1932), entitled *Junior Certificate History*. This turn of events was a change for the better and there was soon a focus on the Senior Certificate history which covered the period from the Napoleonic Wars up to the formation of the League of Nations in 1919. The relevance of such history was questioned, particularly as it ignored African history. It must be noted that teachers were not prepared to be taken for granted insofar as history teaching was concerned, and there was a demand for involvement at both the writing and teaching stages.

It was Grant's article which appeared in *The Teacher,* the Botswana Teachers' Union Magazine in December 1969 that provoked the teachers' doubts about the relevance and the adequacy of that textbook. In that article, *The Beast is Still With Us* he stated:

> 'The beast is still with us. Some time ago I did my best to kill it but it will survive as long as the syllabus remains unchanged' (*The Teacher,* 1969)

What was of interest though, was that in the new edition of the book that had been revised in order to remove the grosser features, there still remained some ugly features as can be seen below:

> 'But the book is so bad that a change here and there cannot really improve it nor make it any less irrelevant. One could recommend it for its comic value but so long as it is backed by the full weight of the Examinations Council and education authorities here and there is less of the comic than the tragic about it' (*The Teacher,* 1970).

Such remarks put the finger on the trouble spot, for as long as the awareness about the irrelevance and the inappropriateness of the book was not shared by the examinations controlling body, there was little chance to address the problem squarely. It is even fair to mention that many teachers themselves had never critically examined the textbook. The teachers of the subject had never realised that the future careers of thousands of students rested on their ability to assimilate and regurgitate such meaningless stuff. The greatest criticism was that the Junior Certificate examination in history determined the teaching approach and there was no effort to make students analyse the subject matter critically. There was little in-depth thinking in the materials covered by the syllabus. Truly, the examination was meant to help the crammer to succeed and de Villiers was a crammer's textbook. For instance, the section dealing with the ancient world started with the rise of the early civilisations along the River Nile and the banks of the Euphrates and Tigris Rivers. There was no attempt to explain the underlying factors. The fall of the Roman Empire was dealt with in an unrealistic fashion, not relating events to the local history that pupils were familiar with. Nowhere in that textbook was there reference to the local history of the pupils studying history, let alone mentioning the structures of local administration. No mention was made of the role of the Village Boards, the Headman, the traditional ruler and his Kgotla/Nkundla. According to the prevailing thought, that was not history worth reading. When local history was done in one section, it was that of South Africa, and everything started with Jan van Riebeeck in 1652. The assumption before that was that there was nothing to know about the original inhabitants. The examinations based on that book leaned heavily on dates and events. At examination time the pupil was faced with either a long list of events to be matched with dates or vice versa. For example to give dates for the following events: the Battle of Zama, the Death of Julius Caesar, the Wreck of the Stavenisse. The dates would be: 202 BC, 1486 AD, 707 BC. As can be imagined there was a great deal of guesswork and that was a waste of pupils' precious time.

Once again, the unfortunate BP and her sister territories had no alternative, as the examination headquarters was outside the country in South Africa, which had a longer educational experience. Another disturbing factor about the book was the repetition of the obvious which made reading uninteresting. For instance, the use of the word 'actual' a word that should be used with care was randomly used in the Junior Certificate history paper. For example, 'apparently the Egyptians had "an actual" religion', 'actually the City of Rome developed...' and worst of all, 'the Cretans apparently, actually worshipped a goddess.' All this was uninspiring to the young pupils at the JC level, particularly, since the subject matter was extremely foreign.

The strangest section of the book related to the settlement of Southern Africa. To tell the world that the history of South Africa started with the arrival of the Dutch, sounds ridiculous in the light of the new research information about the early settlers. The most unpardonable transgression was to make generations of African children recite such garbage as 'the thieving propensities of the natives.' Many students in this region were taught to despise their people in an unbecoming fashion. To read in this region the corrupt practices of Willem Adriaan van der Stel, and that in 1655 Annatjie de Boerin, the wife of Hendrik Boom, the head gardener, was given a monopoly to sell milk was just ridiculous and of no consequence. What of the dances, and which were in vogue at the time, such as the minuet, the quadrille and the cotillion which had no meaning to us as students and later as teachers?

With the appearance of *From Stone Axe to Space Age* (Blake and Haliburton, 1972), there was a more urgent call for a comprehensive text, since the latter publication was equally inadequate in many ways. The attack on the new book came from Ron Pahl's article which appeared in the *The Teacher* in 1971 entitled *A Critique on Part II of the Blake-Haliburton Text – From Stone Axe to Space Age*. Ron Pahl was a history teacher at Seepapitso Secondary School and had come to the country under the auspices of the American Peace Corps. His was an additional voice added to a barrage of criticisms of the book. The main criticism was that its bias was strongly in favour of Europe and only 40 out of 375 pages of the text dealt with the history of Africa, excluding European exploitations, conversions or colonisations in Africa. The authors of the book evidently believed strongly that African history 'consists of little more than a history of European involvement on our continent' (*The Teacher*, 1970). What was covered within those 40 pages of the text that covered African history, the author of the particular section (Dr Haliburton), was 'outdated and ill-informed in writing a book to be first published in 1970' (*The Teacher*, 1970).

The second issue which was a cause of concern was the shallowness of the book and lack of depth in dealing with sections considered important in dealing with local history. The book tended to be a narrative account without any attempt to interpret events and showed a lack of imagination and, as a result, important aspects of our history were glossed over. In addition to that, the vocabulary of Part II was hopelessly mixed in South African terminology and antiquated colonial concepts of Africa (*The Teacher*, 1970). For instance, that detestable word 'Bantu' which carries a political stigma in the South African context was the major example and was used continually throughout Part II. It was absolutely futile on the part of the author of the section to point out that it had been used only in its linguistic sense. Unfortunately, he had forgotten, that regardless of intellectual rationalisation the majority of the population of Botswana and the region as a whole know the term only in its racial context in South Africa. The terms *Nguni* and *Sotho-Tswana* adequately describe the African population South of the Limpopo and have no racial connotation. It was, therefore, appropriate to use the term 'African' in place of the word 'Bantu'.

The use of the words 'Hottentot' and 'Bushmen' were another source of criticism since these were in contrast with the terms used by Isaac Schapera such as Khoi-Khoi for Hottentot and San for 'Bushman'. 'Such terms were more acceptable as they had fewer racial overtones attached to them' (*The Teacher*, 1970).

In an effort to depict the 19th century European infatuation with their 'great' deeds on the 'Dark-Continent', the African was completely forgotten as the European slavers, missionaries, explorers, voortrekkers and British settlers pushed into Africa. The pictures and texts were dominated by Rhodes, Kruger, Livingstone, Jameson, Lugard, Botha, Smuts and even Ian Smith.

Pahl's final thrust was that the greatest distortion of the book related to the interpretation given to the black-white interaction in Southern Africa. His conclusion was that the author's proximity to the Republic of South Africa (in Lesotho) had led him to follow the South African interpretation that the movement of a few disgruntled Dutch farmers across the Vaal River was the major historical event in South Africa. As a result, Haliburton had overlooked a staggeringly larger event that had a far more profound effect upon the peoples of Southern Africa, that is the 'Zulu Aftermath' as described by Professor Omer-Cooper. He said that 'it was not only a far more cataclysmic event, (but) without it the "Great Trek" likely would never have taken place' (Omer-Cooper, 1966). Without the Zulu Wars to denude the high veld, there would have been no open land for the Voortrekkers to occupy.

Obviously Pahl's criticism of Part II of *From Stone Axe to Space Age* was not to be left unchallenged. Haliburton, then Head of the Department of History at the University of Botswana, Lesotho and Swaziland (UBLS) reacted sharply in defence of the book by stating that he and Pahl fundamentally disagreed on an understanding of what is legitimate African history. His contention was that the exploitation and colonisation of Africa was certainly a major part of the history of modern Africa. For 500 years Africa had been subjected to the pressure of outside forces originating in Europe. It would be very naive to think that the attainment of political independence dissolves the strength of those forces either for the past or at present (*The Teacher*, 1970). The argument continued that the story of the Sotho-Tswana and Nguni in the past 200 years was one of adjustment to the intrusion of the white settlers from Europe. A part of that population lives in Botswana, Lesotho and Swaziland, politically independent but economically part of the economic union dominated by the white politicians in Pretoria. Above all, the rest of the black population was politically subordinate to these whites and the policy of 'apartheid' had been framed with them in mind. Haliburton made bold that:

> 'It would be criminal, I believe, to write history for pupils in our schools which did not give full treatment to the expansion of the white population, the political and economic changes which came in its wake and the whole development of the

racial theory which has culminated in the apartheid system and the creation of Bantustans' (*The Teacher*, 1970).

He lamented the fact that Pahl did not see it that way, for he (Pahl) had suggested that *Difeqane-Mfecane* was more important than the movement of a few thousand disgruntled Dutch farmers across the Vaal, but that one must remember that the effects of the coming of those settlers overshadowed every diplomatic manoeuvre of the three governments as well as many of their internal decisions and practices. The figures indicating the male working population of the three countries in South Africa, for example, 22% from Botswana, 18% from Swaziland and 36% from Lesotho suggested the overwhelming presence of South Africa in all that affects the three countries. It was a great wonder how Pahl could dismiss those white farmers so lightly (*The Teacher*, 1970). The children who undertook the Junior Certificate work were entitled to know those things about the world they would earn a living in.

But how did the debate end, some have asked? It is more accurate to say it has not ended, but its concerns may be different. The concrete evidence to its partial decline was the appearance of a series of history books on Southern African history written by teachers and university lecturers from Botswana, Lesotho and Swaziland in the first half of the 1980s. The text *From Stone Axe to Space Age* has died a natural death. Pahl's ideas may have been mistaken, for instance, in thinking that an event like the Great Trek could be swept under the carpet, for it affected the history of South Africa and beyond. Today, the descendants of those Trekkers claim the regions they occupied beyond the borders of the Cape are legitimately their own fatherland. The idea of 'Boerestaat' even at the negotiation conference table in the envisaged 'new South Africa', has its roots in the claims on the land settled by those disgruntled Boers. This is not in any event an attempt to legitimise their claim but merely to state the fact.

Nonetheless, Haliburton's view is unacceptable when he stated that Pahl objected to certain terms used to identify racial or sub-racial groups. He did not see the insult in such terms as 'Hottentot', 'Bushman' and 'Hamite'. He stated that he was at a loss when he was asked to apologise for the use of these terms, or what the advantage would be in using other terms. This was completely naive for a historian of Haliburton's calibre, and he of all people should have known better. To address people correctly is to give them dignity. One wonders how he would justify such terms as 'Kaffir' and 'Rooinek'. There is no sense in telling the people that the term 'Bantu' is accepted in the world of scholarship. It is to be extremely insensitive to the feelings of others.

Whatever can be said of these frank discussions on historiography and our reactions, the discussion revealed the concern of teachers and the desire to contribute to the writing of a relevant and meaningful history. The teachers found *From Stone Axe to Space Age* extremely inadequate and lacking in depth. Many topics that are considered important such as the African migrations were treated superficially. The teachers of different persuasions in the three countries were, to put it simply, disappointed with the new history text. That was revealed by their readiness to write alternative history texts. These discussions helped to clear the air and the Botswana Historical Association, under the wing of the BTU, helped to keep the debate alive and encouraged the teachers to address the problem squarely.

The BTU and the Teaching of English

It is appropriate to mention at this point some rumblings on the teaching of English. There were teachers, particularly foreign white teachers who were unhappy about the handling of the subject. Literature, for instance, that was studied by the pupils in this region was considered rather Eurocentrically biased. Our pupils were made to recite poems such as the *Daffodils* by Wordsworth, *Lycidas* by Tennyson, *The Grecian Urn, The Reaper* and many others. Many of those generations of pupils had never seen a daffodil or the Italian cyclamen. What then was the point? Why were we teaching the Shakespearean plays that derived from a foreign or more specifically English culture? Why did we teach our pupils the novels of Dickens, Thomas Hardy, Jane Austin? The questions were challenging enough, but many of the teachers who graduated from those schools valued the joys of reading that literature and the values they imparted. But more crucially, many African authors of verses, plays and novels had not been surveyed and some might not have emerged. Perhaps even the political climate and change were still in the making. It might also have been the idea of 'the devil you know is better than the angel you don't know'. While many teachers may have accepted the arguments for change, there was little they could do. The teachers did raise their objections when they heard that the teaching of grammar as they knew it was to be dropped. There was a strong belief that a clear grasp of grammar laid the foundation for the comprehension of language. The face of literature has changed with African poetry, novels and dramas introduced into our curriculum. Language (grammar) has also undergone some change, but it is hard to state categorically what the effect of these changes have been.

The BTU Magazine

The establishment of the BTU magazine, *The Teacher,* was a remarkable achievement for the organisation, for not only did it keep up the debate on educational matters in general, it also contributed to the ongoing debate to which reference has already been made. It made the teachers think seriously about their profession and contribute articles on any field in education. As a result of that, matters of interest ranging from the curriculum, examinations, teaching methods, and administrative concerns were openly discussed in *The Teacher*. Apart from that, and since the magazine enjoyed wide readership, teachers discussed such subjects as the conditions of service, salaries, the equipment in the schools, and the delivery of reading materials including books. From time to time, they complained about the attitude and the unfair treatment they received from the inspectors, later, education officers. They literally saw them as policemen who wanted to do them down. From the majority of the education officers they received no help except criticism. The magazine in someways, however, became the teachers' forum through which they exchanged ideas.

The Teacher was to make sure that contact was maintained with the membership all year round, rather than waiting for the General Conference at the end of the year. The magazine was equally given a boost by the then Minister of Education, Dr Thema. He expressed his appreciation for the teachers' magazine which he saw as a powerful instrument of education. He held this belief because he was convinced '...that of the many factors that go towards building a sound system of education *The Teacher* is, by a wide margin the most important factor' (*The Teacher*, 1970). *The Teacher,* according to him, was directly involved in the actual educative process, in the imparting of knowledge to the young, and in that difficult but intrinsic function of education, the moulding of character and the development of personality.

Quite logically he stated that the magazine would join in the struggle for the improvement of the teachers' conditions of service as other organs of teachers' magazines have done the world over. It would be expected to take up the old dialogue and advocate better scales for the teaching profession. Yet there were other values and principles for which teachers' organisations exist, or for which they should exist, and which the organisation's magazine should be used to advocate, to implement and publicise. 'These are the professional values – as distinct from the object of collective bargaining towards the betterment of the lot of the members of the Association' (*The Teacher*, 1970). Finally, the Minister expressed the hope that the BTU magazine would provide generous space in its columns for professional matters and for critical appraisal and constructive examination of our curriculum and syllabuses. That it would be used as a medium for constructive criticism of the many innovations that had been introduced into our education system and of putting forward suggestions towards improving the system for our examination and evaluation was obvious.

In keeping with the Minister's exhortation, many notable articles were contributed by teachers on various subject areas for publication in the magazine. One of these was outlined in a chapter on history, written by Sandy Grant. The other thought provoking article was on 'New Maths', a subject with a new approach which had just emerged in this part of the world, and written by Jerry Hirata – an American Peace Corps teacher of mathematics at St. Joseph's College in Kgale. It will be remembered that the appearance of 'New Maths' had generated heated arguments for and against it. The protagonists of traditional mathematics argued that such a move would weaken the study of the 'real' subject. Some even claimed that this region including Botswana, Lesotho and Swaziland would not be able to produce mathematicians, engineers and scientists of standing. But the younger teachers of mathematics saw hope in the new subject and encouraged its introduction. At the moment this writer is not sure whether the prophets of doom have been supported by facts. Nonetheless, mathematics features in our curricula from primary to university level, although it has not been possible to testify to its quality.

In his refreshing article in *The Teacher* published in 1972 Hirata recalled that among many teachers there was widespread dissatisfaction in the teaching of the syllabus and in the performance of their students. One must appreciate the fact that Hirata's problem was minimised by the fact that he was schooled in the 'New Maths' tradition. His contention was that mathematics in schools was basically designed to meet the computational (ability to handle figures) needs of the ordinary person. Education in numbers, therefore, 'must pass on a certain kind of skill that can be useful to anyone who is to live a productive life' (*The Teacher*, 1972). With the arrival of 'New Maths' came a wave of change; in fact he recounts that 'new' is a misnomer because mathematics is an ancient subject and 'new' means only new in approach, such as the introduction of new topics into the standard curriculum, fresh methods in teaching of the subject, and shifting emphasis towards learning by the discovery of the theory and concepts underlying the method. He encouraged teachers to accept 'New Maths' without question or hesitation and to reassure themselves that the change was worthwhile.

The message was that for any subject to be useful and relevant to our daily lives, what was learned should be applicable to the practical situations outside of school. Many teachers argued that traditional maths had adequately achieved that for what was learned could be easily transformed to everyday life, while on the other hand, the contention was that students doing new mathematics could not even add straight – a gross exaggeration to some extent. Hirata readily conceded that new maths students were ineffective and slow in solving simple arithmetic problems. But that was because new maths does not have enough computational drill to enable them to perform unfailingly. There was less emphasis on repetitions, drills, memorising formulae or using standard methods (*The Teacher*, 1972). The role of new maths was to place more emphasis on an intuitive understanding of different methods and patterns and on an abstract, deductive kind of reasoning through discovery of concepts and theory. This aspect of new maths strikes a familiar note in educational circles, that of understanding and discovery as crucial to learning situations. It is akin to the Montessorian belief that the learner should find out for himself, for learning is a personal thing.

Hirata's ideas on new mathematics coincided with those of David Jenkins, who was employed by the Government as Director of the Regional Testing Centre in Gaborone. In his article 'We Educate Through The Approach' (*The Teacher*, 1970) he raised questions of educational importance. He preferred to regard new mathematics as 'embodying both a change and content'. The change was a departure from the purely instructional to a more flexible one of active investigation. The change was to ensure that pupils were actually doing something to encourage investigation, arouse curiosity and foster self-discovery. In a lighter vein he warned that self-discovery did not mean that teachers were absolved from their responsibility that enabled them to tiptoe to the nearest Kgotla meeting or a neighbour's *mantsho* ceremony. On the contrary, the demands on him were heavier, and instead of instructing, he guided by questioning, dropping hints and arranging the situation for the child to discover for himself (*The Teacher*, 1970). This process lay deep in John Dewey's theory of education 'in that we learn best by finding out ourselves' (Smith, 1965). These are the foundations of his Project Method which has become the rallying point in many educational circles. Dewey, by the way, believed that experience is the best teacher. The awakening on the part of the teachers in their inquiry into the various subject areas helped to enhance the interests and contributions of the Union in the development of education in this country. The dialogue to which Thema had referred to in the *The Teacher* had blossomed and the Union from this stage never looked back.

Music Competitions

An equally fascinating development was the attention paid by the Union to music. Music as we know plays a very important role in society in the education of the young. One may ask what it was that inclined the organisation this way. All societies irrespective of the level of development have sung to either express joy over their jobs or anger, stress and sorrow. Batswana, like many peoples of this region, are known for their singing and their various forms of music. The truth of the matter is that music, like language, has its roots in a people's culture and through singing they express their culture. But how did it originate? The answer is that there is evidence that music was performed for dancing, and in various activities and traditional games as well. Singing then is most probably the oldest musical activity. In almost all cultures the singer has had a special, defined position. At the places of work such as ploughing and hoeing *(ilima/letsema)*, at the thrashing of wheat or corn, during initiation ceremonies our people have been known to sing. Such songs have symbolic meaning both to the young and old. In times of war, turmoil and conflict, warriors were accompanied out of the village by songs and at a distance from their homes, the deep sounds of the drum still accompanied their singing.

The BTU must have been influenced by these thoughts in devoting so much of their time in the schools to make the young sing in order to embrace the cultural values of the societies from which they come. The music that they introduced ranged from local to international forms. The idea was that local music had a particular attraction to the young which carries some lyrics they have listened to as young children at home before they entered the formal education system. These were selected with care in keeping with the physical and mental development of the young. Even international songs, particularly English ones, were chosen with care in order to relate them to the experiences of the children. The purpose of the exercise was to present and render music in an enjoyable fashion. Some of the early compositions sung by our school and adult choirs has had a great influence on later composers trying their hand at the writing of music. A good example is that of Ricks Morake, a composer who has made some contribution to the culture of Batswana. All that he needs to do to improve his skill is to get more exposure and introduce a bit of originality. Beyond our borders there has been a fund of music sung from the composers of different language groups in South Africa, Lesotho and Swaziland. This was encouraged by the BTU as it tended not only to enrich the local cultural outlook but to weave us into a common cultural union. In fact, through this practice we have learned to know and appreciate better our own music.

Furthermore, it was through the organisation of music workshops by the BTU and the invitations to prominent musicians in this region, that we learned about our own creative musical styles. For instance, we have learned of music in traditional societies that evolved several ways to relieve the monotony of one person's singing. 'A principal device is called antiphony which involved two groups that sang in alternation or a leader who sang and was answered by a group of singers' (New Encyclopaedia Britannica, 1991). This type of music is prevalent in this region and in Botswana in particular it is associated with ceremony. The chanting young girls accompanied by young boys in traditional attire are a pleasure to see. According to the Encyclopaedia Britannica, in antiphony 'may be seen the origin of responsorial singing which continues today and which may be the point of origin of several types of musical phrase structures. The polyphony was also anticipated in traditional musical performances and is said to have come through haphazard rather than intentional manifestations, such as the singing of the same melody with parts starting on different pitches or at different times (New Encyclopaedia Britannica, 1991).

In order for the BTU to fulfil its programme and make music part of the curriculum in the schools, a Music Committee was established with Kgeledi Kgoroba, a teacher of science at Moeding College as its first chairperson, followed in those formative years by Peter Tlhophane and P.A.M. Qobo. It was through the efforts of these pioneers that many schools were brought into the singing fold. It was during the chairmanship of Qobo that the country was divided into regions and emerged with complicated name combinations such as LOBANGWE (which stood for Lobatse, Barolong and Ngwaketse), SEMABOTSWA (for Serowe, Mahalapye, Bobonong and Tswapong), FRABOTATO (for Francistown, Bokalaka, Tati and Tonota).

Though the music competitions were well received and attracted donors of trophies such as the late President Sir Seretse Khama, Mohumagadi Gagoumakwe Sechele and Mrs Rita Brink, there were a number of problems that faced the BTU. The major problem was the failure on the part of the Ministry of Education to include music in the curriculum and make it compulsory like many other subjects at the Primary Teacher Training Colleges (PTTC). The argument at some point was the difficulty of recruiting teachers of music, but that was unacceptable since positions that could not be filled locally, such as positions of art and religious studies were filled by expatriates. The same could have been done with music. Music, as we know, is an instrument for teaching and learning, particularly at the lower primary level. After the affiliation of the Primary Teacher Training Colleges in the mid 1970s to the University of Botswana, the final assessment reports raised the lack of teaching of music at the PTTCs as it denied the trainees of an important skill. As a result of this practice music had degenerated into mere singing. At present, it is gratifying to note that this neglect has been addressed squarely by sending abroad our local teachers to study music. It is hoped that new heights will be scaled in the field of music. The BTU's efforts will be enhanced by ensuring that every diplomate from our PTTCs will be music literate. The importance of music in education has been demonstrated by the recruitment of excellent lecturers in music at our Colleges of Education at Molepolole and Tonota. Messrs Springer and Molefe have infused a new outlook into music with their enthusiasm and impeccable style of rendition. One believes that the day is not very far away when the University of Botswana will introduce a Chair of Music.

Despite the early problems to which reference has been made we witnessed the emergence of a crop of excellent young conductors such as Tebogo Lesolle, Sethokgo Sechele, V.K. Monno, Mandie Vanqa, 'Lady' Lecha, Hope Phillips then Principal of Nyangagwe Primary School, Moagi S. Moagi of Kanye, P.A.M. Qobo, N. Momoti, Dijang and Ricks Morake. Among these promising conductors were two seasoned conductors namely McDonald Maleke of Sechele Secondary School and T.J. Molefhe of Serowe Teacher Training College. These two conductors helped to sharpen the conducting skills of the young and promising conductors and thereby contributed to the quality of music at competitions. Through their constructive criticism they urged even novices in the game to improve their efforts. This helped not only teachers to see the value of music but enabled pupils to develop pride in their local music.

However successful, the BTU's attempts to improve the standard of music in the country, their efforts were frustrated by the exaggerated competitiveness on the part of the schools. Some schools clearly missed the point and adopted a win at all cost attitude as if they had never heard that cooperation is an essential element of competition. There was undue mud-slinging from competition to competition. In the midst of this frenzy the children were involved and competitions ceased to be a source of joy. In short, the educational element was destroyed as the pupils were not made to learn from others. The other cause for the unpleasant wrangling was the requirement by the Music Committee that before a school could participate at all levels of competition, more than half of the staff in any school should become subscribers to the BTU. This was hard to realise since some schools, particularly the secondary schools had a large contingent of expatriate teachers who were not necessarily interested in the affairs of the BTU.

There were also some local teachers who did not wish to associate themselves with the BTU as they did not appreciate its role. Nonetheless, the Union needed funds to run its programmes and the competitions were the only viable source for their finances. At times, the tension was so high between the regions within the BTU, that even the Ministry of Local Government and Lands had to intervene. The clash was triggered at one stage by some schools in the Northern Region which were consequently debarred from taking part in that year's competition. The BTU Executive Committee was summoned by the Permanent Secretary to explain their arbitrary action. The BTU was saved from humiliation by the stubborn and fearless young Keetla Masogo, the President, fresh from the University, who was a teacher at Gaborone Secondary School. Finally, the matter of excluding northern schools participation was resolved amicably but one thing came out clearly; the Union could not be taken lightly and their decision would set a precedence. In fact, if the BTU had wavered they would have lost face and would not have been able to enforce discipline among its members. At some quarters, the view that competitions should be sandwiched with festivals gained some ground. The festivals, it was believed, would placate the endemic spirit of competition and make the teachers and pupils work to-

K.M. Masogo

wards a common goal. Importantly, in that case, there would neither be winners or losers and all would be enriched by the sense of achievement.

The teachers' music 'renaissance' went beyond the school environment to the community at large. Music came to be appreciated as a way of life, and no occasion, as in the days of old, passed without music. It is even possible that the encouragement of music at our schools had an impact on our traditional music in style and rendition. There is a fund of music in this country and in the region, which expresses the peoples cultural outlook. This can be improved by modernising some aspects of it through effective and artistic arrangement as we have seen happen beyond our immediate borders. Our budding composers should not be preoccupied with adopting melodies of yesteryear through defective translation. Let us be proud of what is ours though we learn some lessons from others. We would in that case earn the respect of all music lovers.

The BTU Conferences at Mochudi (1968) and Lobatse TTC (1969)

The two conferences held towards the close of the 1960s were a milestone in the history of the Union in that they helped to enhance the image of the BTU in the eyes of the public, including the parents, at a time when the credibility of teachers and the respect the profession had enjoyed was on the decline. This state of affairs could be traced to the emergence of more prestigious professions such as law, accountancy and so on. Kgosi Linchwe's address at the conference held at Mochudi was touched on earlier. It gave recognition to the role that the teachers were expected to play in the development of education in the new Republic. So many, including the Kgosi, believed that our education system was riddled with foreign values to the exclusion of the ways of life of Batswana. He called for the 'decolonialisation of our education and the need to relate our education to the needs and problems of our developing country' (Kutlwano, 1968). He reminded the conference that in the past teachers dwelt on salaries and conditions of service but that it was equally important for them to look at the re-orientation of education policy. He wondered if it was not time after the independence of Botswana to depart from colonial education. In the past, a great portion of the syllabus was devoted to the teaching of what was foreign. For instance, he pointed out that the teaching of history in the schools ignored the African heroes such as Chaka, Dingaan, Linchwe I and a host of other heroes who struggled against the colonisers.

Kgosi Linchwe's point was commendable and made him stand out as a far-sighted leader who was not only concerned with brilliant school results but was concerned with the quality and goals of the Botswana education system. He stressed the restoration of our cultural values and civilisation and the effort to give prominence to our history and the struggle of our own people. In fact, the whole re-orientation of our educational strategies was among the major tasks that should occupy the teachers in their deliberations at such conferences.

Another example of Kgosi Linchwe's vision can be gleaned from his concern for the Standard 7 Leavers' difficulty in finding places for higher education and employment opportunities. To the majority of those children, primary education was the only formal education they would receive, but the education that was given to them did not prepare them for life. He felt that since this was all they would attain, it was important 'to equip these young people with useful skills in agriculture and animal husbandry, domestic science, community development in theory and practice, civics, first aid and development studies' (BTU Conference, 1968).

As previously noted the image of the Union was further heightened by the epoch making address delivered by the late Sir Seretse Khama at the BTU Conference at Lobatse in 1969. It was a most fitting speech at the close of the 1960s entitled the *Nation Building Role of Botswana Teachers*. The conference was honoured to be addressed by a man of vision who was sensitive to the suffering of teachers. He praised the teachers for not simply discussing 'pay and conditions of service' but considering how, as teachers, they could contribute to the development of Botswana. His was a fair assessment of the role of the Union, for while the teachers concerned themselves with the conditions of service, it was not uppermost in their deliberations. That was a clear acknowledgement of the role teachers had played and were to play later, and, above all a recognition of the BTU as a partner in the difficult task of nation building.

He commended the mutual understanding and cooperation that existed between the Union and the Department of Education. For the first time, the President declared his awareness of the enthusiasm shown by Botswana's teachers in attending many courses organised by the Department at the national, regional and local level. 'I appreciate that this involves efforts and sacrifice on the part of the teachers, and that often vacation plans are given up in order to attend courses arranged at short notice' (BTU Conference, 1969). So close did he monitor the teachers activities that he even confirmed his awareness that some teachers took the initiative themselves in requesting that short weekend courses be organised for them. Such weekend courses included book-keeping for the treasurers at the regional and branch level, the teaching of science, the new approach to social studies as spearheaded by the African social studies programme based in Nairobi, and in addition to that, the interest shown by teachers in attending the upgrading courses at Francistown.

He also touched on his favourite subject, Botswana's national principles of democracy, development, self reliance and unity which formed the basis of a guide in shaping our approach to education. The teachers, as he put it, had a singular opportunity to put these principles into practice: 'You have a unique and challenging nation building role' (Khama, 1969). Democracy to him was not just a political concept, it was something which everyone had to apply in their daily lives if they were to have full meaning. Democracy depended on understanding, and that in turn depended on education in the widest sense. Teachers, therefore, were of immense help to political leaders who were concerned to maintain and develop democracy as was the case in Botswana.

He saw development in which the teachers were involved as inextricably bound up with education. For him development meant 'change, not in our own way of life, but in the attitudes and values, the ways of thinking which underlie that way of life' (Khama, 1969). If people were to be persuaded to change their ways they had to understand why they were being asked to change. Development, therefore, was best based on consent and understanding and not compulsion. Nonetheless, in this task we tend to become impatient and arrogant when others fail to see reasons for such a change. 'It then becomes essential to explain these reasons, because we can only go as far as the people allow us' (Khama, 1969).

It emerged clearly in the address that we were being challenged to move forward and plan an education system which from primary school to university would reflect Botswana's social and economic aspirations and which would be related to Botswana's development needs. It was imperative for us to ensure that the education our children received would enable them to help Botswana achieve an economic revolution. This meant that our education system must not only be expanded but reformed. In this respect the President stated:

> 'We are beginning to move away from the academic curriculum designed in the colonial period to supply a handful of teachers and clerks. Industrial expansion demands that the schools introduce more practical subjects in the curriculum' (Khama, 1969).

No doubt these were truths and predictions held highly by the teachers. They had earlier sounded their discomfort with some aspects of the colonial system of education. The address stimulated them to diversify their approach and the need to develop in our future leaders not only a spirit of community service but an awareness of life. That could be done by a curriculum reform which would introduce innovations like development studies at Swaneng and Shashe schools and the introduction of agriculture and domestic science at Kgale (St Joseph's College). It will be recalled that the Swaneng Hill School established by Patrick van Rensburg was the first institution to call a halt to an education system that did not relate to the aspirations of Batswana, an education system that was elitist.

Typical of Sir Seretse's sense of justice, equity and broadness of outlook, he touched a sensitive chord when he referred to the unbearable and demeaning discrimination and handicaps borne by the teachers.

When he finally said, 'we know that we can improve our performance with your help', he gave the teaching profession dignity. In fact, so great was the impact and recognition of the role of the BTU in nation building through curricula reform that a proposal was put forward of additional subjects to be introduced at the primary level including woodwork, domestic science and animal husbandry. The recommendations were conveyed to the Director of Education and at the same time the Union expressed its concern on the problem of automatic promotion. The teachers decided to study the problem before making their recommendations for improvement or change.

The address by the President was appropriate in every respect for through the Union the teachers had, even before the independence of Botswana in 1966, geared themselves for change. Earlier on this had been demonstrated by their persistent inquiry into the curriculum they taught in schools. This was preaching to the converted but it is fair to remark that some saw no necessity for change. The challenge was acceptable to all forward looking teachers and was amply demonstrated by their unswerving devotion in the face of adversity. The returns were extremely disappointing and sometimes the attitude of those in authority during colonial rule left much to be desired. Of interest again, though the address had made an impact, there still remained those brutally discriminatory practices. For instance, the Okoh Commission to which the President had made reference at the BTU Conference at Lobatse in 1969 was the letdown of all time. The Report was awaited with anxiety, for Commissions had come and gone before and recommendations had been made and had gone unheeded. The importance of the Okoh Commission lay in the that for the first time the salaries and conditions of service of the Civil Service, the Teaching Service and Industrial Class were considered simultaneously. The Okoh report was a progressive document, but what made it a detestable thing was its interpretation which discriminated against the bulk of secondary school teachers, particularly those who had been teaching in local schools. This singular event hardened the attitude of many teachers.

Coming soon after the Okoh disappointment was an announcement on the sale of houses through the house ownership scheme. Its stated aim was to encourage home ownership and to meet the needs of commerce and industry in the medium cost housing area. Once again, the Teaching Service was ignored and that was a bitter pill to swallow, particularly in the wake of so many assurances to better the lot of the teachers' conditions. So when the teachers assembled at the Gaborone Secondary School in December 1972 they were prepared to make their grievances known to the Ministry of Education beyond doubt. On that occasion they demonstrated what they called 'an end of the road of negotiation' with the Ministry of Education. The teachers expressed their disgust at the poor conditions of service, the dismissal or termination of teacher's services, housing conditions and the bad treatment of teachers by the officers of the Ministry of Education over the various personal issues presented by the teachers to the Ministry. The demonstration was a great shock in some circles and from that date the BTU was never the same as they could no longer be taken for granted.

The BTU in the 1970s (And Beyond)

However successful the 1960s were for the BTU, the following decade started on a sad note. Phillip Matoane who had been the President of the Association/Union for almost ten years was declared a prohibited immigrant by Presidential Decree on 28 January 1970. The news shook the BTU to its foundations. The Union lost a fine leader, a dauntless fighter for the rights of the teachers, a forthright, dedicated and articulate man. He was appreciated by both friend and foe. To the teachers he was a great friend and defender, and to the establishment he was a nuisance who constantly rocked the educational boat. Some high ranking person in the office of the Director of Education described him as 'one who had maintained careful control of the Association and helped to make it a responsible body of opinion' (S284/2/1). He was even described as a good organiser who had held office for at least four years.

The question that weighed heavily on the Union was, who would succeed Matoane, for that seat had become extremely hot. The BTU Executive Committee sought audience with Sir Seretse on the Matoane issue. Without hesitation, in what was considered a democratic approach, permission was granted for the Executive Committee to discuss the deportation order with His Excellency. On the appointed day the BTU team converged on State House and was received courteously by the President and some Government officials. The teachers' delegation, led by George Kgeledi Kgoroba, included Gogoa Kgomanyane, G.N. Kgotlane, J.B. Gabaake and Temba P. Vanqa. The team was not at ease since most of the delegates were not Batswana and were, on principle, arguing on behalf of a South African teacher employed by the Botswana Government. Despite the delegates' fears, the discussions were frank and cordial but the Government was unmoved by our arguments and the matter ended there (Meeting of President Seretse Khama with the BTU Executive Committee, 1970).

It is possible that during those weeks and months of uncertainty some individuals may have made representations on Matoane's behalf but it is not certain. The only voice that pleaded on behalf of Matoane was that of L.H. 'Sandy' Grant. He decided to take the bull by the horns by writing a letter dated 24 February 1970 to the President asking him to temper the storm for the shorn lamb. He accepted that as a resident visitor in the country he had no right or wish to concern himself with those decisions which could rightly only be taken by the President and Batswana themselves as a people.

It was appropriate for Grant who had known Phillip Matoane as a member of the Teachers' Union to express his shock and plead for a colleague in his hour of need. He had a lot of respect for Matoane, whose contribution to the country he appreciated, noting that, 'He has brought to the Union a dedication which has undoubtedly helped it to develop into a maturing organisation – and one thinks particularly of its leadership in the fields of music and sport' (Grant, 1970). Grant admitted that he was not aware of the actions which had brought Matoane to that situation and it was no intention of his to exculpate him from them, but 'like all of us he has his failings but this particular one, whatever it may be, should be seen against the background of his long service to the Union, to the teachers and education' (Grant, 1970). The Government was not prepared to change their mind and Matoane left the country.

Reference has already been made to the Okoh Commission to which the President had referred at the Lobatse conference. It was an event that aroused a lot of interest throughout Botswana. Okoh had a mammoth task and something which had never been attempted before. He had to relate the salaries and conditions of service of the Teaching Service to those of the Civil Service. This was borne out of the concern in both Government and non-Government circles at the disparity in salary scales between teachers and civil servants. It was stressed that he should address such recommendations as would encourage the recruitment of new teachers and also persuade existing teachers to stay in the Teaching Service. Admittedly, the point at issue was that the recruitment of Batswana as teachers or civil servants was made from the same pool of educated manpower. The manpower and localisation problems of Botswana could be seen in their true light only by taking the staffing of Civil Service and Teaching Service together.

Okoh accepted the endless anomalies which persisted as many of them had been inherited from the colonial times. It was therefore, necessary to remove the discrepancies between the salary structures of the teaching service and the public service by lowering the entry points of graduate recruits to the public service to a more realistic level, for that action 'would reduce the large differentiation between the emoluments of qualified teachers and those of the officers in the Central Government' (Okoh, 1970). On the supply of secondary level teachers he recommended that 'immediate steps be taken to create approximate parity in salaries between graduate secondary school teachers and new entrants into the civil service holding equivalent qualifications recommended in the Development Plan' (Okoh, 1970). No doubt such a recommendation was warmly received by the Union, for disparity had been a sore point for many years. Though parity in salaries was not necessarily a solution to the problem of teacher shortages, it created the conditions which would in future permit a solution to be found. In keeping with his broad experience in both services he recommended that since promotion posts were inevitably fewer in the teaching service than in the civil service he advised that a strategy of reconciliation of the two services be carried out. It would be based on a reduction of gross differences of salary, a re-statement of the basic entry qualification, provision of fair opportunities for existing civil servants and teachers alike to improve their qualifications and a better balancing of the services on respective general conditions. It would, 'go far to lift this discontent which weighs so heavily upon the Teaching Service' (Okoh, 1970). All in all, that would free teachers to align themselves with Civil Servants in devoting their combined efforts to the great task of nation building.

As can be imagined, the BTU Executive Committee accepted the opportunity to talk to the Commissioner and make their submissions. A high powered delegation that went to see Mr Okoh consisted of P.M. Matoane (President), G. Kgoroba (Secretary), G.N. Kgotlana (Treasurer), G. Kgomanyane, J. Moilwa and J.B. Gabaake. The whole burden of the teachers' evidence was that their salaries and other conditions of service should be 'at least equivalent to the salaries of the Civil Service, and that the conventional view to regard teachers as "missionaries", which still lingers on, is an inexcusable anachronism which merits immediate abandonment' (Okoh, 1970).

What was gratifying about the teachers' submission was that they did not just pour out a barrage of grievances, but also made recommendations. To many it was clear that the profession had been degraded to the limit. There was need to resuscitate the image of the organisation through a campaign of information, including systematic career advice in secondary schools. Other suggestions for enhancing the teaching profession ranged from the introduction of the probationary period of service for all teachers of say fifteen months following first appointment, to the provision of demonstration primary schools with well equipped and well paid teachers at each Teacher Training College. These were commendable proposals and were conveyed by the Commissioner to the Teaching Service Committee.

The BPATA and Women's Issues

Perhaps there are few organisations in this country that have fought for women's rights so vehemently as the BTU. The campaign was started by the BPATA, later BTU, to appeal to the Department of Education to treat women teachers with respect and dignity. The most thorny question related to maternity leave and as this chapter is being written it has defied solution within the Civil Service.

The teachers made representations to the Commission for the amendment so as to allow the grant of up to 30 days paid maternity leave. Before that, women teachers who took maternity leave were not eligible for pay, a most insensitive practice of denying these teachers financial support when they needed it most. Of interest, earlier recommendations made from the Surridge Review of 1958–59 and Skinner in 1964, recommended that maternity leave should not exceed 90 days and should not be paid except that leave earned should be utilised against it. For the pensionable officers, the unpaid leave should be considered as 'not in the public interest' so that it does not count as pensionable service.

On the other hand, because of discriminatory practices which had existed for many years, women teachers were subject to the provisions of Section

29 of the Teaching Service Law which provided that a female teacher may be granted up to three months confinement leave without pay. Okoh recommended no change, but suggested its application should not be restricted to married teachers. Unmarried women teachers, like unmarried officers in the Civil Service, were eligible for unpaid leave. What remained to be addressed was that women teachers were not paid salary when their maternity fell within school holidays, an extremely untidy and insensitive practice. In fact, one has never been able to find a reason for this heartless arrangement. Okoh had come to heal wounds that had been gaping for a considerable period of time.

The story of pregnancy among unmarried teachers, mark you, not just married women teachers, must have agitated the minds of the officers in the Department of Education and many school committees scattered throughout the country. Some of the schools were the creations of various church denominations, and the founders of these schools were not prepared to countenance behaviour they considered immoral. The community primary school committees consisted of the District Commissioner, the missionary who acted as secretary, the Chief and some prominent members. Invariably all these individuals acted as guardians or custodians of tradition and morality. Sometimes they were judged harshly on the treatment they meted out to our women teachers. Obviously they belonged to a different age whose norms we considered irrational. Theirs was the golden age of high morality which was fast disappearing. Without condoning the act, the Union saw it as a social problem whose solution did not lie in the chastising of women teachers. The problem had to be addressed in the light of social realities.

The concern which has been referred to, as manifested in high offices, was exemplified by a circular letter dated 20 April 1967 sent to the District Secretaries and Town Clerks and copied to the Permanent Secretary of the Ministry of Local Government and Lands, the Attorney General, Education Officers and District Commissioners. The letter was a request for advice on this 'all too important question' of pregnancy among unmarried teachers. The point at issue was that before the Teaching Service Law No. 34/64 came into force in 1966, it was 'administratively' correct to suspend pregnant unmarried teachers for two years. In the Teaching Service Law the penalty of suspension was retained in the form of an interdiction which might be followed by dismissal assuming that unmarried pregnancy indicated misconduct. Disciplinary action had to be taken under Section 20 of the Teaching Service Law and might culminate in dismissal by the Director of Education.

However, the Director of Education seemed to see the light, for he pointed out that there were other considerations to be borne in mind when dealing with this controversial subject. For instance, experience had shown that the practice of suspension for two years did not seem to have diminished the number of unmarried teachers becoming pregnant, and that pregnancy out of wedlock was a common occurrence in Botswana and was not confined to teachers. This was a prejudicial statement and he might have added that it was a universal social problem. He further touched on a controversial issue which had been raised on a number of occasions – if a pregnant unmarried woman teacher was punished, was it not proper to subject the male teacher responsible for the pregnancy to such punishment? There existed no comparable machinery to discipline male teachers who practised pre-marital or extra-marital sex. It is readily assumed that even if such punitive measures were taken against male friends, the practice would not have lessened the problem. On a more liberal approach there were other equally interesting arguments raised, such as the various means of avoiding pregnancy. It was possible that there were unmarried teachers who practiced contraception without much risk of being disciplined. The important question raised was that, if in the Government clerical service, unmarried women who became pregnant continued in service without punishment and without interruption of service why were women teachers then singled out? On a rational note, the Director of Education argued that an unmarried mother needed wages more than a single woman or a married female employee. But above all, Botswana could ill-afford to do without teachers' services especially if they had been trained at Government expense.

It was the ruthless discrimination against women teachers that prompted Sandy Grant, then engaged in Rural Development work and teaching at Mochudi, to write an open letter to all the members of the Legislative Assembly, the President of the Botswana Teachers Union, the Botswana Christian Council and the Director of Education in October 1967. Sandy Grant held that the only possible reason for the establishment and continuance of the humiliating policy of suspension must concern the national moral order. It could not concern discipline since the supposed crime would not, in the majority of cases, have been committed within the school premises and would not have anything to do with professional behaviour and standards. Since the Education Department had chosen to condemn and punish for offences that were not committed within the confines of school, it had to be taken for granted that they did so in an attempt to support certain moral values.

What was strange was that morality only became the concern of the Education Department when it infringed on education. 'The Department may deplore widespread promiscuity since it is bound to affect the character of society as a whole' (Grant, 1967). In order to change the situation, it was imperative to provide sound education. There was no need to impose certain moral standards on society as a whole, although it could punish for fragrant offences committed within the schools themselves. Suspending a teacher was abhorrent, particularly if there was nothing to show that the punishment acted as a deterrent. Who, in any event gained by this archaic policy? Certainly not the women. What the women remembered was the ugly and unfair treatment meted out to them. Those who returned to teaching after the humiliation saw their employers as arrogant bullies. The Department of Education gained nothing, but they lost teachers they needed so badly. The children who invariably lost a teacher were 'treated to a vivid demonstration of the folly of becoming teachers themselves' (Grant, 1967).

The years following the publication of the Hutton Report set in motion a barrage of issues that had not been resolved earlier. One of the greatest achievements of the BTU was its recognition beyond any doubt, by the Administration that they were its partners in the difficult task of nation building. The recognition brought in its train the implementation of such structures as would enable the teachers' organisation to bargain meaningfully with the Government. For instance, there was a determination to install all those structures that would encourage conditions of service for the Teaching Service as well. The teachers as we have seen took advantage of the trust bestowed on them by making a constructive contribution to the improvement of the curriculum in different subject areas. In other words, while they continued to press for their rights, they squarely met their responsibilities as professionals. The resultant attitude, the participation of teachers in the development of education and the granting of membership to them by the Administration/Government can all be attributed to the Hutton Commission, its report, and later Commissions. The Hutton Report triggered many changes that had not been thought of earlier and therein lay its importance.

CHAPTER FIVE

The Search for a Philosophy of Education: The 1970s and 1980s, Decades of Change

The early 1970s were years of promise as we have seen in the previous Chapter. The Union had made gigantic strides in their professional effort and had come to be recognised by the government as having a significant role to play towards the betterment of education in Botswana. The Okoh Report, despite the snags brought about by its implementation, promised a better future for the Teaching Service. The long pending conditions of service accompanied by a salary review for teachers were due for implementation. Both President Khama and Kgosi Linchwe had challenged the teachers to look beyond the narrow confines of personal interests at broader issues such as the reform of education in its entirety. The teachers were called upon to widen their horizons and consider matters of national importance that were likely to be affected by education.

The Common View of Education

The question to ask is, what is it that constitutes the broad ideal we hold about education? Is it the mere transmission of moribund and defunct ideas that have no relevance to our situation? That was the challenge to the organisation – to look beyond teaching strategies within the classroom and to examine and assess the goals of our education system and to determine what type of citizens we want to produce at our schools. Even then, our schools were to comply with the National Development Plans, which rightly tended to stress the link between education and manpower needs. This was no longer the main concern, instead 'the primary aim in the field of education is to create in the shortest possible time, with such financial means as may be available, a stock of trained local manpower capable of serving the country's economy (NDP, 1968–73). In this respect, there was no lack of consideration of what we thought our education system should be. In short, what was our philosophy of education? While we conceded that there is 'an inevitable universal element in such disciplines as philosophy, there is no doubt that philosophy and philosophy of education can also be culturally influenced' (Akinpelu, 1981). In other words, while we could borrow ideas elsewhere we needed something that was truly our own. This Chapter will examine some of the thoughts of local thinkers, such as Dr Kenneth Koma, and other thinkers of international repute such as Paulo Freire and Julius Nyerere. Some of their thoughts on education for self reliance, education for all, and education with equity, have found root in our society, but some of their ideas however plausible have not been acceptable, for the government of the day does not share the same philosophy. What was needed was an outlook on education consistent with practical means and beliefs. Sir Seretse, in his address at the Teachers' Conference at Lobatse in 1969, gave us a glimpse of his own vision of what education should be. When he mentioned the national principles of democracy, development, self reliance and unity, he urged the conference to see them 'as a guide in shaping their approach to education' (Khama, 1969). Botswana's philosophy of education is encapsulated in the word Kagisano – social harmony. It is a concept based on respect for others and in such terms implies that no one should be denied access to education on the grounds of race, colour and creed. In short, education is an inalienable right. Above all, education was bound to society with every member making a contribution.

As noted previously, despite the progress made early in 1970, the organisation lost its President, Phillip Matoane, who had reigned for a number of years of illustrious leadership. The Vice-President, Gogoa Kgomanyane took over the leadership. Everyone was aware of the risk, for what happened to Matoane, could also happen to him. There was, therefore, a reluctance on the part of the foreign teachers to assume positions of leadership in the organisation, and those who continued to, did so at their peril. It was not surprising then that at the next conference held at St. Joseph's, Kgale in December 1970, Kgomanyane did not stand for election. It was the young Keetla Masogo, a young graduate from the University of Botswana, Lesotho and Swaziland, then teaching at the Gaborone Secondary School, who took the challenge and was elected President. Everyone was pleased with the outcome of the election for two reasons. First, Masogo being a Motswana would be able to stand his ground, and secondly, he was known for his sharp wit coupled with forthrightness and fearlessness. In him, we had a young teacher who did not pull his punches when the interests of teachers were threatened. All in all, the organisation was in good hands once more. Earlier it was shown how he rescued the organisation from humiliation as a result of clashes of interests within the organisation. Through his skilful debate he weathered a few storms that could have slowed down the work of the teachers' organisation. One of these was the reluctance to allow the use of school premises for teachers' meetings, including the organisations' Executive Committee. In Kweneng District, this became extremely contentious when the Executive Committee took a visitor, Dr Don M'Timkulu from the WCOTP to Molepolole to talk to the BTU branch there. The Secretary to the School Board wrote a fiery letter to the then Director of Education and blamed the BTU Executive Committee for disrupting afternoon classes.

The President, Keetla Masogo and his Executive Committee, were rebuked for the alleged unfortunate act. Masogo once more handled the case with assiduous competence and good relations were once more established between the teachers' body and the Ministry of Education. This event and many others earned the teachers a lot of respect and it became known that no one could intimidate them. The teachers were prepared to serve to the utmost of their ability but not on their knees. Another interesting element which had been simmering in the background and surfaced at the St. Joseph's Conference was that young Batswana graduates from the UBLS were evidently aspiring to executive positions within the Union. Many acknowledged and encouraged this trend, for it was considered legitimate for capable Batswana teachers to be involved in the shaping of the education of their nationals. There were also disgruntled 'old horses' within the Union who had contributed to the growth of the organisation. Such teachers deserved consideration in being elected into responsible positions, but their aspirations had to be matched with ability. The foreign teachers who held executive positions welcomed the move as legitimate, and a good call for change.

The New Executive: Its Link, Its Problems and the Years of Enlightenment

At election time, the wishes of the local teachers were taken into account, but the outcome was not far removed from their wishes. Among the elected teachers there were four local teachers on the National Executive Committee. The results of the election were as follows: Keetla Masogo, a local (President), Molemane Molefe, a local (Vice-President), George Kgoroba (General Secretary), Diamond Selema, a local, (Assistant General Secretary), G.N. Kgotlane, a local, (Treasurer), James Moilwa (Education Committee Chairman), Temba Vanqa, (Editor: *The Teacher*) (Minutes of the Botswana Teachers' Union Conference, 1970).

The year 1970 was also eventful in that the Union was beginning not only to look beyond the borders of Botswana and joining hands with other teachers' organisations within Southern Africa, but beyond Africa. Mention has been made of how in the 1960s the HCTFTA was formed with Lesotho and Swaziland. The Association with the two countries enabled the BTU to exchange ideas with other organisations on professional matters. The desire, for instance, to join hands with an international organisation (WCOTP), brought to the conference at St. Joseph's College, Raymond Smyke, then the Assistant General Secretary of WCOTP. Raymond Smyke came at the invitation of the BTU to brief the membership on issues relating to the policies and procedures for joining the organisation. Smyke's attendance helped to clear the air as there were some members of the Union who wanted the local organisation to join the World Association of the Eastern Block, while others had their eyes fixed on the WCOTP. As a result of Smyke's address and discussion, the overwhelming majority pressed for joining the WCOTP. The thinking at the time was that we understood better the philosophy that underpinned the western system of education from which ours derived. It was only in 1972 at the WCOTP Conference in London, that the Union was finally granted membership status (Source: Minutes of the WCOTP Conference, 1972). On that occasion, the BTU emerged on the international scene and interacted with other teacher organisations throughout the world. Raymond Smyke deserves special mention because it was through his untiring efforts and advice that the Union was admitted to the WCOTP ranks. During the early years of our membership, he helped and provided the Union with funds to travel to the Conferences of the Confederation in different parts of the world. The Union places great value on this membership.

At that conference, Smyke addressed the issues of sound administration within the Union at national, regional and local branch levels. He shared his vast experience of administration by stressing the need to cultivate a meaningful relationship between the Union and the Ministries of Education and Local Government and Lands if the Union was to make a lasting contribution to the development of education in Botswana (Source: Minutes of the BTU Conference, at St. Joseph's College, 1972). However, he warned that if the BTU was to earn the respect of Government, it had to demonstrate its ability to do its job so that when they went to the authorities for the improvement of their conditions of service and salaries, its members were to do so from a position of strength. His was a welcome visit, for he christened the Union with a new concept of 'eyeball to eyeball' in dealing with Government (BTU Conference, 1972). These challenging words fell on the eager ears of young Batswana graduates from the Universities who were very critical of the Government's treatment of teachers in regard to salaries and conditions of service enjoyed by Civil Servants. In fact, some of the students engaged in studies at UBLS had expressed their discomfort about the education system of Botswana and the plight of the teaching profession in the local press. A good example of the students' concern was their communication to the President, Sir Seretse Khama, raising their misgivings about the establishment of Maru-A-Pula Secondary School. From its inception, there was a view that Maru-A-Pula was a prestigious private elite school catering for the needs of the upper crust of society. The main concern was the divisive nature it would have on Batswana children (UBLS, 1970). The students also complained to the Minister of Education, B.C. Thema (later Dr Thema) about the cavalier treatment of teachers in Botswana. They pointed out that they observed glaring signs of inequality between teachers and their counterparts in the Civil Service. They pointed out that the unfair treatment had been there for too long and lack of attention to this malady was because it affected teachers who were not nationals of Botswana. They felt that as nationals 'and as people who were going to stay in Botswana they should make that stay as comfortable and as fruitful as possible' (UBLS, 1970). They also referred to what they called 'soccer fever' whereby teachers were transferred to satisfy football needs. They decried the ill treatment of teachers by the District Councils. They also complained about the poor housing of teachers, the inhuman treatment of unmarried lady teachers who fell pregnant, and the traumatic handling of their cases. Legitimately they asked 'if the pregnant lady teacher is a bad example to the pupils, what about the typist who works in the same school and who is seen by the pupils everyday' (UBLS, 1970). To the students, that was morally indefensible and a manifestation of 'distorted thinking' (UBLS, 1970). They also complained about what they called stringent teaching laws, which affected teachers under what was called 'misconduct', lack of promotion hopes, (almost nil in the Teaching Service), and the absence of opportunities for serving teachers to further their studies. 'It does not only alienate the teachers concerned from the service but it also shows how little is attached to the quality of teachers and teaching in Botswana' (UBLS, 1970).

As a result of this breath of fresh ideas from within and abroad, the early 1970s saw an intensification of workshops designed to help put the BTU on a sound organisational footing at the branch and regional levels. To broaden the scope of the regional organisers, north and south workshops were mounted. That was an old strategy which had been adopted from the early days of the BPATA, later BTU, to cope with the large numbers of teachers scattered throughout the country. Earlier, mention was made of the efforts of Patrick Motsumi, then a teacher at Ramotswa, who was organiser for the south and how he had harnessed, not only the services of other teachers, but local administrators and in particular Kgosi Kgolo Bathoen II of the Bangwaketse. Later came the stalwarts of the BTU including the late Daniel Kwele in the north and the evergreen, T.T. Mosimakoko in the south. Both the organisers had a long teaching service and were familiar with the problems of their fellow teachers. Kwele was for many years a Principal of Nyangabgwe Primary School, and had from time to time served as a member of the BPATA's Executive Committee. Kwele as we know, tried his hand at politics and won many hearts through his oratory. He even rose to the rank of Cabinet Minister in the Botswana Democratic Party. The teachers had been wise in their choice to harness the services of such a talented person. Mosimakoko served in a number of schools as principal, among them, the Bangwaketse School. He also held responsible positions in the BTU including Chaplaincy and the Chairmanship of the Setswana Curriculum. These organisers worked quietly in the most remote parts of the country and helped to keep the Union intact. The workshops were also organised to help chairpersons and treasurers at the local level on procedures relating to their responsibilities. The strategy was vital if one considers the problem of raising funds and the fact that the Union's finances were very low. Every precaution had to be taken to ensure that monies were accounted for. The other workshops concentrated on educational matters such as encouraging subject panels to examine closely the objectives of the education system. There was a well specified search for relevance in what we offered without necessarily rejecting what we considered important even if it was foreign in origin. Teachers were fully aware that education requires a measure of adaptation and adjustment. Though criticism was mounting particularly with regard to our primary education, we could not throw out what we knew and opt for the unknown. Herein lay the root problem – the country's search for our philosophy of education. There was equally a call at that stage for the administration to concentrate on the improvement of the quality of primary education rather than dissipating its energy on a dramatic but deceptive expansion. This was itself dependent on the calibre of the teacher, since it had the most critical influence on the quality of education.

A Call for Appropriate Education

It will be recalled that the founding of the Francistown Teacher Training College, funded by the Government of Sweden, joined it to the older Colleges at Lobatse and Serowe and was intended to mount a five year upgrading of teachers in correspondence work, residential study and radio programmes. Pre-service and in-service training was strengthened with a new emphasis on practical subjects such as home economics, wood and metal work, agriculture, science, mathematics and social studies (NDP, 1968–73). This approach had been reinforced at Swaneng Hill School where it was pointed out that it was not only in formal teaching situations that young people learn. 'Much can be learnt from practical work...' (van Rensburg, 1974). Yet what could not be ignored at this level was that despite these improvements, there were a large number of primary school leavers who were not only unable to enter secondary schools but unemployed in the conventional sense, and while it was difficult for the primary schools to provide young children with specific skills, it was important for teachers and parents to help to understand their country's situation and the basic principles on which its development is based. The aim was to introduce young people to a wider range of learning experiences.

With regard to secondary schools, in addition to home economics, wood and metal work, arts and craft work were offered in all schools. The natural sciences, agricultural science, development studies and commercial courses were offered at some schools. Meanwhile a desire was expressed to extend practical courses into the secondary school curriculum. This was a realistic approach in terms of the manpower needs of Botswana. 'The primary aim in the field of education is to create in the shortest possible time, with such financial means as may be available, a stock of trained local manpower capable of serving the country's economy' (NDP, 1968–73). What was disturbing was that the curriculum in the secondary schools was narrow and not well suited to Botswana's needs. 'The curriculum is academic and little attention is given to practical and cultural activities or subjects related to Botswana's main industries – arable farming and cattle raising' (NDP, 1968–73). But caution was made that secondary education should not be expanded in order to create an unhappy collection of frustrated and unemployed would be white-collar workers. The message was that the product of our secondary schools must be prepared for responsibility in industrial expansion and rural development. Added to that the secondary schools were required to 'produce qualified students capable of being trained not only to replace expatriates, but also to occupy new posts resulting from development and to meet the normal requirements arising from natural replacement' (NDP, 1968–73). Equally, a need was felt to speed up progress in technical and vocational education to benefit from industrial expansion. Happily the programme on technical and vocational education is in place today and is receiving optimum Government support. The emergence of such institutions as the Polytechnic, Vocational Training Centres, Automotive Trade School and other related schools are a fulfilment of this dream. It was a realisation that people with vocational and technical skills play a vital role in the process of development. 'Hence, it is important that young Batswana are trained and equipped with appropriate technical and vocational skills which enable them to contribute to Botswana's development' (NDP, 1976–81).

Birth of Botswana's Philosophy of Education

Basic to the questions and the queries raised by the teachers and the public relating to Botswana's education system, was an unmistakable search for a philosophy of education that would reflect our national goals. Beyond the normal expectations there were those who felt that need to measure the effects in terms of individual outcomes. In other words what type of person was our education intended to produce. Perhaps the teachers and the public in this country were fortunate to have a government that had identified the four national principles of democracy, development, self-reliance and unity. These served as a basic framework on which their philosophic thoughts found support. Yet it must be stated clearly that the Union did not necessarily see these as a philosophy but as a means by which a balanced philosophy of education could be attained. What essentially constituted our philosophy of education? In Professor J.A. Akinpelu's *Introduction to Philosophy of Education*, three elements of a philosophy of education illustrated the Union's goal. The Union's philosophy was 'based on the nature and of the society as conceived by that society' (Akinpelu, 1981). The Union deliberately sought an education that would first produce individuals who were conscious of their environment and work for the betterment of their fellowmen. In Botswana, we were in this respect influenced by the thoughts of Patrick van Rensburg at Swaneng Hill School who had with a small band of teachers in 1966 established what was known as the basic quests of that school. One of these 'was how to inculcate a commitment to social justice among the educated minority and how to equip them with the knowledge and skills needed for development' (van Rensburg, 1974). The aim here was to sensitise the young to concern themselves with the plight of their less privileged fellowmen and make the school less exclusive and available to a greater number of people.

Put in a straightforward fashion, education was not to be used as a ladder to success at the expense of their less fortunate brothers and sisters. The strategy was to achieve these ideas through the life and activities of the school and through its curriculum (van Rensburg, 1974). However difficult the goal was, efforts were to be made to resist the compulsion to create a status in our society. Education was to be based on what the society considered the type of knowledge worth having, how it was acquired and a genuine love for ones culture.

Whilst it was thought proper to examine what constituted other people's philosophies of education, there was need to come up with something that is our own, something that the Union could be proud of. It was also true to say that while such beliefs and policies might be suitable for the countries in which they had developed, they did not necessarily suit our situation. In this respect, Sir Seretse Khama, when he addressed the eleventh Annual Conference of the Botswana Democratic Party in Francistown on 1 April 1972 hit the nail on the head as far as the Union was concerned. His theme on that occasion was the *Philosophy of Kagisano*. To that end he sounded a caution to our world view of what education is. Hence he claimed: 'But our aspirations, our goals, our policies and our principles must be identified and expressed in terms which our people understand. This means that we must build them on the foundations provided by Botswana's culture, Botswana's values and tradition' (Khama, 1971).

His emphasis was based on the view that there can be no worthwhile education free from a people's cultural influence. This becomes crystal clear if one takes into consideration that the curriculum is a selection from culture. Since we cannot teach everything, we need to select those elements in culture that should not be lost to posterity. President Khama conceded that this had been done and it had been recognised that stable and sustained development of Botswana must be guided by national principles. These were, *Puso ya batho ka batho* – democracy, *ditiro tsa ditlhabololo* – development, *boipelego* – self-reliance, and *popagano ya sechaba* – unity. In the educational context, the implementation of these principles would lead to *Kagisano* – which has been described 'as the totality of the four national principles...' (Report of the NCE, 1977). *Kagisano* is concerned first with the idea of social justice, which implies fairness and equity. This must not be confused with equality but should concern itself with fair or equitable distribution by providing equal opportunities. Secondly, the sense of community and social responsibility deserves emphasis in the context of education since 'community feeling is at the root of African culture and the education system must preserve and foster it' (Report of the NCE, 1977). To meet this requirement, arrangements should be effected whereby community responsibility for education can be embodied in the system for governing schools. In addition, the curriculum of the schools should be so structured as to emphasise compassion and mutual responsibility. Above all, schools and colleges must operate as a community in order to realise *Kagisano*. That was what Patrick van Rensburg envisaged when he expressed the view 'that the secondary school in a developing country can be a focal point for development in the surrounding community' (van Rensburg, 1974). However, President Khama had warned that *Kagisano* should not be a slogan, 'but [an] ideal for our nation' (Khama, 1971).

Drake Selwe Becomes the President

It was at Francistown that the BTU held its conference in December 1971 under the leadership of a young but capable Drake Selwe, a headteacher of the Bakwena National School at Molepolole. It will be remembered that Kgomanyane, who had succeeded Matoane, did not stand at election time at St. Joseph's in 1970, and on that occasion Masogo was elected President of the Union. Masogo did not complete even a year as he had to leave to pursue further studies. Drake Selwe then became the President, and in him the Union found a steady and determined man whose talent for leadership was to blossom with time. His performance at the first conference was excellent in the light of the endemic and increasing problems of the Union. It was obvious that in his maiden Presidential address he dwelt on the difficulties experienced in the Union and of the limitations imposed on the progress of the organisation. The greatest limiting factor was the paucity of financial resources because of the inability of members at the branch level to pay subscriptions. The majority of teachers were paid very low salaries and hence their reluctance to meet their financial obligations towards the Union. However, the situation improved towards the end of the year by making subscription payment a passport to the popular music competitions (BTU Minutes of the Music Committee, 1971).

Selwe's address, based on the theme of the conference, was *The Organisational Structure of the Union and its Influence on the National Education Policy,* covered a large range of burning issues. The first of these was the housing problem for teachers. It will be remembered that coming soon after the Okoh Report's disappointment, an announcement was made to put houses up for sale – the house ownership scheme. Its stated aim was to encourage home ownership and to meet the needs of commerce and industry in the medium cost housing range. Once again, the Teaching Service was left out in the cold and this was a bitter pill to swallow, particularly in the wake of so many assurances from high offices, to not only better the lot of teachers but to incorporate their service in nation building through education. The formulation of a philosophy of education by the teachers was a call for commitment and dedication towards their service. First of all, the teachers had to be proud of their profession in order to give their very best. But if they were treated so shabbily that the communities they served despised them, how were they expected to portray a respectable image? Theirs was a lost cause, and the exodus of teachers from the profession to other attractive sectors of the Government was not unexpected. An uninspired and disheartened team could not pull together. What was needed in order to keep a committed cadre of teachers within the education system was to match our philosophic ideals with action.

For instance, President Selwe in his address referred to the speech made by the Minister of Local Government and Lands at the opening of schools at Machaneng and Makobeng where he stressed the need for teachers to lead exemplary lives in the eyes of the public and the pupils. Such words of exhortation were appreciated, but one wonders how teachers could gain the respect of their pupils and the public when each morning or as they went to work 'they literally crawled out of a shanty or hovel, while next door officers working at the Post Office, Police Force, Public Works ... leave for work from a dwelling place' (BTU Conference, 1971). At least it is gratifying to think that 20 years after that conference the housing of teachers has improved tremendously even if some problems remain. What is crucial at this point and worth noting is that our philosophy strategy meant different things to different people. To talk of equity and fair play had nothing to do with practices. How were teachers expected to infuse the concepts of equality and community experience through the curriculum if they were degraded in the eyes of those communities.

Of interest, teachers were not only ignored when others were showered with benefits, but they were constantly subjected to humiliating harassment. For instance, on 8 November 1971 a month before Selwe opened the conference on housing, the *Daily News* (a local paper) carried a story by the Kgatleng Council Secretary warning teachers to pay rent retrospectively from 1 January 1971 to the end of November 1971. The stern warning stated that 'any teacher who fails to pay rent within that time will be expelled from the Council quarters' (Daily News, 1971). Sometimes, on issues of this type it is difficult to make a judgement without the risk of being biased. One needs to get the facts straight. One of the Kgatleng teachers told the Daily News reporter that the teachers were not unwilling to pay rentals, 'but only that they were against the principle followed by the Council when assessing rent' (Daily News, 1971). There was, as one could discern, a fundamental difference between the teachers and the Council in determining the terms of the procedure on rental. Teachers themselves were not free from blame if one considers the occupancy of the Council's property and the refusal to pay rent in whatever circumstances. At one point it was even pointed out that in an effort to rectify what the teachers considered houses without proper amenities, including the absence of sanitation, it was then decided by the District Development Committee to acquire the services of a competent house evaluator in order to evaluate each Council house (Daily News, 1971). Before the decision was implemented, the teachers received the warning referred to above. As would have been expected, the District Council Secretary was quick to discuss the teachers' argument that all rentals should be based on a legitimate assessment of every property taking into account all the essentials and personal amenities. What is fair to note is that the story of the Kgatleng District Councils and the teachers was not confined to that area alone. Similar arguments and counter-arguments were heard from time to time from different District Councils. However, what is important was not the arguments themselves, but their effect on the morale of the teaching force in Botswana.

Selwe had one thing in mind, and this was to inspire and keep the morale of the teachers high and the reiteration of the question of low salaries seemed the most obvious means of keeping the bonds of unity alive. This point served at many teachers' gatherings as a rallying point. He reminded all that the Okoh Commission's terms of reference had been met and that the Government White paper would go a long way to ameliorating the suffering of teachers. 'To the dismay of all, instead of improving, things became worse, to the extent that an Anomalies Committee was set up...' (BTU Conference, 1971). Since the White Paper ignored a number of important issues, there was a general feeling of despondency. The attitude of the administration towards the teachers left much to be desired since they had for a long time borne the burden of discrimination. The fact that the Government continued to drag its feet helped to bring the teachers together including the 'doubting Thomases'.

The Coming of the Education Law

Sometimes in depicting the plight of the BTU, it is forgotten that within the government circles, there were many supporters of the teachers. These friends had campaigned before for a humane treatment of teachers irrespective of their employment agency. M.K. Segokgo, who was then the Parliamentary Secretary to the Ministry of Labour and Social Services, was among that band of friends. Since the start of the 1960s he and many other office bearers of the BPATA were anxious to see the implementation of the Education Law. At the BTU Conference at the Botswana Training Centre (BTC) in 1965, he sensed the urgency of the law, and promised that the teachers comments would be invited when the final document was drafted for submission to the Assembly in 1966. That was possible since the Teachers' Association had earlier had discussions with Her Majesty's Commissioner, Peter Fawcus (later Sir Peter Fawcus) of the need for an Education Law. When the Teaching

Service Law No. 35 of 1964 was promulgated, the BPATA Executive Committee was swift in its reaction and criticised it in a letter to the Minister of Labour and Social Services dated, 30 October 1965.

The teachers were absolutely correct in their rejection of the law because it was extremely difficult to understand fully the provisions of the Bill in the absence of any statement underlying its clauses. The teachers believed that these were the necessary ingredients of a sound and comprehensive Education Law. To justify their criticism, the teachers put forward what they considered the appropriate elements of a Bill providing for education in an emergent and democratic state. Under basic principles they raised two points. The points underpinned the teachers vigilance and determination to make some contribution to a law that would affect them as professionals. First, they called for universal education – which would embody the best that culture and civilisation had produced over the ages. Secondly, the teachers touched on a critical note, for they called for education for good citizenship. This point came to be this country's philosophy of education. The concern of all those entrusted with the education of the young was to turn out of our schools citizens who are aware of their responsibilities. Today this is the ongoing theme of the social studies programme which stresses that education should be directed towards the development of the human personality to the maximum (BTU Communication to the Minister of Labour and Social Services, 1965).

The Union obviously had their own ideas on what constituted a sound system of education. Its success lay in the broadest possible participation by the teachers and parents. The same approach was extolled by the NCE (1977).

The Union was critical of the power that the Minister and Director of Education exercised, thereby ignoring the creative role which the teachers and parents had to play in training children for citizenship. It is fair to note that through the bill, and for first time, an opportunity had presented itself for Batswana to help direct the development of future citizens of Botswana. As Bechuanaland was proceeding orderly towards independence, some of the provisions of the Bill were out of step with the democratic processes developing in the country. The Bill was dominated at all levels by the power of the Minister to nominate, even at the level of School Committees when the trend at local and national levels was towards elections paying heed to the wishes of the people. While it was acceptable to have the Minister's representative in some of these bodies, the presence of the representatives of the parents and teachers was desirable. This was a trend that was to be emphasised by the NCE in its Report of 1977. The idea of community participation in primary education has become a central point in the running of our education system through the Ministry of Local Government and Lands and Housing and the Ministry of Education respectively and the community junior secondary school education system.

The coming of the Local Education Authorities, the establishment of the Appeal Tribunal, and the unlimited powers of the Director and the Minister of Education in particular, received severe criticism. First the local education authorities posed a number of problems. For instance, the principle of nomination instead of election. Why were local authorities in the first place entrusted with the job of raising finances since the poorer areas generally in greater need of funds would not be able to meet their needs. Whereas if such responsibility lay with the central authority, funds would be directed to the areas that needed it most. The teachers were convinced of the need and importance of a direct connection between the schools and district committees elected by teachers and parents, the Department and the Ministry. If such links were instituted, the democratic process established in the political field would be reflected in the educational field (BTU, 1965).

With regard to the establishment of the Appeal Tribunal, the teachers were equally concerned that it was created in order to dispense with the courts as institutions to deal with the problems arising from operations of the Education Bill. The teachers felt that the courts were there to dispense justice and traditionally were known as guardians of liberty of the individual against the arbitrary actions of officialdom. They believed that the Appeal Board would not necessarily be bound by legal procedure. For instance, Law No. 35 of 1964 Part VII, Section 25(7) stated that, 'The Board ... shall not be bound to receive and consider only evidence admissible in a court of law' (Laws of Botswana, 1974). The most logical thing was to use an already established institution rather than create one that was considered rather dubious.

The powers of the Director of Education and Minister of Education were the subject of much discussion in the BTU. For instance, the power of the Minister to close schools was considered drastic and unnecessary. When a school was 'ordered to be closed and remained closed for a consecutive period of six months or more, the Chief Education Officer shall remove the name of the school from the register...' (Laws of Botswana, 1974). While not advocating chaos in the operations of the Ministry, such a measure and related ones were considered harsh. The greatest challenge facing Botswana was to establish schools and not to close them. The thirst for education in the whole of Africa since independence and in Botswana, in particular, had to be taken into account by establishing technical and vocational schools in addition to the present academic schools so that the many and varied talents of the people could be developed to the full. There was a great need, instead, to encourage local initiative. The Administration had to be reminded that many schools that started privately in a small way later became Government-aided schools. Too often, groups of individuals inspired by the ideal of self-reliance went out to demonstrate their contribution to development by starting bookkeeping classes, building extra classrooms and so on, but their hopes were invariably frustrated by bureaucratic requirements so that by the time the expected reply was received, time had been lost. However, it should be pointed out that while doubts were raised on some practices which exceeded expectations, the teachers concurred with legitimate control on the part of the Minister and Director of Education. For instance, the Union was in full agreement that if the Minister was satisfied that if a school was operated in a manner that was calculated to be 'detrimental to the physical, mental or moral welfare of the pupils attending thereat...' (Laws of Botswana, 1974). In addition, any person who had been convicted of an offence while managing or assisting in the managing of any school, might be ordered to close the school. That was an important move, for as a result of the demand for education, fraudulent acts might be committed in the name of assisting the needy.

With regard to the prohibition of publications, the teachers again queried the extensive powers of the Minister and the Director. It was pointed out that such control was symptomatic of a Government that, seized with fear and frustration, might resort to legislation. Of course, the surest way of popularising ideas was to ban them. Over and above this, the function of banning publications was too weighty to be left in the hands of one person – the Minister. This responsibility was given as follows: 'The Minister may by notice in the Gazette declare any publication or periodical publication to be undesirable for use in schools ... and shall be deemed to extend to all copies, in whatever language of such publication or periodical publication' (Laws of Botswana, 1974).

The teachers warned, that the clause, if left unchecked, would defeat the basic principles on which free and liberal education stand. Section 24 of the Bill cut across the tenets of true liberal education, which must train the individual to think critically.

The Minister's powers of nomination were also criticised by the teachers as it did not give the opportunity to elect suitable members to school committees, which is the inalienable right of the community. If the community were given the chance to elect they might at first falter, but might later learn the proper procedure of managing their affairs. Through participation, consultation and coordination, Batswana it was felt, would develop a sense of pride.

Other matters which agitated the minds of the teachers included the non-reference to housing for its members in all categories of schools. Teachers also took the opportunity to raise the issue of compulsory education for the entire primary course. There was a feeling that since Botswana was independent, it was important to raise the degree of literacy in order to curb delinquency. As we know today, Botswana has been preoccupied with literacy programmes for a long time, and this effort can be seen as a literacy campaign leading to the establishment of the Botswana Extension College (BEC) in 1973. 'BEC will be established in 1973, and it will use correspondence courses, radio and face-to-face methods to teach a wide range of subjects, ...

It is planned that the College should eventually run a variety of courses, for example, Junior Certificate subjects leading to formal examinations – courses of upgrading and retraining' (NDP, 1973–78).

To enhance literacy and thereby contribute to manpower development, BEC worked closely with other extension departments and agencies including the Division of Extra Mural Services (DEMS), now the Institute of Adult Education (IAE) at the University of Botswana. As we now know, out of the Botswana Extension College was born the Department of Non-Formal Education (DNFE) in 1978. The teachers did, at the same time, recognise the need for adult education and literacy in a country where the majority of the people were illiterate. 'The successful promotion of development especially in the rural context, rests heavily upon the ability of people to communicate. The high illiteracy rate in Botswana makes it difficult to disseminate information and general educational materials' (NDP, 1973–78). The importance of these concerns lay deep in the teachers' view of education – a right to which all, young and old should have access. It was an attempt to address the sins of omission of the colonial administration. The teachers accepted the view that for a nation to be democratic it needs to embrace the educational process. Illiteracy tends to delay the process of change. It is interesting to note that the NCE (1977) recommended that literacy should be given priority in Botswana's non formal education programme in that 'a literate population is an important long term objective if Botswana's other national objectives are to be met' (NCE, 1977). Perhaps what is significant about the teachers' thoughts is that their outlook on education, and what it should be, touched on the concerns of the Government. Their utterances no doubt fuelled the need to examine our education system in some depth. Such thoughts called for a clear statement on the National Education Policy. There was a concern at that time that our education should not only meet the needs of the minority. In the context of the post independent Botswana such an ideal had no place.

Such claims, for instance, that universal education was impracticable in Botswana's economic situation were rejected as unfounded. The teachers urged for a concerted effort by all to plan education according to our needs and situation. The challenge that faced Botswana was to work out a system of education based on our philosophy of life. This included the eradication of illiteracy, for to keep people illiterate was to opt for inequality and discrimination in the long run. Illiteracy was considered the main obstacle to the principle of equality and to that end the Union was opposed to the establishment of institutions that perpetuate class differences in a democratic Botswana. The Union unequivocally condemned the mushrooming of schools that charged exorbitant fees which could only be afforded by a few parents, while hundreds of Batswana children roamed the streets without education.

The simmering discontent continued in its entirety up to 1972, and there seemed no attempt to address these problems. So, when the teachers assembled at the Gaborone Secondary School in December 1972 for their conference, as stated before, they were without doubt prepared to make their grievances known to the Ministry of Education. On 13 December 1972 the teachers marched through the centre of Gaborone to the Ministry of Education. What was most gratifying on that momentous occasion, was the fact that one spotted some UBLS students marching with the teachers as a mark of solidarity. These were the same students who had earlier sent the Minister of Education (B.C. Thema) a petition querying the improper treatment of teachers in the field. 'This negligence by the Ministry of the conditions of Batswana teachers is perpetuated by the presence of expatriate teachers. These teachers from outside are induced to come into the country by being offered higher salaries than nationals and given subsidiary allowances' (UBLS, 1970).

On that day, all business at the Ministry of Education came to a halt because of the unprecedented step taken by the teachers. Both the Government and the local community were taken by surprise, but the Government adopted a low profile for it was a peaceful demonstration. Even the police within the Government enclave showed no particular interest but simply went on with their regular chores. The teachers' patience had run out and it marked what they called 'an end of the road to negotiation' with the Ministry of Education. The Ministry's lack of care coupled with the absence of appropriate conditions of service, the dismissal and termination of teachers services without valid reasons, poor housing and the generally poor treatment of teachers by the Ministry of Education had led them to the impasse. The resolutions that the Union subsequently passed included the demand for a reshuffle of the Ministry of Education and a greater say and influence on education by the teachers. The conference closed with the Union more prepared to forge ahead with their struggle for what they termed legitimate rights. On reflection, one must say that a new culture began to emerge from the 1972 demonstration, and compelled the administration to listen to the views of the teachers. It was during this time that many subject panels were born and were largely manned by the teachers. Other structures like the National Council for Teacher Education, the Consultative Committee and the formation of the Task Forces during the NCE (1977) symbolised the acceptance of the role the teachers could play in the evolution of education in Botswana.

The new Executive Committee was thus saddled with the big challenge of organising the Union into a formidable fighting force in order to carry on where the 1972 Conference had left off. The Executive Committee consisted of the following: President, George Kgoroba; Vice–President, Drake Selwe; General Secretary, Temba Vanqa; Assistant Secretary, M.S. Maoto; Treasurer, J.O. Rammekwa and Editor of *The Teacher,* T.S. Motshwane (BTU Conference, 1972).

In George Kgoroba, the Union found a dauntless leader, a debater and clear thinker. The soft spoken Kgoroba turned out to be a ruthless and hard puncher whenever the rights of the teachers were tampered with. He knew the problems of the organisation well, for before he was called upon to lead it, he had served in various positions as the General Secretary, Chairman of the Music Committee and in many other ad hoc committees. The Union, therefore, could not have elected a better leader. The two years he spent in office were crucial for he pulled the organisation firmly upwards following the Gaborone demonstration by the teachers. He soon earned the respect of friend and foe, for his sound principles, courage and forthrightness. His hand was strengthened by the fact that the teachers' call for a careful examination of the educational ills led to some progressive Members of Parliament demanding a major shake up in the Ministry of Education. To drive the point home, the President, in his address at the Annual Conference of the BTU in 1973, called for an inquiry into how the Ministry was run. Taking his cue from the conference theme – 'Curriculum Development as a Basis for a Sound Education', the President advocated a thorough scrutiny of the country's education machinery which, as he put it 'was pulling at a low gear' (BTU Conference, 1973).

The conference in its further deliberations expressed concern that our education, to a large extent, reflected foreign influence and was geared to produce white-collar workers. Looking back though, this author feels that these were legitimate sentiments, expressed by teachers, yet there was a mistake in thinking that the colonial system could, in its entirety, be thrown out the window in favour of education that was considered relevant in all respects. It takes time to change from one system of education to another because educational change is a steady and slow process. In fact, it had been shown that many independent countries have become more steeped in colonial systems of education long after colonial administration had come to an end. What teachers had in mind was to introduce technical and vocational education. This outlook had leanings to what the Swaneng Hill School had set out to do. It was to become a model of a system of secondary education which 'widened the curriculum to include other technical subjects' (van Rensburg, 1974). To curb some of the foreign influences it was important to rethink our curriculum in order to meet Botswana's genuine needs. Among other burning issues discussed at length was the double shift system in primary schools. The shift system was an arrangement whereby primary pupils were taught in two groups, one in the morning and the other in the afternoon because of large classes which among other things had led to a lack of classroom space. The arrangement was intended as a temporary relief measure, but seemed to continue indefinitely. Fortunately, the system had been abandoned by at least 90% of primary schools and this may have been the result of an improvement due to the provision of additional classrooms and an increase in the number of trained teachers.

Contributors to Botswana's Philosophy of Education
  (a) Patrick van Rensburg
  (b) Paulo Freire
  (c) Kenneth Koma
  (d) Julius Nyerere

Another boost to the teachers' search for Botswana's philosophy of education was the emergence during the mid-1960s and continuing through to the end of the 1970s, of literature which set out to examine closely the educational dilemma in the developing world. Sometimes it is difficult to say to what extent the Union's efforts were fuelled by the new literature, but it is fair to assume that they managed to steal a leaf from this breath of fresh ideas. The writers who featured prominently were Patrick van Rensburg, the founder of Swaneng Hill School, Julius Nyerere then the President of the Republic of Tanzania, Kenneth Koma, leader of the Botswana National Front and Paulo Freire of Brazil. One thing in common held by these writers is that their experiences on education derived from the Third World. All of them had known the educational ravages of colonial domination. They were, therefore, concerned about the nature of education in the developing countries and they in different ways called for an education system that was community based or oriented. Their perception of education and the community involvement in the education of children must have influenced the Report of the NCE. 'Not only were schools to be community centres but that the education of the young is a joint responsibility of the school ... and parents ... parental encouragement contributes importantly to progress in schools' (NCE, 1977). They all advocated a drastic departure from the colonial education which, according to Nyerere, was not designed to prepare young people for the service of their own country and their people, but 'was motivated by the desire to inculcate the values of the colonial society and to train individuals for the service of the colonial state' (Akinpelu, 1981).

PATRICK VAN RENSBURG

A brief examination of these writers and their thoughts on education is relevant. First, Patrick van Rensburg's ideas. He has been associated with education in this country from the early 1960s when he settled here. He gives a vivid picture of the problems that the Standard 6 school leavers faced. The primary school pupils he taught at one school in Serowe were hopeful that they might succeed in starting their own secondary school. They were aware of the difficulties of getting into a secondary school, but they might not have known what type of education they wanted. It was van Rensburg, among others who saw the purpose of education as 'the fullest development of the individual human personality and intellect, liberated from the basic want' (van Rensburg, 1974). Education is intended to prepare people for life but above all in emerging countries it is to make the educated concerned with the political, cultural and material progress of all the people. It was necessary to look forward to a time when every young person could have an equal opportunity of developing his talents to the full.

A new approach was also effected in thinking about education, and its purpose was to promote development 'based on the character, traditions and culture of the people, the existing state of the country's development, its educational, technological and scientific progress and its economic resources' (van Rensburg, 1974). Basic to this was an attempt to break away from the colonial set up where education was seen as the key to the betterment of living conditions, prosperity and a way of escaping from poverty and drudgery on the land. The material success of the coloniser was seen in terms of his academic acquisition.

Patrick van Rensburg

One of the stumbling blocks to progress in the developing countries was the idea of seeing primary education as a logical step to secondary and further education. 'There are large numbers of pupils at primary schools which are simply a catchment for secondary schools' (van Rensburg, 1974). Even the curriculum was designed as the initial part of a longer programme. What was missing was an attempt to cater for those who would not proceed beyond primary education. Primary education made such little impact that it was not able to support those who left school at that stage. What also complicated the problem was the preponderance of unqualified teachers, so that when the pupils finished primary schooling they had no technical skills. In order to remedy the situation, the primary course had to be reorganised so as to cater for the needs of the large number for whom primary education would be terminal.

It was in the light of these problems that van Rensburg backed his educational theory with practical activities and brought the Brigades Movement into existence. Those who joined the Brigades were required to give their labour in exchange for food, technical instruction and about two hours of teaching a day in general subjects. On the academic level, efforts were made to formulate syllabuses in Setswana, English, civics, mathematics and science, and the stress was on their relevance to those young people. 'The syllabus we evolve will, we hope, cater especially for their needs but we will aim at quality' (van Rensburg, 1974). It was with the advent of the Brigades that the idea of self-sufficiency in terms of food supply by the school for its own needs and creating a market in the neighbouring communities found root.

Since there were no viable industries in the country to provide employment, agriculture attracted good attention. It had to be revitalised by introducing new ideas and techniques. The aim was to make it more profitable for those who engage in it and make it more attractive to young people and especially the literate youth. One should comment that in this country, however well intended the idea, there are two factors which militated against it. First, faced with harsh climatic conditions, there was a need to upgrade our technology in order to cope with such climatic conditions. Secondly, even those who advocated agricultural programmes saw it in terms of other people's children and not theirs.

The idea of education oriented towards development by Swaneng Hill School must be seen as van Rensburg's greatest contribution. It was an attempt to stem a trend in developing countries including Botswana where only a tiny minority of the population managed to complete secondary education at the expense of the tax payer. This invariably led to the creation of a small privileged elite that aimed at material prosperity through the exclusion of their fellowmen. Swaneng's philosophy sought 'to discourage the notion that education is a ladder on which ambition climbs to privilege' (van Rensburg, 1974). It was imperative that the educated minority in a developing country should be made aware that their role was to make more people share the benefits of development. The aim of the school was to ensure that as their students left, 'they will feel under some compulsion from within themselves, through sympathy and fellow feeling with the poor and the hungry, to fight want, ignorance and disease in their country' (van Rensburg, 1974). The horizon-widening effect of education was to enable those who received it to play a much more effective part as decision makers in the development of their country.

THE CONTRIBUTION OF PAULO FREIRE

Another thinker who made a valid contribution to education in the developing world is Paulo Freire, a national of Brazil. He was mainly concerned with the education of adults. In his approach to education, he started from the premise that there was no neutral education; education to him is either for liberation or domination. He, therefore, advocated education for liberation which was directed at the physical and mental liberation of the colonised communities, a liberation from the subtleties of colonial domination. He called for a complete rejection of foreign structures which have rendered the colonised person rootless. He believed that no one was capable of freeing the oppressed except the oppressed (Freire, 1972). How can this educational ideal be attained? Freire saw this in what he called cultural action for freedom which was the appropriate process of humanisation. Humanisation is the ultimate goal and according to one of Freire's main themes, it is the pursuit of full humanity. The pursuit of full humanity cannot be effected in isolation but only in fellowship and solidarity. It is through problem posing education that humanisation can be attained. It is the oppressed who must fight for liberation. This points the way to the teachers and students to become subjects of educational process by rejecting authoritarianism. To achieve this position, the genuine educator must be dialogical from the beginning. He has to enter into a dialogue with the learner. This is the horizontal relationship between persons. Without the deep love for the individual and the world, it would be impossible to name the world which is the basis of creation. Central to dialogue is the love of man. Freire claimed that in order to work with the peasants and other workers we have to believe in them. 'We have to establish real communication with the people in order to know what we have to learn with them in order to teach with them' (Freire, 1972).

Both van Rensburg and Freire advocated interesting insights into education. The former's approach is basic and down to earth and is in line with the process of change in developing countries. The attempt to universalise education is welcome. There is today talk about basic education for all, which fully embraces the idea of equity and justice. Resources must be used judiciously to meet the needs of the majority of children, particularly the underprivileged. Central to this philosophy is that education should not be used as the passport to privilege but that the skills acquired through education should uplift the community as a whole. One of the basic quests of Swaneng Hill School sought to 'inculcate a commitment to social justice among the educated minority and – equip them with knowledge and skills needed for development' (van Rensburg, 1974). The aim was to make the school a focal point for development in the community. Freire's theory of education of the adult does not lend itself easily to comprehension because of its subtlety. Central to his approach is the attempt to diminish the dominating role of the teachers in the learning situation for the teacher must himself also learn as he teaches. There is a need to create a sound relationship between the teacher and the learner, but above all the learner's ability to acquire knowledge must not be undermined, for his learning must derive from his environmental situation.

Education therefore, seen in this way, stresses empathy between the educator and the educatee. Its implication is understood by those who see that the teacher can be a learner and the learner a teacher. In this view it is the equality of the learner with the teacher, for the teacher is no longer merely one who teaches but one who is himself taught in dialogue with the student, who in turn, while being taught, also teaches. The point is that when we all learn and share common ideas and values, myths cannot find a place in such a learning situation. No one volunteers to know everything while the rest are ignorant. The reverse of this would be to treat students as passive recipients and the teacher the fountain of all knowledge. The monologue has an equivalent of what Freire calls the 'banking' concept of education which fits well with the idea of cultural action for domination. The teacher must not aim to 'fill' the learner with contents that are detached from reality, for such a procedure turns learners into genuine repositories of education. The student-teacher contradiction must be solved so that both are simultaneously teachers and students. It is not the role of the educator to regulate the way the world enters into the students (Freire, 1972).

For one who has spent a lifetime in the classroom, Freire's ideas are most plausible. They are an attempt to relegate to the background attempts to memorise stagnant facts that do not relate to life situations of the learners. Adults as well as young learners are concerned with information that solves their problems. Equally important, our educational strategies should avoid the absolute domination of the learning environment by the teacher. There is evidence of this in our local schools from both the primary and secondary levels, and efforts should be made to allow the learner to find out for himself with minimum guidance. The mug and jug situation is rejected. Nonetheless this is not to say this approach is not without problems. The first one is that teachers tend to be very conservative and do not want to accept insecurity. There is no greater truth than that old dogs cannot learn new tricks. What is needed is to instil these concepts into our pre-service trainees and make them part and parcel of the in-service programmes for adult educators. Secondly, in most situations our system is so examination oriented that we have hardly time to think of the implications of our style of teaching and the harm it can cause.

Koma's Contribution to Philosophy of Education

Kenneth Koma has contributed to the dialogue in post-independence education in this country. He rightly states that education is not a luxury but an essential part of the basic equipment of a country. Without education as a starting point all other forms of investment turn out to be a big loss. It is absolutely necessary that the development of human resources must precede all other forms of investment (Koma, 1982). Koma like Abdou Moumouni (a Cameroonian educationist) is highly critical of colonial education. Like Moumouni, he contends that the abolition of illiteracy in developing countries is a temporary task, but education necessitates an articulate system. It requires a system that is implemented by qualified cadres who have a definite orientation and a clear and well defined perception. The teachers and cadres who received their schooling in the colonial-type system need to be re-educated and reorientated. Crash programmes of re-education for teachers will be one of the ways to achieve this re-orientation.

Since the colonial system of education was an imported system brought by the colonisers, it was superimposed on the traditional informal African system of education of pre-colonial Africa. The colonial education depersonalised and marginalised the African culturally. Indigenous culture was 'submerged and many Batswana were encouraged to believe that their own cultural inheritance was inferior to that imported by the British' (Report of the NCE, 1977). That is why there has been a search for an appropriate system of education of real independent Africa which must borrow certain elements from the traditional pre-colonial African education. These borrowings could be integrated and incorporated into a new concept of education which is both modern and advanced (Vanqa, 1979).

Whatever the shortcomings of traditional education, it developed the body and the mind as well as imparting moral responsibility and character to the individual at the centre within the community of society. The main problem and inadequacy in the present system is that it is not adapted to present the needs and requirements of the problems and tasks in developing countries. A worthwhile education must place the community before the individual. Koma has condemned Botswana's education as it is influenced largely by class differentiation which favours those who are decision-makers to the disadvantage of the subordinate groups. He concluded in the paper which he presented at the Symposium on Education for Development in Botswana in August 1983 by saying: 'when we speak of illiteracy in Botswana, and in fact when we speak generally about the problems of education, we really speak about the education of the poorer classes and the education of the second or third class citizens. The most socially despised ethnic groups are also the poorest. The most under-privileged classes are also the poorest and the poorest are also the groups which receive the least and sometimes none of the benefits of our educational efforts' (Crowder, 1984).

Perhaps one of the most fascinating contributions to serious thought about post-independence education by Dr Koma relates to his question of whether we can have education that is community centred while we allow the economy to encourage individualism? He readily accepted the fact that man is the deciding factor and if one succeeds in changing man, 'he will ultimately change his material world' (Koma, 1982). He conceded that there is a constant interplay of influence between the base and the superstructure. In order to change the superstructure, we must change the base. If we apply this to education we should be aware that it is not the only aspect of society, for man has ideas and institutions and above all material existence. 'To change man effectively, you have to change not only his ideas and institutions, you have to change also his material world' (Koma, 1982). For instance, if we teach man to live in harmony with other men, we should provide an environment where he can live in harmony with other men. Koma concluded that 'it is vital to teach man that there is a need to live in harmony and cooperation with his fellow men. But it is even better, in addition, to teach him this if an environment in which his daily life will be lived in cooperation with other men' (Koma, 1982).

These sentiments were also expressed by the outgoing President of the

BTU, George Kgoroba when he addressed the BTU conference at Lobatse Secondary School in 1974. He based his talk on the theme of the conference *Education for a Purpose*. He told the teachers that 'Our system is irrelevant, outdated and ... a system borrowed from our colonial masters' (BTU Conference, 1974). He expressed his rejection of an education system which he considered out of step with the wishes and aspirations of Batswana. He appreciated that many leaders were wrestling with the problems of poverty, disease and ignorance. But the progress was extremely slow partly due to the fact that they were trying to solve their problems by relying on an old an unsuitable type of education. It was, therefore, impossible 'to use yesterday's tool for today's job and expect to be in business tomorrow'. He noted that the changes that had taken place in politics and in government had not been matched in education, and while many independent African states had severed political ties with their rulers, they continued to lean heavily on those countries' educational patterns. What African states needed urgently was a revolution of their education systems to take place at the following levels:

(a) universal education and education for life;
(b) elementary and secondary school curricula;
(c) the emphasis on science and technology;
(d) adult education;
(e) general culture of the people;
(f) craft work or practical subjects; and
(g) teacher education.

An urgent call was made to develop a built-in science attitude in our youth and the people as a whole in our education system. There was great need to adapt and reconcile traditional values to meet the demands of modern society. If the stated policy of the ruling party was to provide the type of education which sought to create social justice, the existence of differentiated schools for the rich on the one hand and the poor on the other made nonsense of the ideal and was morally indefensible. It was wrong to encourage a system of education that prepared only a privileged few to occupy prestigious positions. This differentiation in primary education manifested itself in the dismal Standard 7 results where out of 13 453 who sat the examination, only 2841 secured places at our secondary schools, while those who found no places at the Brigades would roam the streets (Standard 7 Results, 1973).

In conclusion, the President made some far-reaching recommendations. One of these recommendations was the appointment of a National Education Commission to review the whole system of Botswana's Education, composed mainly of Batswana and led by a Motswana. It is interesting to note that two years later in 1976, the Government appointed a Commission to look at our education and make the necessary recommendations. The report *Education for Kagisano* was published in 1977. The second recommendation called for the reorganisation of the Ministry of Education. In this respect sufficient staff were to be employed to develop efficiency in the construction, expansion and administration of sound educational policies. Government was implored to recruit young Batswana university graduates into the Ministry of Education which was the only sector of Government where young Batswana were conspicuously absent.

Another important recommendation was education for social justice as a Government's goal. It was imperative to introduce equal educational opportunities in rural and urban areas and that free and compulsory education should be implemented at the primary level. In this connection, there was need to overhaul the existing primary and secondary school curricula as well as teacher training education.

If the concept of social justice meant anything, Kgoroba called for the complete and immediate abolition of the artificial division of schools into Tswana medium and English medium schools and establish a uniform primary school system which would offer equal opportunities to all Batswana children. Tied up with this was the call to transfer all primary education to central Government.

Among other recommendations was the need to change the unsatisfactory system of education through curriculum reform, including the teaching of science, mathematics and arts and crafts. This called for the redoubling of efforts on teacher training programmes as well as in-service courses.

The 1974 Conference signalled the close of an era for President Kgoroba as he came to the end of his term and was succeed by Drake Selwe. The year 1974 was significant in that it can be safely said that it marked the improvement of relations between the Ministry of Education and the BTU. The presidency of Selwe was to witness unprecedented changes which no doubt put the Union in better stead.

Perhaps at this point, it is proper to pause and ask to what extent have the ideas of van Rensburg, Freire, Koma and Nyerere been incorporated into our education system? Or, to what extent does our education system reflect these ideas? First, it is important to remember that education is a sensitive subject which touches the lives of all people. Therefore, there is need to take precautions and scrutinise very closely any ideas that impinge on established or accepted educational thought. Secondly, it is important to remember that however plausible and convincing are the arguments for new ideas, they do not necessarily lend themselves to acceptance if the Government of the day is not convinced of their benefits and validity. Coupled with that, the establishment, whether social or political, tends to move very cautiously.

If we examine Freire's ideas such as humanisation, dialectics and conscientisation, all have a place in our education system and have influenced our thinking. Humanisation is tied to man's pursuit of full humanity in order to interact with other humans effectively. The pursuit for full humanity cannot be effected in isolation but only in fellowship and solidarity. This is consistent with the view that 'no one can be authentically human while he prevents others from being so' (Freire, 1972). According to our educational philosophy this is the basis for social justice. All the people must be accorded the opportunity to become human. Problem-posing education requires that man subjected to domination must fight for liberation. If we see education as a liberating agent we then see the role of education throughout the cycles of our education system including adult education. Through dialogue in the teaching approach we come to understand others by exchanging ideas with them. This calls for the horizontal relations between persons. 'We have to establish real communication with the people, we have to be humble, we have to know what we have to learn with them in order to teach them' (Freire, 1972). In such a teaching system the teacher cannot treat students as passive recipients while he sees himself as the fountain of all knowledge. The new teaching methods including the project method which have become so common in our schools point to this necessity. Conscientisation which encompasses Freire's philosophy of education implies overcoming 'false consciousness' and also means 'the critical insertion of the conscientised person into demythologised reality' (Freire, 1972). It is only through a radical denunciation of dehumanising structures that conscientisation can become viable. Education is to overcome the mythicisation of the reality of the oppressor. Perhaps this approach is more closely observed in literature, history, mathematics and sciences. The developing world is aware of its potential through a revolutionary approach in local literature, history and other disciplines.

On turning to van Rensburg, we are aware of how some of the ideas hatched at Swaneng Hill School in the early 1960s have found place in our education system. Initially the Swaneng Hill School ideal was to ensure that all children, and not a select few have access to schooling. It was a break from the elitist education which found root during the colonial era. The Swaneng Hill School flame never died and many have come to accept the reality of such a strategy. Education has come to be accepted as a right and not a privilege. Today the idea of basic education for all is on everybody's lips. Nonetheless, it would be erroneous to believe that all these ideas emanated from Swaneng Hill School, but they did help to champion the cause by example. Children who had no chance of entering regular secondary schools earlier were accepted at Swaneng. Some of those 'rejects' now hold responsible positions within Government and private sector.

The other ideas which found expression at Swaneng Hill School included the introduction of meaningful practical subjects and the involvement of the community in the life of the school. Some of these ideas had been considered elsewhere on a theoretical plain. At Swaneng they became a reality through the cooperatives. Some of the students acquired skills that have enabled them to live fuller lives. One should not think that these novel ideas were accepted without question, for many battles were fought. The likes of van Rensburg were attacked openly in high places. As one can see, this was a bold attack. 'van Rensburg's claims were aimed at perverting our youth and retarding the progress of the country...' (Daily News, 1977). At the same time there were those who hailed the brilliance of van Rensburg's efforts. The 'greatest contribution made by Swaneng Hill School to rural development in Botswana was the Brigade Movement, fathered by van Rensburg' (Daily News, 1983). At the same time it is fair to state that the Government itself partly embraced these ideas by establishing the Brigades Development Centre (BRIDEC) and spreading the Brigade movement across the country through the establishment of the Polytechnic and Vocational Training Centres.

THE CONTRIBUTION OF JULIUS NYERERE

The ideas of Julius Nyerere have a bearing on education for almost all countries in the developing world. Nonetheless, it should not be assumed that everything he espoused found ready acceptance. He perceived the education system as an instrument of society to re-inforce the ideals of society. Before education can be restructured the social reorganisation of the community should take place first. 'Only when we are clear about the kind of society we are trying to build can we design our educational service to serve our goals' (Nyerere, 1968). Education should be used as a means to mobilise communal cooperation and not individual success at the expense of others. He projected the idea of Ujamaa commonly referred to as 'familyhood' which is characterised by work by everyone in order to be self-reliant and to develop equality and respect for human dignity. These ideas are reflected in our education system. Nyerere posited that, 'Our education must inculcate a sense of commitment to the total community, and help the pupils to accept the values appropriate to our kind of future, not those appropriate to our colonial past' (Nyerere, 1968). Perhaps the most outstanding contribution of Nyerere to education in the developing world was his insistence that education must prepare young people for work in a rural society where development depends largely upon the efforts of the people in agriculture and village development. The involvement of young people in development is vividly illustrated in our *Tirelo Sechaba* commonly called National Service. Earlier, Nyerere had condemned the 'locking' up of youth in prestigious institutions to continue consuming what had been produced by old and frail people. This, tied up with schools being reorganised to 'become communities – which practice the precept of self reliance' (Nyerere, 1968) was what was important. We support the idea of schools becoming community centres and this is exemplified by the primary and junior community secondary schools in Botswana.

Conclusion
It was the teachers within and beyond the confines of the BTU who popularised the ideas of thinkers like van Rensburg, Julius Nyerere, Kenneth Koma and Paulo Freire. It was teachers particularly at secondary schools and at the tertiary level who gave meaning to these philosophies within the classroom. The BTU with other teacher organisations in Botswana gave expression to such thoughts. That education is a right and not a privilege may have been popularised by the teachers with support from the Government of the day.

Chapter Six

A New Direction Towards Education: Advice and Inspection

It is fitting at this stage to pause and examine briefly the nature and the format of the Education Department reports submitted by the Director of Education, School Inspectors, Education Officers and Sub-Inspectors from the late 1930s to the present. It is also fitting to examine the impact of these on the development of education both in the BP and then in Botswana. It should be through the gallant stand of the teachers and through their organisations that they pressed for the humanisation of the teaching service. The Administration, with the help of teachers, set out to broaden the outlook of the Education Officer, to see teachers as allies and the teachers to see him as a friend and a helper.

The purpose of this Chapter is to look at the transformation of the relationship between the Department (later Ministry) of Education officials and the teachers in the schools. What comes out clearly is that whatever the Inspectors and Education Officers pronounced on the teaching force, their comments reflected badly on the organisation of the education system ranging from the teacher training programmes to the paucity of equipment at the schools and other facilities. In this respect, it is clear that the BTU and its predecessor the BPATA reacted sharply to the naked accusations by some rash and little discerning inspectors who later became Education Officers. The spate of condemnations that followed some inspection visitations resulted in a barrage of threats and sometimes dismissals. The BTU frequently came to the rescue of teachers, particularly when such measures were considered unfair. For instance, at that time there were a large proportion of untrained teachers who not only lacked professional training but had low qualifications. Such teachers needed help and not condemnation. Some schools lacked equipment and teaching materials to such an extent that children never got decent tuition, and therefore, inspectors and education officers were called upon to show empathy and to give a helping hand – very few of course, exercised that option. At the same time, we should remember that there were teachers who did not pull their weight, and therefore deserved strengthening up. There were of course, negligent teachers who deserved to be punished, but even they needed humane treatment as some of them were ignorant of their rights as well as their responsibilities.

The Early Reports in the Protectorate

The early reports in the 1940s were dominated by negative reports in subjects such as English and Setswana at Mmopane School: 'there pupils read English and Setswana with difficulty and spelling is poor' (Report of the Education Dept. 1947). But there was acknowledgement where good work was done. 'The standard of work throughout the schools showed slight improvement on that of the previous years and more care was taken to answer the question set (Report of the Education Dept. 1949). But there were instances where some officers reached a point of despair. 'Because of chaotic conditions in many schools it is correct to say that a great deal of the money spent on primary education is completely wasted' (Report of the Education Dept. 1965 and 1966). The report went on talking of the fantastically high rate of wastage in primary schools and of the very small number of pupils who managed to struggle through the course from year to year. Coupled with this rather unsatisfactory situation was the slow start of secondary education. The first venture into secondary education was made in 1944, when a junior secondary course was begun at St. Joseph's College near Gaborone. The other aspect of this section will examine how the teachers' cases arose, their nature and what impact they had on the difficult managerial system with the preponderance of 'teachers whose qualification is a mediocre pass in the primary school certificate examination' (Report of the Education Dept. 1965 and 1966). One should point out from the outset that some teachers' cases were serious, ranging from negligence at work and unbecoming conduct, to trivial ones including late arrival at the beginning of the school term and truancy. What is also fascinating was how the cases were settled and the procedures adopted. Some decisions were fair but others where shockingly bizarre and sometimes taken at the village level by people to whom the teachers where not directly responsible.

It should also be mentioned that the problems that engulfed teachers were absolutely unnecessary. Teachers on the whole showed unbelievable ignorance of their rights and procedures generally. They tended to expose themselves to slander and recrimination and of course some of them learned the hard way. It is again easy to see the predicament of the teachers in the absence of conditions of service.

Things however, have not remained so, the inspector of schools and education officer who were once seen as a terror of the schools have become friends who help and advise teachers. The circumstances have so changed that even school children are at home with the education officers. The teachers too have been given the chance to speak to the education officer with confidence and exchange ideas about the work they are all interested in. They talk about cooperation and not confrontation. Of interest was the fact that both the BPATA and what came to be the BTU intervened when they felt that the school reports were unfair and biased. Equally, they reacted sharply when the teachers were victimised.

The Bechuanaland Protectorate Act No. 26 of 1938 promulgated on 15 July 1938, and entitled the 'BP Native Schools Proclamation of 1938', defined 'native schools' as a school devoted entirely or partly to the education of 'natives' (Report of the Education Dept., 1965 and 1966). The proclamation went on to say that 'every "native" school shall be subject to inspection by the Director of Education or by the Inspector of Schools or other authorised officer who shall have the right of entering such a school at any time during school hours, of examining the state of school buildings and equipment, of ascertaining the progress of the pupils and enquiring generally into the standing and qualifications of the teachers, the nature of instruction given and such other matters as may be relevant to the conduct and discipline of the school, and may call for such returns as he may require in order to obtain information on the aforesaid' (Report on the Dept. of Education, 1965 and 1966).

It is clear, therefore, that the world of the teaching profession would be incomplete without the annual departmental report and the reports by the inspectors in the field after visits to the schools rendered under their supervision. Why were these departmental reports so important? Like all reports they were a yardstick of the Protectorate's progress on the all too often difficult portfolio of education. All the stake-holders like the Government, parents and tax payers generally were keen to know if their money was spent effectively. Obviously negative reports cast a gloomy picture while promising reports obviously elicited favourable responses.

At the same time we should remember that the reports we shall refer to in this section had a long history. The first of these reports according to B.C. Thema (later Dr Thema) in his unpublished thesis, was dated 10 June 1901 by the Acting Assistant Resident Commissioner, Ellenberger. For obvious reasons it may be asked why did it take so long for this type of exercise to take place when 'the first schools were established in about the year 1840 by the London Missionary Society' (Report of the Dept. of Education, 1965 and 1966). Also, why was the report undertaken by a non-educationist? It does show in a sense that the Colonial Administration did not take Ellenberger's report seriously, for it dealt only with education in the Southern Protectorate comprising the areas of the Bakwena, Bakgatla, Bamalete and Bangwaketse. It gave a comprehensive review of the extent of the work undertaken by the missionary bodies. It was rather unfortunate that the Northern part of the country was not covered by the report, for such omission did not give a complete picture of the state of education in the whole territory. The second report was submitted by James Burns in 1904. This was prompted by Ellenberger's recommendation that the efforts of those 'natives' who sacrificed so much for education should be given more recognition by the Government by giving a small grant towards improving 'native' education. The recommendation was heeded, for in 1904 the Government gave the first grant towards 'native' education in the Territory (Thema, 1947). When the first grant was paid, the Government was keen to know more of what the missionary bodies in the country were doing. As a result of this, in 1904 the Board of Directors of the London Missionary Society (LMS) sent out James Burns from Tiger Kloof on a tour of inspection of the Society's schools in the Protectorate. The report was tabled on 14 December 1904. The significance of the report was that it gave a clear account of the extent and nature of work done in the LMS schools. No doubt such concern by the LMS must have nudged the Colonial Administration into action and prompted them to assume full responsibility for education in this country. But it appears that the Administration was not impressed by what was taking place after 100 years since the founding of the first school in this country by David Livingstone at Kolobeng. In 1965 there were 247 primary schools of which only 96 offered a full seven year primary course. The only Government secondary school was built at Gaborone in 1964 two years before the independence of Botswana in 1966. This shows the heavy burden that lay on the new Government in order to develop a sound system of education at all levels.

Later Reports and Their Significance

The most far reaching report was that written by E.B. Sargent, Education Advisor to the High Commissioner from 1904 to 1905 which followed James Burns' report. The move on the part of the Administration was commendable, as it showed their concern for the education of Batswana even if that move was not supported by a positive policy. Sargent's report was important for its comprehensive investigation into the education system of the BP. What made his report more comprehensive than those undertaken by Ellenberger and Burns was that he visited schools belonging to all denominations throughout the BP. The report was also significant for the recommendations it made for the improvement of education in the territory. For instance, he recommended the creation of a central authority which would have avoided control by different authorities. According to Thema, if the recommendation had been adopted it would have built for Bechuanaland an excellent system of education. Because Sargent was an experienced educationalist he had a clear insight into the establishment of a viable programme of education. Other recommendations included the establishment of a Central Board of Advice in which the LMS, Dutch Reformed Church and Hermannsburg Mission would be represented with the Government Secretary as Chairman. On local control, he called for the establishment of 'some elementary form of local control' for the day schools at the principal villages (Thema, 1947). At this stage a vital point needs to be raised. Generally, if there is a lesson which we have learned thoroughly, it is the art of criticising the colonial administration for educational negligence in the Protectorate. The communities under the leadership of the Dikgosi showed even less interest in the education of their children. There is an allegation that the indifference to missionary schools showed itself through the weakening of popular support given to such schools in the Protectorate with the exception of those under Kgosi Linchwe of the Bakgatla and the Dutch Reformed Church.

It is quite clear that the Administration was not happy about the state of education and the current problems except for the occasional reports which we have referred to. However useful those reports might have been, they could easily have been ignored if there was no one to follow them up. The first Inspector of Schools for the High Commission Territories was F.H. Dutton who was appointed in 1905. His visits came at yearly intervals and were hurriedly made over a short period, the rest of his time was as Inspector of Education for the other two High Commission Territories. For that reason 'he came regularly every year, went his rounds of inspection, wrote and filed his reports in the Resident Commissioner's Office and went back to his office in Maseru' (Thema, 1947). He examined and reported on work for which there was no one to direct, and as a result his reports and recommendations could not be followed up and worked upon in order to improve the work of the schools.

Dumbrell's Directorship

Until the appointment of H.J.E. Dumbrell as Inspector of Education for Bechuanaland and Swaziland on 1 December 1928, the officers who came to inspect the schools in the BP came from outside, and they obviously were not familiar with the conditions in the country. Their reports did not meet the Administration's expectations for they tended to be general. When Dumbrell was appointed there were high hopes that he would help the advancement of education in the territory for before him the 'Director of Education at Maseru ... inspected the Protectorate schools only when he could spare the time from his regular duties in Basutoland. His visits had latterly to be confined to a few weeks a year' (Thema, 1947).

It was to be expected that Dumbrell's first report would point out a variety of flaws in the education system because of the unsystematic manner education reports were handled. He therefore came up with far-reaching recommendations. Of course, he did not start from scratch for he leaned heavily on Sargent's report. He was not happy with the many authorities that governed the schools and to obviate that he stressed the need for the comprehensive control of education through the Board of Advice. It was, therefore, logical for him to call for the reorganisation of school work, the School Leaving Certificate Examinations and the Bursary Scheme. So inventive and full of initiative was he that he was the first to introduce the idea of cattlepost schools. Dumbrell's invention was commendable in that it sought to take education to the herd-boys scattered all over the country tending domestic animals. The chosen teachers were expected to follow their 'students' from one watering point to another. This must have been a wearisome exercise for the teacher who moved in the wilds carrying a chalkboard to interest herd-boys and who may not have been interested in his mission since they had a different agenda. Dumbrell's recommendations went further than that, and included teachers' salaries and he submitted a tentative scale to the Board of Advice at its meeting held on 10 and 11 November 1930 (Thema, 1947).

By 1935 when Dumbrell was appointed as Director of Education he was a permanent resident in the country and it must have been his presence that led to new changes. For instance, as a result of the need for the supervision of the schools, the first Inspector of Schools was appointed in 1938. Before that in about 1929, there were two Tribal Reserves and each had an officer designated Sub-Inspector who was appointed and paid by the Tribal School Committee. Outside these Reserves, there was no supervision apart from visits undertaken by Dutton. In order to improve the supervision of schools, Dumbrell made a recommendation in his first report in 1929 that provision be made in the next estimates for two supervisors of schools. By 1935, there were four such officers in addition to the two sub-inspectors and in 1946 there were eight of them. They devoted their time to inspectoral work and very little to supervision and demonstration. The inspectorate consisted largely of local teachers who had trained in Southern Rhodesia (Zimbabwe) and South Africa from such institutions as Lovedale, Healdtown, Tiger Kloof and other institutions that offered teacher training. The majority of these inspectors had only a Standard 7 qualification, which was followed by a two year teachers' course, generally referred to as Native Primary Lower Certificate (NPLC). Only a few had the Junior Certificate after which the trainees took the Native Primary Higher Certificate (NPH). Their appointment depended on length of service, and sound and efficient service as heads of schools. There was also provision for the appointment of European Officers, the ones responsible for some special subjects and who were recruited to teach agriculture and for educational work. Their work was to be chiefly connected with the training of teachers, the development of work in the middle school, and the development of agricultural work at central and village schools. Dumbrell from the outset intended to bring these men and women together in order to provide opportunities for pooling experiences and exchanging ideas. The measures made for better supervision and more regular inspections of schools.

Dumbrell again aimed 'to turn these officers into a band of responsible men whose duties will not be confined to the writing of reports but who will be fully aware of and sympathetic towards the aspirations of their Department' (Thema, 1947). What he hoped for was to remove the police element in the inspectors job and render him a friend and a helper of the teacher. Unfortunately, this trend was lost and many school inspectors became the tyrants of their times. The teachers were talked to but were never listened to as some unsympathetic inspectors knew everything, and had nothing to learn from the teachers. There were many examples of this tyranny, but the outstanding ones were the three inspections conducted at Seepapitso Secondary School in Kanye in 1963, Camp School in Gaborone in 1963, and Moeng College in 1965. Some teachers were singled out for thorough chastisement. This attitude on the part of the inspectors was keenly felt in those formative years when there were large numbers of unqualified teachers. In order to create a better image of the inspector, Dumbrell changed the designation 'Supervisor' to 'Assistant Education Officer'. For instance, in the Annual Report of the Department of Education in 1942 it was revealed that of the 291 African teachers employed at the primary schools, 188 were unqualified. Some of these untrained teachers were committed and they had made a genuine and praiseworthy effort to master their environment.

> 'In this connection the regular inspections made by the African supervisors, the following up of their reports by letters of advice and encouragement visits paid by the Director of Education and the Inspector of Schools ... are effective means of helping the teachers along the right path' (Report of the Department of Education, 1942).

This trend was supported by H. Jowitt who succeeded Dumbrell as Director of Education in 1946. His view of the Education Officer was one who would desist from condemnation and assist the unqualified teacher in a meaningful manner. At the same time an idea was expressed that although every sympathy was felt for the teachers because of the acute difficulties with which they were contending, some of them had to accept a measure of responsibility.

The Early Reports

The Annual Reports of the Department of Education were not necessarily confined to teaching in the classroom or related matters. The Department equally showed interest in the general welfare of the teachers and their extra-curricular activities. For instance, the Report of 1946 made reference to the BPATA Conference that was held at Ramotswa from which a number of resolutions were forwarded to the Department for discussion at a later stage. The Report also commented favourably on the Association's maturity and seriousness in the types of topics they tackled such as the professional growth of the teachers. There was ample evidence shown in the general welfare of the teachers and the teachers obviously deserved this change of attitude.

There was yet another type of report which was issued yearly by the examiners at the end of the written examinations, usually accompanied by the Standard 6 results and later the Junior Certificate results. These make interesting reading, and give a clear perception of how the examiners saw their role in education, and how the teachers and the pupils were expected to perform. To a large extent one gleans the weakness of the administration of education of the time exacerbated by a horde of unqualified teachers and poor equipment in the schools. Some examiners gave sound and valid suggestions while others appreciated nothing that was done and their criticisms were harsh. These were the most feared examiners for continued criticism threatened the teachers' tenure. Nonetheless, one is inclined to feel that their criticism was out of place if one considered the educational environment of the time.

Interesting examples of some insensitive reporting have been excerpted from the Examiners' Reports (1946), and are shown below.

English Language Spelling: The Report in a stern tone started by saying: 'This deserves strong criticism. There has been no improvement since last year and the previous years – an evidence of a want of systematic teaching of this subject in our schools. Carelessness was common and it was all too common to come across words incorrectly copied from the examination question'.

The instances of carelessness given were 'buck' for 'bucket', 'riaway' for 'railway'. While one may be impressed with the enthusiasm of the examiners, one wonders what such examples of carelessness served. These were foreign words with which the community from which the children came were not familiar.

Language Work: 'The questions on the use of words', continued the report, was a cause of embarrassment to all students. This should, however, be an urge towards encouraging wider reading than remaining within the limited pole of a single reader'.

English Composition: General: The standard of English was considered very low. The outstanding errors found were in connection with spelling and use of punctuation marks. As for language use it 'varied from a form of Tswana to kitchen English'.

Letter Writing: This criticism was even more harsh and uncompromising, even exaggerated at times. One feels the examiners' reports looked for minor things instead of looking across the spectrum of the handling of the language and the environment in which it operated. Some examiners seemed to have forgotten that English is a foreign language, particularly in those days when the language did not touch, to any considerable extent, the lives of the people. For instance, the report stated that 'very few centres ever taught their pupils the correct method of writing a letter on the lines asked under this heading' (Examiners Reports, 1946) Mention was made of such endings as: 'I am finishing with regards'. Again it was common to find such mistakes as 'I am youth faithful.' While not condoning these errors the reports tended to be stereotyped.

Setswana Language and Composition: On this subject comments were favourable. For instance, it was noted that there was marked improvement in the writing of the language compared with previous years. The teachers for once were praised for having studied the earlier comments from the examiners. There was good work in word division, paragraphing and punctuation. In a lighter vein, warning was given against the influence of tribal dialect 'Candidates ... were completely confused over the correct usage of *tla* and *ta*. The word *tau* was sometimes spelt *tlau* and *ruta* as *rutla'* (Examiners Reports, 1946).

Arithmetic: Performance was reported as poor and showed that the previous years' remarks were not taken notice of as mistakes made were still of the same type.

Geography: Candidates displayed complete ignorance of (a) mapwork, and (b) knowledge of the three High Commission Territories. The report went on to say, quite correctly, that geography did not necessarily mean knowledge of say, a list of railway stations between Bulawayo and Durban. The information which a pupil acquires should be that which helps him to form the attitudes and skills which he should use to control the understanding of his own life in its relation to the rest of the world. The report showed a balanced approach of the examiner to the subject.

History: Here the examiner showed a glaring lack of insight into the subject and a narrow view of history. For instance, what the examiner found disappointing was that candidates did not know 'such South African celebrities as Robert Moffat, David Livingstone, Jan van Riebeeck and Paul Kruger' (Examiners Reports, 1946). Furthermore, some candidates' knowledge of Julius Caesar was limited to Caesar having said *et tu brute* or 'Caesar crossed the Rubicon'. These comments were not helpful to anyone and at the very least were trivial. The examiner was not concerned that the pupils were not taught local civics which included the child's immediate environment such as the *Kgotla* and the School Committee. All that the examiner was concerned with was the pupils reciting the names of van Reebeeck's three vessels and his date of arrival at the Cape which were so prominent in South African history books. Suppose a pupil had never heard of Jan van Riebeeck. What difference would this make to a Motswana child? There was perhaps every reason to know everything about Robert Moffat because of his contribution to the early establishment of western education in the Bechuanaland Protectorate. Furthermore, the comment that history and geography 'as taught in Bechuanaland African Schools at present are of no educational value' (Examiners Reports, 1946) was extremely short sighted and showed a lack of understanding. History can be badly taught and so can geography, but what is taught, except by ignorant people cannot be said to be void of all educational value. If teachers of history and geography were poor, one had to examine their training programmes even if these were conducted outside the Bechuanaland Protectorate. At the same time, one had to consider the level of training of these teachers and the paucity of teaching materials at the time. Since the examiners and the inspectors were not so close and helpful to the teachers, one reads a lot of bias in their reports. Because teachers were not given meaningful assistance they were bound to repeat their mistakes the following year.

Another interesting style of reporting followed visits to schools by inspectors/education officers. This type of report went into minute details and gave a full picture. Such a report came after a visit to Sikwane school in the Kgatleng area in 1950. It started with routine issues such as pupils' attendance on the day of the visit (this was important for it could be that on such a day pupils did not come to school as they were helping parents tend cattle at the posts, *morakeng*, or harvesting at the lands, *masimo*, and was followed by an examination of the staff, their qualifications, the school buildings, their state of repair, the registers and the timetable. Schemes and records of work, textbooks, notebooks and corrections followed. It was on the notebooks and corrections that stress fell and adverse comments were made. The report revealed that the children's books had very little work to show for the first half of the year (District Commissioner: Kgatleng (Mochudi) 1950). Concerning the corrections of children's compositions, teachers were advised to avoid comments/remarks such as 'Try again' or 'Improve your handwriting' when the work was in need of more constructive criticism. The teachers were perfectly correct to urge their pupils to improve their work in every direction. Perhaps they could have given a more comprehensive approach to corrections. It is true that sometimes the mistakes that the teachers made were easily copied by their pupils and internalised. For instance, in one class the teacher was reported to be largely responsible for the inaccurate spelling in children's books, of words like 'marridge' for 'marriage' and 'soljers' for 'soldiers'. Without being too critical or condoning such glaring errors, one should remember that English is and remains a foreign language. Even if it is Botswana's official language such mistakes continue to dog our footsteps. This matter, of course, is now complicated by American spellings which have found their place in our written English.

On the thorny question of teachers' quarters, it was reported that there was no sign of change in spite of the appeal made by the Education Officer after his last visit. One should remember how hard the assignment was for the local communities that lacked the necessary funds. But there was an expectation that since the school was being given considerable recognition by transferring Mabalane to the Sikwane Centre, and if the community hoped for more stabilised staff, or for improved staff conditions, they were urged to do their share towards making their living conditions more attractive. The report no doubt was unique in so far that it even concerned itself with staff housing.

Then the report dealt with individual staff members. The Headteacher was showered with praise and was described as having 'ability combined with an alive personality'. His class control was considered excellent but he was advised to discourage chorus answers by his pupils in class. The criticism was fair, since chorus answers can make the less or uninformed pupils hide behind collective answering. One woman teacher was said to display little energy in her teaching and 'probably pays more attention to her own knitting than she does to preparation' (DC Mochudi, 1950). A comment on another woman teacher's performance was that she 'has the strange belief ... that teachers always sit and teach' (DC Mochudi, 1950). She was said to be capable of better work but had to move around in the classroom in order to familiarise herself with the individual's needs which warranted individual attention. To be honest, some of these criticisms were too personal and trivial to say the least.

The report on Morwa School again in Kgatleng had this to say of the Headteacher. He was a man with 'a very good presence in the classroom and his influence is not only confined to the classroom and the teaching day, but he is a keen scout leader in the community as well' (DC , Mochudi, 1950). The two women teachers in the same school were not so lucky. One of them was said to lack imagination despite her many years of service. For instance, in an arithmetic lesson she puts sums all having an answer of 18 – a rather hard example to believe, however, confused the teacher was. In other subjects her lessons were 'sketchy and contained very little substance for a 30 minute period' (DC Mochudi, 1950). The report described the other lady as 'extremely immature' and found it difficult to handle the two classes for which she was responsible. Even at this point, there is something to say in favour of the teachers. Considering the low level of training of some of the teachers at this time, some of them without professional training, one had to be circumspect and realistic in criticism of teachers. The management of more than one class by an ill-equipped teacher is no easy task.

The report on a visit to the National School in Mochudi in 1950 was general and did not single out the members of staff. On staffing, the school was said to be one of the best schools in the Protectorate, with six qualified teachers out of a total of ten. For that reason alone, a high standard of work was expected from the staff. The only subjects that came under fire were handiwork and needlework. Handiwork, done in the school was said to be most disappointing, and did not justify the amount of time spent on it. The criticism on needlework was severe, for it described it as the worst kind seen at any school in the Protectorate. Such harsh criticism was accompanied with threats that verged on unparalleled intimidation. The report concluded by saying that 'unless there is a change of tone in this subject by the end of this year, we will have to replace the present staff with teachers who are more conscientious about the work' (Education Officer's Report: Mochudi, 1950).

Because of the severity of the criticism that followed visits to some schools by supervisors and education officers, the response sometimes from headteachers was equally vicious. In some cases the District Commissioners, who were Chairmen of School Committees, responded on behalf of their schools. For example, in 1951 the District Commissioner at Mochudi responded to the foregoing reports on Bakgatla schools and wrote a letter to the Director of Education and pointed out that in spite of the limited funds he was determined to implement some of the recommendations made by the Education Officer (DC Mochudi, 1951). Equally, the office of the Director of Education also responded to the Education Officers' reports on schools visited. The responses, of course, were very moderate as he did not want to be embroiled in trivialities and petty gossip. What is clear of course, was that the supervisors/education officers saw themselves as 'little policemen', who had to keep the teachers in the schools on their toes by inspiring fear. Inspectors of those days were even feared by school chairmen.

However, there was also a brighter side to these reports, for the benevolent and broad-minded supervisors occasionally congratulated and suggested better organisation of headteachers when a good report was issued. This was the case in 1947, when the sub-inspector reported favourably on the Kumakwane School in the Kweneng Reserve: 'It is hoped that your work will be further enhanced by the appointment of a third teacher. Alternatively and probably a better arrangement, you should not cater for Standard V' (DC, Molepolole, 1947). The letter was copied to the District Commissioner in Gaborone and the Rev. S.A. Thobega of Molepolole. In this case, there was an effort to give a progressive and enlightened approach to the often difficult educational situation.

One of the few magnanimous supervisors of the time sought to be constructive in his criticism of teachers in schools, helped them and made friends with them. Maybe he was ahead of his time, for this attitude was only given expression in the 1980s as a breakthrough in the new education officer-teacher-pupil relationship. The Education Officer is both a friend and a helper in what has been called 'new directions in education'. K.K. Baruti was praised by the agriculture Officer, W.H. Turnbull in a letter written to him. His encouragement of teachers at Kumakwane in spite of the inadequate equipment and difficult season the school garden had, produced a large variety of vegetable crops. Turnbull concluded by saying that 'the Director of Education has asked me to commend you [K.K. Baruti] for the high standard of composition of your report and for the clear way in which the various matters have been presented' (DC Kanye, 1947). The headteacher was assured of attempts to be made to solve the staffing problem in what was considered a deserving school indeed. This was encouraging.

Because K.K. Baruti was praised for his positive and helpful report, it did not mean that shoddy work would escape his keen, careful and searching scrutiny. When faults and carelessness were spotted, he did not pull his punches. When he visited Mankgodi School in Kweneng in 1947, it was just the opposite of the report he gave on Kumakwane School. Nothing favourable was said of the teachers' performance and their pupils throughout the school. His criticism pinpointed the weaknesses in the administration and indifference of the teachers to their work. For instance, he laid a finger on the trouble spot by denouncing the lack of preparation by the teachers which resulted in ineffective teaching. The unprepared lessons by the teachers were a serious indictment indeed.

The importance of the report on Mankgodi School is that, of all the reports consulted, it was at this school that the Assistant Education Officer mentioned music in his report. Of music, he commented that 'the children sing fairly sweetly, but the attack is poor, due to the fact that the choristers do not sound the chord of the given voice pitch before they start singing, and the teacher does not stand in front of them to conduct the song' (DC, Molepolole, 1947). Of note here, is that Baruti displayed his sound background of music. It is not surprising that one of his daughters Mrs Kealeboga Makhwade (nee Baruti) emerged as the song bird of Tiger Kloof Institution where she obtained her Cape Senior Certificate – an equivalent of our present Cambridge Overseas School Certificate (COSC). The only fly in the ointment according to Baruti was that too many Xhosa songs had been taught. 'The principal needs to discourage the singing of songs in languages which are neither English nor Setswana' (DC Molepolole, 1947). Perhaps Baruti committed an error here, for if he wanted to hear more Setswana songs sung he should have encouraged Batswana to compose their own music. This could be treated as 'healthy jealousy', for K.K. as Baruti was fondly called, was broad-minded and far seeing. Maybe the reasons why Xhosa songs were sung in the BP schools was because in those days there were a fair sprinkling of Xhosa teachers in the country, and above all a good number of qualified Batswana teachers were trained in South Africa at institutions like Lovedale, Healdtown and Bensonvale and Tiger Kloof in the Cape where early Xhosa composers had made an impact in music circles. Perhaps many familiar songs were written in this language. Even Baruti went to Healdtown Institution in the Cape for teacher training. But what is still fascinating is the present attitude that Nguni music must not be used in our school competitions. These advocates seem to be out of step and forget that the world in which we live has become smaller, and that cross cultural fertilisation is the order of the day. The little window of cultural exchange is likely to influence young Batswana composers.

The New Approach of Inspection

There was also another brand of school inspector or educational officer who was prepared to come to grips with the problems in the schools visited. This type of inspector was not only concerned with blanket criticism, but was prepared to listen to the teachers' points of view and possibly exchange ideas.

This was a forward looking approach which came to be accepted, for it shows that the education officer has nothing to hide. Such a report was produced by a panel of education officers who visited Mochudi Middle School in 1948. The report followed routine headings such as timetable, buildings and their state of repair, equipment, pupils and the subjects offered.

All these were followed by well thought out and fruitful recommendations to which the teachers responded before the education officers left the school. The main criticism related to the neglect in preparation which was a common fault. It might have been lack of preparation at the training level and in some instances, it might have been the fact that a large number of teachers had no professional training and, therefore, lacked the skill. The second point emphasised the weakness of pupils in both written and spoken English. Since English was the medium of instruction the teachers were encouraged to intensify work in this subject. It does appear that Setswana had posed a big problem for a long time. The problem centred on terminology in the teaching of Setswana grammar. Again, in this instance, the panel advised the use of available Tswana terms and if these were not readily available they could use English. The staff at the school were so encouraged by the open and friendly discussion with panel of education officers that they voluntarily undertook to conduct extra afternoon classes in order to assist slow pupils to revise work of the lower classes which the middle school staff considered to be weak (DC Mochudi, 1948).

The panel not only made recommendations to the teaching staff at the school, they also met the Bakgatla School Committee. They (the panel) believed that projects within the school would succeed only if they had the support of the School Committee. It was explained to the Committee that the recommendations made were chiefly of a pedagogical nature and that teachers had been given full instructions at a staff meeting. Furthermore, the Committee was informed that the weaknesses at the Middle School were due almost entirely to the shortcomings of the teachers who showed little interest in their school work. The headteacher was castigated for misdirecting his efforts in an attempt to solve the problem by teaching all day in preference to supervising his assistants' work. Naturally this might have been due to lack of guidance at the time of appointment. With regard to the shortage of textbooks, the panel advised that the problem might be solved by the Department of Education buying texts on behalf of the Bakgatla schools, provided that a requisition list was submitted towards the end of the year. An encouraging report on staff at the Kweneng Reserve was recorded. At Kopong School, the Education Officer was puzzled by the fact that the onerous task of heading a school was simply that Kopong being an isolated place, the teacher was unable to obtain professional supervision and advice. The remark was legitimate in that the 'young teacher lacks the technique that can be acquired only by the training and advice of qualified, experienced professional colleagues' (DC,

Molepolole, 1948). Perhaps to remove this handicap, the Education Department was prepared to sponsor him to a teacher training institution through a bursary. At Lentswe-le-Tau School came another encouraging report. In 1948, in the Bakwena Reserve the headteachers' performance was considered outstanding, and his influence in the community was considered excellent. He 'enjoyed the confidence of the local headman Makgasana Kgosidintsi, a sound and experienced teacher' (DC, Molepolole, 1948). A woman teacher was praised for the sympathetic and efficient handling of young children, 'something which enabled her to retain both control over and affection for her children' (DC, Molepolole, 1948).

The other reports including the one given by the Director of Education, J.H.E. Dumbrell in 1942, tended to be comprehensive for they covered a large range of topics including the 'Double Shift System' which was in operation and said to be satisfactorily organised. The tone of the school and general discipline also came under focus. What was equally noticeable was that some reports showed a high standard of professionalism which had not been noticeable since then through to the early 1970s. Even the methods of teaching were considered effective and depicted a clear adherence to the education code. These latter reports considered broader principles on which depended school success – such as to secure from all pupils greater speed in all forms of written work. In addition to this was the necessity to impress upon the pupils the need to learn to obtain information for themselves, and that use should be made of works of reference and exercise sets which would require such work. 'Much of time given by teachers to imparting knowledge could be saved by the pupils finding out information themselves' (DC, Mochudi, 1942). This is the present day strategy in teaching and so influential is this approach that today we talk of the project method. In this learning situation the pupils look for information on their own. English which received a wide coverage in many reports was considered to be well handled but more effort was required to facilitate communication through the written and spoken word. The School Committee at Kgatleng which took keen interest in the work of the schools in their charge were commended for their solid support. All in all, the reports had their strengths and weaknesses but what was most needed was an enlightened approach from those who dealt with teachers.

The Dismal Reports of the 1960s

The 1960s for some reason stand out as portraying a singularly sad image of the approach by some education authorities towards inspection and the role teachers could play to improve the quality of education in this country. One should appreciate the fact that positive and helpful reports tended to urge teachers to better effort, while negative ones dampened the spirit and turned the teachers against the Department of Education. If anything, to live with encouragement is to learn to be confident. The prejudicial approach to inspection reports was not only confined to the primary schools It will be recalled that some secondary schools were managed by communities and some churches, including the Roman Catholic Church, and this was quite noticeable from the end of the 1940s to the early 1950s. One also needs to understand the dilemma of the Education Officer at that stage. They had dealt to a large extent with the primary school teachers who they dominated because of low qualifications. The secondary schools in the BP during the 1960s boasted of a sprinkle of graduate teachers who were reasonably grounded in their disciplines. Therein lay the problem, for these teachers could not accept blind and vague criticism, and the fact that Education Officer was to be seen as a know-it-all of some kind.

To drive the point home, let us look at the inspection report of July 1963 on Camp School in Gaborone. The naked bias could not be hidden at any point for the report was blunt. The opening sentence read like some verdict from some small court of law. 'The classes performed badly in English' and the class teacher of Standard 5 and 6 was advised to give more attention to oral English (DC, Gaborone, 1963). It is strange that all classes, from Standard 4 to sub-standards and the beginners, were reported as poor, ranging from oral to written work. The only class which emerged with a positive report was sub-standard B. In this class, oral English was reported good and the Inspector was impressed by the mental alertness of the pupils. Anyway the report did indicate how unsatisfactory the pupils' writing was, and this linked with the teachers poor blackboard work where she was said 'to have no idea of the sizes and shapes of capitals and small letters' (DC Gaborone, 1963).

Nothing again seemed to go smoothly with regard to the school records and administration. In this respect, it would appear that the headteacher, who was the General Secretary of the BPATA, was on trial. For instance, it was reported that the log book showed that the last entry was made in April and the visit was in July 1963. The headteachers' plight was so serious that he was threatened with demotion if he did not set a better example for the rest of the staff. The Education Officers' criticism of the headteacher surprisingly did not take into account that he alone in the school was responsible for two senior classes of 30 pupils and in addition he handled all the administration – a taxing job by any standard. Proof of this heavy burden on the headteacher was borne out in a letter written on 19 July 1963 by the Director of Education to the Headteacher of Camp School to the effect that the Education Office in Lobatse was being asked 'to appoint a suitably qualified, preferably male teacher to your school if one is available' (DCK 10/4). The letter stated that the arrangement would make it 'possible for you to teach Standard VI only, and attend to administrative and supervisory duties' (DCK 10/4 1963).

One cannot help feeling that some Education Officers had a complex when dealing with staff at some secondary schools in the country. It seemed that the same Education Officers were at pains to show how knowledgeable and versatile they were. For instance, some believed that they could evaluate teachers from English to physical science, a level that was impossible if a good job was to be done. Science as well as arts subjects needed specialised knowledge and skills to make a fair assessment of teaching in those disciplines. Some education officers felt they could do everything, and therein lay the problem. When they inspected Seepapitso Secondary School in 1963, their report resembled the Inspectors' report at Camp School and that of Moeng College three years later. The reports had one thing in common, namely a harsh and intimidating tone, characterised by the lack of valid suggestions and helpful tips for the teachers. The remarks were sour with generalisations and innuendoes. It would have been helpful if the panel of inspectors had discussed and exchanged ideas with the staff at the schools they visited in order to make them aware of their shortcomings.

At Seepapitso Secondary School all was well as far as administration and professional performance were concerned, except for the teacher of domestic science. The report verged on a complete diatribe, for she was accused of interesting herself with the work of the cook and 'attends to the cleanliness of the lavatories' (DCK 10/4, 1963). The only valid criticism related to needlework which was neglected despite the fact that six brand new Singer sewing machines had been provided but had never been used since the inauguration of the Department. The laundry section of the Department was not functioning either: 'actually the room reserved for this was full of cobwebs, grime and dirt' (DC, Kanye 1963). The panel even suggested that serious thought should be given by the Department to 'close (the school) and the equipment ... be transferred to another school where it can be used' (DCK 10/4, 1963).

The comments on the individual teachers and their teaching was equally caustic, a situation which could have been avoided if the panel talked to the staff and ascertained their problems and came up with solutions. One teacher's performance was 'marred by his attitude towards students' and that he used threats to his students and his remarks were in bad taste. It is clear that one member of the panel had fallen in love with the term lackadaisical, for it was levelled at one teacher at Seepapitso Secondary School and was repeated again at Moeng College. What incensed the staff at Seepapitso Secondary School were the adverse and unhelpful comments on the domestic science teacher. 'A very energetic and active teacher but these qualities are frittered away because of her unstable nature...' (DCK 10/4, 1963) which compelled her to dissipate her energies in other directions.

The Moeng College report in 1966 once more revealed the inspector's wrath. But before that year, visits to the College were encouraging and the language was mild. For instance, in 1963 the inspection reported fairly on the staff performance, and of interest the word 'confidence' was used six times to describe the performance of six teachers out of ten. The only exception was a teacher whose performance was described as 'dull and lackadaisical and another one whose teaching was described as unsatisfactory' (EDI24/10, 1966).

The report that followed the 1966 inspection caused the principal and the staff at the College sleepless nights. The report was so harsh that one got the impression that nothing was right at the College. The staffing position was the one that prompted a lot of debate, for it was felt that the turnover of staff was abnormal. The state of affairs was unsatisfactory and the panel concluded that it 'must have contributed ... to the generally unsatisfactory state of the school' (S384/1/4). There were indeed some problems at Moeng College, including the isolated nature of the College far from the main centres, including Palapye and above all poor roads. It was extremely difficult to retain teachers at the College. There were other factors such as the absence of the conditions of service and the 'inconsistency of policy and administration of our Governing Council so that its actions have become unpredictable' (S386/1/2). The accusation was contained in a memorandum addressed to the Government Secretary of the BP by the Moeng staff in 1962. Like the BPATA earlier complained, the Ramage Report recommendations had strengthened their contention that the teaching staff were excluded from its terms of reference and they found the position untenable. They continued in that vein to tabulate their problems, for instance, 'the Governing Council compares the amount of work done by our officers with the amount of work done by the employees in the tribal offices...' (S386/1/2). The Department of Education was so incensed that in the process they lost reason. It was no sound argument to state 'that anomalies do exist but it is equally clear that they are not confined to staff at Moeng ... for teachers employed in tribal secondary schools and at St. Joseph's College and Moeding College are equally affected' (S386/1/2). The wrath of the Department was clearly stated when the closing remark stated that 'I dislike round robins of this nature ... complaints should be submitted by individuals to the Principal for consideration by the Executive Committee or the Governing Council' (S386/1/2). The report did not spare the staff generally for it stated that 'none impressed us as outstanding, most were lacking personality and drive both in and out of the classroom' (S384/1/11). The headmaster responded to these condemnatory remarks furiously as he considered them meaningless and prejudicial.

The criticism of administration centred on the lack of supervision, which was described as disastrous at all levels. The timetable showed a large number of private study periods which were unsupervised with no work set for the students. In all fairness one must accept that it was an extreme case of carelessness on the part of the school administration if the picture painted was true. The panel concluded rightly when they maintained that the principal was the man in charge and therefore, it was his responsibility to see that the staff obeyed his instructions even if they did not agree with his ideas and 'if they were not prepared to cooperate, they should resign forthwith' (EDI24/10). The laissez-faire policy had brought the school to the brink of disaster.

Obviously something drastic had to be done to save the school from neglect and malpractice. Hence it was recommended that the principal and staff should institute adequate supervision at all times since the poor state of discipline was due to the prevalent slackness. If the principal was 'unable to exercise the required supervision, he should be offered employment more suited to his talent' (EDI24/10). The principal was so incensed by the panel's remark that he wrote to the Director of Education and implored him to expunge the statement from the report. A more drastic recommendation was that the school should be gradually phased out as more space became available in schools that were more centrally situated. The officers even suggested that the buildings and the site be offered 'to various institutions ranging from an experimental agriculture farm, medical department, TB hospital, leprosarium, community development or to the Prisons Department – as an open farm prison where prisoners could do a useful job' (EDI24/10).

Several points need to be raised at this stage. How far sighted and sensitive were these Education Officers to the political developments that were taking place, and what were the implications for education in this country? It should be noted that when Moeng College was inspected in 1963, the team consisted of six high powered officers who did not breathe a word about the closure of the institution. In the same year, the final Cambridge Overseas School Certificate results were commendable, if one takes into account the high turnover of staff at the time. There was one first class, a couple of second classes, and some third classes and only one failure out of a class of 13. That was an achievement indeed, and it was unthinkable at that stage to close Moeng. Above all, some of the founders of Moeng, who had since passed to the beyond, might have turned in their graves. First and foremost, Moeng College had been established to serve the Bangwato. How justified and realistic were these two Education Offices in their recommendation in 1966, when Botswana was on the verge of independence, and the emphasis on education particularly, at secondary level was the Government's priority in order to develop manpower to replace expatriate personnel. The second point is, why were things allowed to deteriorate to this extent in so short a space of time, when in 1963 the College was doing so well? If the panel of six in 1963 took three days to do their work so meticulously, how possible was it for two to take the same amount of time, do a good job, and even to come up with such an assumption of an unsatisfactory position both in quality and quantity? (This statement was in reference to the staff who were lacking personality and drive). Naturally, such a report left a trail of animosities – the principal and staff were estranged, and even the Chairman of the Moeng College Board of Governors was not enthusiastic about the report judging by the letter which he wrote to the Director of Education.

Strangely, for some reason hard to explain, the Director of Education, who informed the Minister of Education of the dismal picture conveyed in the report, was almost in agreement with the phasing out of the College. Yet the Director of Education was aware of the need for secondary education. Hence, on submitting the report to the Minister for his attention, he stated, 'in view of the high priority accorded to secondary education by Government, and of your own long and distinguished association with the College' (EDI24/10). There seemed to be a conflict.

The reply of the Minister, who was the ex-headmaster of Moeng College was hard to understand, for he knew the thirst of Batswana for education. Proof of that was that he himself had acquired his secondary and university education in South Africa, and had taught there for many years. To have concurred with the Director of Education that the report indeed painted a dismal and disturbing picture was one thing, but to concede that his views − closure of Moeng College − were not different from the Directors or on the Education Officers' recommendation was another. However valid the Minister's observation that he had his doubts about the principal being able to exercise required supervision, it did not warrant the closure of an institution which had been built with the sweat of that community. He saw the principal's failure to perform satisfactorily as a 'result of inability to handle and make the best use of the staff' (EDI24/9). His acceptance of the recommendation that the College be gradually phased out and to transfer the ten pupils in Form 4 elsewhere was not reasonably thought out. At the same time, one must take into account the sense of anguish that must have occupied the minds of those who had contributed to the development of the College and had seen it make a steady and commendable progress.

There was great pressure from some quarters that stronger action be taken against the principal and that Form 4s and 5s be removed in January 1967. There was the view that the damage had reached a point of no return and that 'if we wait it will be too late'. This obviously was an overly hasty and emotional outburst which lacked substance as later events were to show. From those dismal years of poor performance, Moeng did come of age and in the past few years has been one of the best schools if good results at COSC are anything to go by. To close Moeng College was unthinkable and that would have been a national disaster. Even the later communications of the Director of Education to the Chairman of the Moeng Governing Council, and copied to the principal, who was asked to comment on the dismal report was ill conceived, for he in no way tried to solve the problem through serious thought. To keep repeating the story that the College had been allowed 'to slide into a state of neglect' was not helpful. If anything, it infuriated both the principal and his staff.

Of interest, the Chairman of the Moeng College Governing Council was more pragmatic in his approach. He was equally unhappy and did not condone the happenings at the College. He argued that the College until a few years ago was famous, and had attained good academic standards which in spite of its inherent disadvantages maintained a satisfactory and sound educational programme. Like anyone else who was discerning enough, he was aware of the increased need for secondary education. This, no doubt, as the tempo for a further increase was sustained – it was imperative to retain Moeng. 'Only a concerted effort therefore, can assure the survival of Moeng College' (EDI24/10). To downgrade the College, the chairman felt would be an unwise step to take and what remained to be done was to overhaul and consolidate the administration. That was a realistic approach rather than endlessly castigating the principal and his staff for reasons that were clear for everyone to see. What was needed was to strengthen all the weak points and overhaul the administration and create an environment that was conducive to the climate of teaching and learning. It was incumbent upon the authorities concerned to do all in their power to attract good staff, make living conditions acceptable and improve the facilities. The principal's rebuttal of the allegations in the report was a natural reaction, but tended to fan the flames of accusation. One thing was clear, and that was that the principal had the backing of the Governing Council.

In fairness to all the parties concerned, one should examine the essence of their rather unusual behaviour in difficult circumstances. One assumed that the Department had a solid code of conduct to which all had to conform. A teacher or any other person employed and paid through public funds was obliged to justify such expenditure. The parents entrust their children to his care and try hard to ensure that their trust is not misplaced. If he falters, since the job places him in the public eye, he must incur the wrath of the Department of Education through the inspectors, parents and the tax payers. Also, what is important is how the case is conducted. The Moeng College report was hurriedly done and lacked the thorough scrutiny of problems surrounding the bad state of affairs. There was no need to be carried away by prejudice and slander.

It is fair again to appreciate the anxiety of some Education Officers since they had a duty to perform. Some of them had come from top schools and universities and were prepared to see nothing but the best. They had also emerged from a tradition where the inspector was not only the most feared man, but an undisputed know-it-all and had no time to share his wealth of information with labouring teachers in classrooms that were sometimes grossly inadequate. Some of the teachers might not have had the exposure which he had enjoyed in the course of his marathon career, even outside Botswana. The inspector poured his 'wisdom' on to his scribbler behind the closed doors of his office and dispatched his findings to the anxiously waiting staff at different schools. If the inspector's findings were favourable, all was well and peace reigned. On the contrary, if these were adverse, there was anxiety and countless accusations. The outcome of all this was that the inspectorate estranged teachers who were such a scarce resource during those years, and created a barrier between itself and the teachers. The inspectorate failed dismally to relate to men and women whose task was to educate their children. In an attempt to do too well, many inspectors exceeded the bounds of propriety and overstepped the limits of professionalism. The Moeng College report was as unacceptable, as it was unjustified. Truly, reason prevailed and the College escaped the vicious onslaught. Thanks to the vigilance of the farseeing who had the interest of our children at heart.

The Teachers' Cases

This section is intended to show how the workings of justice were extremely incomprehensible at that time and how, invariably, the teacher was the loser. The cases in which the teachers were involved sometimes illustrated how insensitive some local authorities were in their dealings with the teachers in their employment. Surprisingly enough, the teachers showed remarkable ignorance of their rights, in that their lives were mysteriously controlled from the Office of the Director of Education, with its host of inspectors, the Superintendent of the Church, the District Commissioner, who was generally the chairperson of the School Committee, to the headman's office in the village. Some 'cases' were so trivial that they were not worth the paper on which they were recorded.

The history of the BPATA is marked by a trail of teachers' cases. The story of such cases dates as far back as the early days of the BPATA. The cases generally were spread throughout the BP, yet Maun in Ngamiland seemed to feature prominently. It is difficult to say why there was such a preponderance of cases in the schools in that area. One of the cases, for instance, was so serious that it drew the London Missionary Society (LMS) personnel into the centre of the storm. The case involved a teacher who became treasurer to the Batawana Tribal Administration, and who was charged with misappropriation of funds from the Batawana Treasury. Of interest, Rev. J.K. Main, stationed at the London Mission station in Maun vouched for the innocence of the teacher in a letter to the Rev. J. Shaw at Kanye, but indicated that he was only guilty of careless book-keeping. Nonetheless, the teacher-treasurer was sentenced to 12 months imprisonment, six months to be suspended if restitution was made within three years. The proceedings were not clear, and as the Rev. Main alluded, he could not preclude the possibility of intrigue for the treasurer apparently was not the only one who had access to the safe. The same view was expressed by the Rev. Shaw, to whom reference has been made above. He stated that the Treasury was unreasonable in that their employee was a teacher turned treasurer. Because he lacked the necessary skills of a treasurer, he should have been monitored very closely within the treasury. The matter was complicated by the fact that, as the Rev. Main seemed to imply, 'there was someone who had only to ask for the key and the treasurer was bound to hand it over' (E/10).

The Director of Education who had been informed of the case by the Rev. Shaw showed a great deal of compassion. He was at pains to find out if the treasurer could not be found a suitable job in one of the Cape schools for some time. He also felt that he should be considered for employment in one of the schools not under the regular school committees. The responsibility fell on the Rev. Main's shoulders to think of some placement. What was equally gratifying in this pathetic case, was that the LMS rallied behind the unfortunate treasurer, and the Principal of Tiger Kloof, the Rev. A.J. Haile, expressed his grief and stated that he could not help feeling that 'Justice had gone astray'. To support the fallen treasurer, Captain Potts, the District Commissioner in Francistown, and the Chairman of the Tati School Committee were asked to secure a place for the young man at one of his schools.

It is true that teachers were sometimes unfairly treated, but at the same time they were often responsible for their woes. The teachers used rather unorthodox tactics in order to secure short-lived benefits. Invariably they were caught flat-footed, and had no one else to blame when they were found out, except themselves. Some teachers used deceit to avoid their responsibility and told untruths which always led to their exposure and punishment. Of course, when the Department of Education discovered such deceitful conduct, it acted swiftly and severely. One of the most bizarre cases involved a teacher at the Batawana National School in 1945. This teacher wrote a letter to the School Secretary in Maun, asking for leave in order to attend to his sister who was ill, and take her to either Mochudi or Zeerust Hospital for treatment. The 'school supervisor was to be asked to set tests for his classes' (E/10). Nonetheless, the applicant's story proved untrue, for on 19 October 1945 it was found that he had written to his sister Jane, asking her to send a telegram telling him to come home immediately, as she was unwell. His mother, who lived at Dinokana was not to be told about the arrangement, as she would not have allowed her (Jane) to comply. At the foot of that ill-fated letter to Jane the wording of the fictitious telegram read:

Tebogo
Maun
Serious illness come (E/10).

The letter containing the instruction was produced by the Supervisor of Schools in Ngamiland. The unanswered question is just how the said officer laid his hands on the said letter. Be that as it may, the teachers plans were irresponsible and negligent. Such downright deceit was just unacceptable for two reasons. First, to lie so blatantly is not a sound policy for a teacher whose function among others is to mould the character of children he teaches. Secondly, the time he chose for his unsavoury mission was unsuitable, as it was towards the end of the year which is usually examination time in our schools. To show how cleverly the teacher had calculated his mischievous strategy, on his return, he did everything to cover his tracks by talking freely about his sister's illness. He wrote to the Secretary of Batawana School Committee to confirm his mission from Dr Delport of Lobatse Hospital. Dr Delport revealed that the teacher's sister was not seriously ill and was never admitted at the hospital. If he wished to visit Johannesburg for medical attention himself as it was learnt later why did he not tell the truth. The story he told earned him suspension.

A very strange case which showed the vulnerability of the teaching profession came from Sehitwa. It illustrated how the life of a teacher could be controlled by anyone in the village. For instance, a teacher from Nokaneng was on transfer to Sehitwa in 1945. He failed to report on time because he was detained by the headman. He had refused to pay a debt of one shilling for some beer he had purchased from some woman in the village. As a result of the headman's intervention, he reported on the 16 instead of 9 July 1945. Again, this case showed how reckless some teachers behaved, for if the story on non-payment was true, he could have saved himself the embarrassment by meeting his obligation. No one can believe that the teacher was unable to pay a sum of one shilling. Perhaps the headman was quite fair in detaining the teacher to protect the community against would be insensitive persons in the village. But equally interesting were the headman's powers to impose a fine for 'the teacher was fined £2.10 for failing to pay' (E/10). That was terribly humiliating for a teacher whose image was irreparably damaged in the eyes of parents and the community generally.

There seemed very little time for serious work at Sehitwa School, for from this school came a number of cases that were finally taken to Maun for settlement. Among these cases, was one involving an injury to a pupil. The pupil was being punished for 'bulliness and disobedience', and when the child was taken to the medical officer he condemned what he called savage punishment. It was admittedly a common belief that those who exceeded the limits of corporal punishment had the view that if one spared the rod one would spoil the child. Many parents accepted that as the norm and at times they volunteered to take the child to the teacher to punish in their place. When the headteacher was summoned to report to the school committee where the Director of Education would be present he realised the seriousness of the case. The teacher was reprimanded by the Batawana School Committee, for they like any responsible body realised how excessive fifteen cuts were for punishment. It is nonetheless gratifying that teachers of that type are not common. With litigation so common nowadays, such a teacher would land in gaol.

What was also disturbing at the time was the attitude of some headteachers, who seemed to think that they owned the teaching staff. What follows could be taken as bizarre behaviour which merited demotion for failure on the part of the headteacher to carry out his job effectively. It is, for instance, unthinkable that a headteacher or principal would fail to inform his staff and children when a school holiday occurred. It was likely to be missed by the teachers and children who came from semi-to-completely illiterate communities. The trouble started when the headteacher failed to inform the staff of a holiday to be observed by the school. He had tucked away the school calendar for fear that the white ants would destroy it if it was pinned on the wall. His predicament was real, but there was no excuse for failing to carry out his responsibility. One female teacher criticised the headteacher vehemently for lack of concentration in his work, because that was the second occasion the school had missed a holiday. Instead of accepting and admitting his inefficiency he became aggressive and threatened assault. The staff in response communicated with the Batawana School Committee and expressed their insecurity. The staff relations were indeed poor and the teachers felt that such an environment would retard progress. The Batawana School Committee acted swiftly by transferring the headteacher from Sehitwa to Batawana National School at Maun, where he could be watched closely. These events, if anything, illustrated a couple of weaknesses. First, it showed an extreme lack of professionalism and commitment among the teachers generally, including some headteachers. Secondly, it could have resulted from insufficient guidance or a lack of conditions of service. Thirdly, the administration of schools was difficult because of a lack of trained manpower and the large distances to be covered to reach the schools on poor roads. Finally, the cases that arose and the way they were dealt with did reflect the thinking at the time and society's perception of teachers.

It was therefore, strange to find cases of similar nature in the 1960s, which were rather more difficult to explain. Moreover, during this time, however defective the regulations were, better conditions prevailed in terms of the qualifications of teachers. The school committees, which were entrusted with administration, were led by enlightened persons. Such leadership should have been more careful in accepting unproven evidence and should not have acted on it so arrogantly. The case in question depended on medical evidence, and it could have been established beyond doubt before inaccurate statements were made that resulted in extreme embarrassment. A woman teacher at Kgomokasitwa School was suspended by the Bangwaketse School Committee on 26 February 1963. The Headteacher had alleged that she was pregnant. The minutes of the Bangwaketse School Committee stated that 'it was agreed that she be suspended ... until she could prove her innocence against the allegations by the headteacher and the doctors report' (DCK 6). Strangely, no attempt was made to get her side of the story.

It was equally not surprising that 'in April 1963, the District Commissioner in Kanye, also chairman of the school committee, wrote a letter to members of the School Committee and copied it to Director of Education to inform them that it could not be substantiated that the said teacher was pregnant. The report from the doctor she visited in Mafikeng did not confirm the allegation of the headteacher, and the doctor in Kanye who was a member of the School Committee stated that from the other doctor's report it could not be ascertained that she was pregnant. In the absence of conclusive evidence, the teacher was reinstated. The event must have been humiliating to the woman teacher. But the most puzzling story was that which was told by the headteacher and yet had no substance. Where did this vendetta originate, for it appears that it was unprovoked. The Bangwaketse School Committee acted rather harshly, without proper investigation. Why were they in such a hurry to suspend the teacher and thereby interfere with the school programme. This was a good example of naked victimisation which should never have been allowed to take place.

Nonetheless, extensive changes have improved the image of the Ministry of Education in dealing with cases affecting teachers. Such arbitrary decisions that characterised the treatment of teachers is a thing of the past. No official, however influential, can throw out a teacher at the stroke of the pen. For instance, under the discipline of the Unified Teaching Service Regulations, it is stated that 'where disciplinary proceedings are to be or may be taken against a teacher the appropriate procedure shall be commenced as soon as possible' (Botswana Unified Teaching Service Regulations, 1976). Above all, the teacher under this law is given the opportunity to defend or to use the popular expression, exculpate himself. This sounds like a leap from the darkness to the glare of light. Equally, the relationship between the teachers in the field and the Education Officers has gone through some transformation. The Education Officer has ceased to be the terror of the schools, and is now a friend and a helper of the teacher. However, this should not be interpreted to mean that these changes have taken place overnight, and that all the Education Officers have seen the light. We all know that things do not happen so easily, for old habits die hard.

New Directions in Inspecting and Advising

It is common knowledge that the approach of inspectors/education officers described above had been a cause of concern to the Department of Education during the colonial era, and to the Ministry of Education after Botswana had attained independence in 1966. The nature of the reports on the schools and the teachers were indicative of grave ills in our education system. What was needed was a thorough rethinking of the country's educational organisation, and above all to change the attitude of education administrators, the education officers and the teachers labouring in the schools.

The breakthrough to the new attitude must be traced to the Lobatse/Serowe Seminars held during August and September 1981 for Education Officers. The seminars dealt with the subject of 'New Directions in Inspecting and Advising.' The mounting of these seminars must be seen in the context of the general and overall development of education in Botswana. There was a realisation that as long as the education officer saw himself as a slave driver, his efforts, however educative, were bound to be counter-productive. If there was to be progress he had to be 'born anew' and virtually immersed in a new tradition whereby he becomes an advisor and helper to the teacher in the classroom.

The tone of the seminars was set by the Acting Permanent Secretary to the Ministry of Education, C.A.R. Motsepe, in his opening address. For instance, when the Department of Primary Education approached him with the rationale for expanding the advising and in-service functions of the inspectorate, and the in-service team, he had been turning the same thoughts in his mind. He told the gathering, 'I was searching for a way to give closer attention to our primary teachers and their classes' (New Directions in Inspecting and Advising, 1981). The basic idea in reorganising the inspectorate was meant to give teachers the constant professional support of trained education officers in order to help them improve the learning environment in their classes. The role of the education officer was to be seen in the context of educational goals of the country. Reminiscent of the times of Dumbrell, Motsepe mentioned that the emphasis was on improving the quality of primary education and to create a different image of the primary teacher. He stated that:

C.A.R. Motsepe

> 'to show the nation and prospective teacher that he/she is not another secondary school student but a future leader of the country, that the Teacher Training Colleges (TTCs) were not institutions resembling a failed secondary school where the losers go when other opportunities fail, but institutions in which valuable public servants are trained to develop the human resources of the nation' (New Directions in Inspecting and Advising, 1981).

To accomplish this programme and to improve the image of the TTC and the Inspectorate, Botswana, in conjunction with the University of Ohio in Athens, had launched a Primary Education Improvement Project (PEIP) which provided pre-service capacities through the Department of Primary Education at the University of Botswana. First, the programme as we know it, was geared towards the improvement of the primary school personnel, and it has done much to enhance the prestige of the primary school teacher who, before, was doomed to stagnate in a primary teaching position. Secondly, the Ministry of Education had strengthened in-service opportunities through the PEIP by increasing the number of teachers' centres and personnel attached to them. Thirdly, the National Council on Teacher Education was asked to approve a plan that required the TTCs to take 80% of its incoming classes from Junior Certificate (JC) and COSC passes, and limit the admission of Standard 7, JC failures and remote area applicants to 20%. It was hoped that this percentage would drop over the years, as more qualified applicants became available. Fourthly, the Ministry of Education studied the offerings at the TTCs to determine their relevance to the classroom situation in which future teachers would be placed. Finally, it was to reorganise the inspectorate, so that education officers 'are advisors to the classroom teachers, and can visit each school at least twice a year and give individual attention to in-service needs as they arise (New Directions in Inspecting and Advising, 1981).

To achieve this new approach, workshops and seminars were to play a major role in order to know what can be expected of a classroom teacher. There was, therefore, need to break away from the traditional classroom arrangement of straight lines of desks with pupils chained to them and turned into passive recipients. Theirs was to change the approach by encouraging group, teaching, encouraging the teacher to spend more time with each small group, and urging him or her to make use of the spontaneous reactions and answers of the pupils.

The clear message was that the Education Officer (EO) in his zeal to change things was not to move quickly but to be 'sensitive to the needs of each teacher, encourage creativity and improvisation in those bound by over organisation and encourage discipline in the disorganised' (New Directions in Inspecting and Advising, 1981). As representatives of the Ministry of Education in whose hands the future of the teachers lay, the EOs had to put them at ease and elicit their trust. Most importantly, the EO was not to see himself as one who wields power, but one whose concern is to improve teaching. 'Keep your eyes and minds on the children and the ways that you and the teacher can improve their learning situation' (New Directions in Inspecting and Advising, 1981).

The heart of the matter was to heighten the sense of responsibility of primary teachers and to impress upon them 'that they are leaders of young people and that their performance or lack of it makes a lasting impression upon children' (New Directions in Inspecting and Advising, 1981). While every effort was made to maintain good relations with teachers, discipline was to be maintained in order to achieve the goal. The change made from inspector to education officer was intended to increase the potential of staff to visit the schools and influence what was happening. For the EO, the change was a challenge in order to create a new image to struggle with new procedures and many other adjustments.

In order to arrive at the crucial change on the role of the EO, the critical areas that were discussed at the seminars included: Criteria for the Selection of Education Officers, The Expectations of an Education Officer, One's Views on One's Role, The EO and the Development of Education, and other such topics concerned with inspecting and advising staff development. These topics were important as they touched on critical aspects of the education system in the country. It was important that leaders in education such as Education Officers were not appointed arbitrarily but displayed or conformed to established criteria. Further, it was important to know from them how they envisaged the essence of their responsibilities including the expectations of teachers in the field, the children in the schools, and the parents in the community. Equally, it is worth noting that most of the subjects discussed were contributed by EOs and were not dictated to them by the resource persons at the seminars. The EOs were reflecting on their past experiences and projecting their new roles.

The paper entitled 'My Expectations of an Education Officer' (New Directions in Inspecting and Advising, 1981) supported by similar papers, saw the EO as one who is skilled in the methods of educating, teaching and one whose purpose is to promote education and be equipped with the necessary skills to do so – a strong criteria for the selection of EOs. The work of EOs demands modesty and a readiness to both teach and learn, while at the same time being approachable. They should refrain from an arrogance and a narrowness of outlook which could create a bar between themselves and the teachers generally. But above all for EOs to perform credibly they need good training which equips them with basic techniques required by the job. Included in their training must be a clear job description advising the teacher on classroom organisation, curriculum development, organising in-service courses and workshops. Looked at closely, the functions of the EOs are to upgrade the standard of classroom teaching, explain the policy of the Ministry to local councils, schools and the general public, enforce Education Law, Primary and Secondary School Regulations and the Unified Teaching Service Regulations.

This no doubt, should teach them about the inspection of schools as a form of communication between the school and authority and not a 'fault finding mission'. It is an exercise to create a dialogue between the EO and the school to share experiences on those aspects that improve teaching and learning. The comprehension of such a deeply laden philosophy on inspecting and guiding by the earlier inspectors (later EOs) would have helped the education in this country to progress meaningfully. The discussion on inspection of schools raised an important point which emphasised the need for inspection records and reports to be as realistic as possible, free from prejudice and to give a true picture of what takes place in a school. 'They should reflect the strengths and weaknesses of a teacher in a fair and balanced manner' (New Directions in Inspecting and Advising, 1981). Since a school report forms a permanent record of a school or a teacher, it should contain and highlight good and bad points. In addition, this was expected to reflect on the character and personality of an EO.

What the discussions also achieved was that for the first time, the EOs aired openly the constraints that militated against their maximum professional potential. For instance, the work of the EO was sometimes handicapped by the lack of supporting staff and as a result information did not reach the schools on time. Sometimes the late arrival of stationery, books and furniture frustrated the teachers, children and the EOs. Another stumbling block to the efficiency of the EOs was sometimes the lack of cooperation of both the headteachers and assistants. It was, therefore, clear that unless the headteachers cooperated, the EOs were bound to make hasty decisions which might be inaccurate due to lack of information. In fact, the main ally was the headteacher who knows the strengths and weaknesses of his staff. Still more frustrating to the functions of the EOs was the lack of communication procedures and the observation of the hierarchy that went with it.

The changes within the inspectorate were discussed at length and centred on the ambiguity of these changes. For instance, during the years 1976 to 1978, field officers were called assistant education officers and at that time it was not clear who they assisted in their job since they worked alone. Perhaps in search for a better label, from 1978 to 1980, they became known as Inspectors of Schools and later the position was designated Education Officer in keeping with Dumbrell's idea in the 1940s.

Why then were these changes made and what was the motive since they caused so much concern? The strangest thing was that no explanations were given to make those involved aware of the significance of the change. 'While the changes in designation have been made, there has not been definite specification of the duties of this officer to go along with new names, except in general terms like, inspect schools, and in-service teachers...' (New Directions in Inspecting and Advising, 1981). But it is clear that for guidance, a paper was prepared in 1978 for the field officers that stated fourteen points as the duties of inspectors under their job description and in comparison with those of his counterpart, the education secretary.

What then was the position of the inspectorate in the past? Before 1981, the Ministry of Education had two functions of the inspectorate. One group was designated 'Inspectors of Schools (field)' while the other was called 'Inspectors of Schools (in-service)'. The functions were different and distinct from each other, and this meant that they did not belong together and logically their functions were different in dealing with teachers. The field officers visited schools for inspection, followed by reports submitted to headteachers, while the in-service staff conducted workshops for teachers and reported to headquarters on what progress was made at such undertakings. As would be expected, the teachers had different perceptions of the two groups of officers. Maybe one of the far reaching recommendations related to the new type of visit to schools, namely group visits, whereby they were brought together to discuss ideas, problems and methods in specific schools. The aim was to help EOs to know their colleagues and learn of their interests and skills. The gatherings were meant to facilitate cooperation and foster a team approach, but were 'on no account to resemble the old panel inspection ambush type' (New Directions in Inspecting and Advising, 1981). Furthermore, to facilitate the flow of ideas and information, it was suggested that regional workshops be arranged for education officers on a rotational basis inviting specialists if necessary and using those EOs with special skills. Included for discussion in such workshops were infant methods, remedial teaching and various subject specialisations. These arrangements helped to clear the air and to some extent reduce the element of suspicion among teachers.

The Lobatse/Serowe seminars brought about a clear statement on the role of the Inspectors/EOs and removed nebulous and indistinct assumptions. Their first responsibility is to guide, so that in executing their duties they have to identify and indicate the directions to be taken by the school events in an advisory manner. Secondly, they have to educate, by giving official instruction, teach laid down procedures and train for deficiencies that come to their notice. Thirdly, to support and be aware that inspection and supervision are two supporting services to education. Fourthly, to evaluate in order to check on the results of investment – the human investment in the name of the school children.

Efforts were also made and issues raised to terminate the EOs isolation and humanise him by establishing contact with pupils. The contact was considered a vital component of their responsibilities. To this end, it was felt that the EOs should visit schools some of the time to work in the classroom with children and discover for themselves that children are not predictable and that their abilities vary. On such occasions, they could be asked to teach demonstration lessons to assist the teachers. Through such exposure, the EOs might discover some strategies which as trainees and later as teachers they might have missed and be able to recognise what is appropriate at different standards. The most progressive and revolutionary suggestion was that the EOs could take some time off to spend in a classroom as a class teacher on secondment or on sabbatical leave. In this way they were bound to empathise with teachers in the schools and approach their work in a realistic manner. The most crucial ingredient of their experience as teachers was a fair evaluation of their teaching by their colleagues and experienced teachers. Such a procedure would broaden their horizons and make them appreciate the problems that teachers face in schools. An experience of that type would give them first hand knowledge of the quality of staff in rural schools that are constantly faced with classroom shortages and a lack of essential facilities.

To crown some of the far reaching recommendations in relation to the status of the EOs and Regional EOs, they were encouraged to visit the Teacher Training Colleges to acquaint themselves with the programmes offered since the teachers they worked with train at these TTCs. It was also crucial that the EOs give feedback to the Colleges on the performance of their graduates. In other words, for the EOs to perform efficiently, they had to be introduced into all the different activities of the country's education system. For instance, they were to participate in the planning of the TTC curriculum, and pay special attention to remedial teaching, teaching infant classes and the teaching of reading. It was equally fitting that the EOs were involved with the practice teaching stages of the TTC students and this could be attended to when the EOs were on secondment or on sabbatical leave.

The examination of the role of the EOs or the search for new directions in inspecting and advising also brought in many other issues of concern to the EOs. The questions relating to this broad topic were philosophical and demanded well thought out responses from the participants. The responses ranged from concerns such as self reliance, personal fulfilment, relevant knowledge to pupils who are unable to find information, from being an authoritarian figure to one of being a team leader and a facilitator. The major breakthrough was that the propositions came from the EOs themselves which was symptomatic of their clear perception of their role and their acquaintance with the broad principles of education.

In conclusion, one should mention that the success of an education programme depends on the training and the effectiveness of the personnel. For teachers to make a meaningful contribution to education they need to grow professionally and the worst thing that can happen to them is stagnation, due to a lack of diversity within the school, region or the system at large. Through the support and dignity accorded them by the system, such cases as we narrated earlier, would hardly surface. Such teachers would not be interfered with by rank and file in the execution of their service. This of course, brings us to the question of staff development, and it is in this respect that the EOs can lend a helping hand. First, they could work alongside colleagues giving demonstration lessons and these could be complimented by headteachers with the promoted staff by mounting workshops in the neighbouring schools. Secondly, the EOs would harness the services of those teachers who have attended in-service courses for monitoring school based courses. To further consolidate the work of the EOs, TTC staff should participate at these school-based courses when time allows. All these issues would help to consolidate the image of the EOs who in turn would have a high regard for the teachers and treat them as fellow workers. Once the EOs insecurities were removed they would work well with teachers who in turn would earn the respect of the community.

Chapter Seven

The BTU: Its Dilemma and the Way Forward

We saw in the last chapter that Kgeledi George Kgoroba was succeeded by Drake Selwe, then Headteacher of the Bakwena National School in Molepolole, at the Lobatse Conference in 1974. Selwe the teacher, the principal, administrator and a graduate of the Kanye Teacher Training College was saddled with the unenviable task of piloting the Botswana Teachers Union (BTU) through difficult times for 12 years. He may not have been blessed with the striking qualities of his predecessor such as debating skill, unbridled energy and fighting spirit, but he was a seasoned negotiator. There is a view that many dreams of the BTU were realised during Selwe's presidency. The fight for better conditions of service which had been going on even before his time came to fruition during the latter part of the 1970s and up to mid the 1980s when he led the Union. Selwe's particular skill weathered the storm and saw the total acceptance and recognition of the BTU by Government. He obviously preferred negotiation to confrontation, and winning friends to making enemies. While this stance was commendable, there was and is, up to this day, a feeling that good relations were not to be secured at any price. This was true particularly at a time when a number of issues including the stop-order arrangement which required the Ministry of Education to concede to the teachers' demand for the monthly deduction for the BTU coffers. It is exactly on the issue of unconditional negotiation that some teachers have held that the BTU lost not only its direction during those years but its very soul. Perhaps the birth of a later organisation such as the Botswana Federation of Secondary Teachers (BOFESETE) who were unhappy about the operations of the BTU, and Job Evaluation Unsatisfied Teachers (JEUT), later termed Botswana Primary Teachers' Association (BOPRITA). They felt that after the Government Job Evaluation exercise the teaching profession had been affected. To crown it all, in the eyes of the primary school teachers, the BTU seemed indifferent to their plight.

Drake Selwe, on assuming office, adopted the recommendation of the outgoing President to bring young Batswana to positions of leadership within the BTU. The Executive consisted of the following: President, D. Selwe; Vice-President, C. Mahube; General Secretary, S. Masina; Treasurer, J.O. Rammekwa; T.S. Motshwane, Editor – *The Teacher;* and D. Selema, Chairman, Education Committee. The only members of the new executive who were not Batswana were S. Masina from Zimbabwe and J.O. Rammekwa a South African.

Selwe's Years of Toil

It was this executive which was under the leadership of Selwe that piloted the BTU through difficult times and secured exciting achievements. It should be mentioned that contributing to a determination to win were two stalwarts of the BTU. First was Joe Rammekwa who served as BTU treasurer for many years, and secondly, L.B. Ramatebele a vigorous and energetic general secretary and loyal friend. What may have helped Selwe and his team was that within the Ministry of Education there was a significant change of attitude towards the BTU. Masogo, who was Permanent Secretary for many years, was a staunch supporter of the BTU and as President, as was noted earlier, had campaigned for the same issues. There was a general realisation that the teachers' organisation was a trustworthy partner in the major task of nation building through education. For instance, at the first meeting of the Consultative Committee, a sub-committee of the Unified Teaching Service (UTS), held in August 1976, the chairman stressed the need to create good working relations within the service with the teachers representatives. The friendly mood within the Ministry of Education such as in the National Council of Teacher Education, the Bursaries Committee, the National Committee on Education Policy and the Secondary School Headmasters Committee and other relevant committees helped pave the way for progress. The coming of the National Council for Teacher Education (NCTE) and vigorous participation of the BTU was another landmark during Selwe's term of office. There was a joint meeting of the Ministry of Education (the physical provider and teachers' employer) and the University of Botswana (the professional custodian and the certificate validation institution) to discuss and confer on the development of Teacher Education. The BTU which is the mouthpiece of teachers was represented. To show how valuable the contribution of the BTU was, it was represented on the University Advisory Committee on Education. The teachers knew that these were policy making structures that would enable them to influence thinking in the Ministry in their favour, and thus help the development of education in Botswana. One of the recommendations that came from the Swaneng conference, in line with the development of education, was the request for the mounting of regular refresher courses for primary school

Drake Selwe

teachers in order to update their skills. These refresher courses were invaluable, particularly in modern mathematics and science, which many teachers had not studied at school. The BTU was assisted in their quest by the WCOTP (later known as Education International) through the efforts of Raymond Smyke and Tom Bediako who were consultants as far back as 1971. The Norwegian Teachers' Union, Danish Teachers Union and Canadian Federation of Teachers helped the BTU to achieve its goal. One of the most far-reaching recommendations called on the Ministry of Education to take over primary education from the Ministry of Local Government in order to ensure uniformity in the implementation of the UTS law.

Ramatebele

The first task of the new Executive Committee was to embark on a recruiting campaign. This was necessitated by the fact that though the BPATA/BTU, which had been in existence for 35 years, was relatively unknown to many teachers, and they were therefore, not involved in the activities of the organisation. The long trips which were undertaken by the Executive Committee to places such as Tsabong, Hukuntsi, Ghanzi, Pitsane-Molopo, Gomare, Kasane and many others, were intended to take the Union to the teachers to the four corners of Botswana. The Union's purpose was also to sensitise the teachers to the greater needs of the country and make them aware that they were partners with the Government in nation-building. Those visits to the schools bore fruit, although not in terms of material gains, but they aroused a new spirit of commitment on the part of the teachers to serve their people. It began to dawn in many quarters that the Union was a valuable ally that could speak unequivocally on their behalf. There was a need to build the morale of teachers who were not only victims of unscrupulous employers, but were beset sometimes by trying conditions in their schools, such as lack of furniture, equipment, poor housing and indifferent committees.

Perhaps the finest breakthrough of all time by the BTU was the coming of the Unified Teaching Service Act of 1975, which was promulgated in 1976, and superseded the Botswana Teaching Service Act. The advent of the Unified Teaching Service (UTS) now called Teaching Service Management (TSM) was an appropriate system for the good management, governance and administration of teachers and teachers' affairs in the country. It made the Ministry of Education answerable to matters regarding the teachers. Above all, it created a common authority for teachers and eliminated a multiplicity of authorities. Above all, it gave birth to the consultative machinery which brought the BTU and the Ministry of Education together for useful talks. The 1950s and the 1960s, it should be recalled, saw the teachers agitating for a common teaching law in order to fall under the control of one employer, and the idea was to discourage different salaries and conditions for teachers serving the same government. Early efforts, as indicated, were made with the coming of the review of salaries by Rusbridger in 1959. Though there was a great deal of change, it fell short of the teachers' expectations. The control of teachers by different employers was considered discriminatory. If all teachers fell under one employer, the conditions of service would be identical and that would ensure that the teachers would earn the same salaries for the same qualifications and experience. Before that there was a hodgepodge of arrangements, such as teachers who were not only in government schools, but in Tribal Administration schools, and a school like Moeng College under the Ngwato Board. The teaching staff in these schools were paid differently and that was a sore point to the teachers who were disadvantaged. Ironically even some teachers who were paid better salaries supported the other teachers, but some did not involve themselves since the majority were expatriate teachers. If anything, the Unified Teaching Service regulations abolished the anomalies which had existed from the colonial administration to post independence Botswana. Once more, the teachers' cause triumphed through pressure and skilful negotiation.

One of the finest aspects of the Unified Teaching Service Act was the section which dealt with discipline. Before the advent of the law, some employers acted arbitrarily in their treatment of teachers. For instance, the act brought in line all procedures in order to obviate some trivial cases and the decisions arrived upon as we saw in Chapter 6. It became possible that in the event of an offence, teachers had to be informed of the measures that were to be taken against them in advance. For instance, in the case of interdiction the teacher was informed of the amount of salary he was entitled to during the period in question. In the event that the supervisor of schools was of the opinion that there was a case against the teacher, the list of charges was sent to the teacher and he was informed of the need to reply or exculpate himself from the charges. Significantly and for the first time, the teacher was allowed to muster all the defences at his disposal.

Another important element of the Unified Teaching Service Law was the establishment of the Unified Teaching Service Consultative Committee in which the BTU was represented. The law states, '...in nominating members to the committee, a registered Teachers' association shall bear in mind the need to represent, as far as possible the interests of teachers employed in various categories of schools' (Unified Teaching Service Act, 1975). So important was the role of the BTU as a member of the Consultative Committee, that the quorum of the committee, among others, included two teachers. With regard to the functions of the Consultative Committee, two stand out as extremely important. First was the maintenance of professional standards, conduct and discipline within the Unified Teaching Service, and second was assistance in the furtherance of good relations between the Government and teachers in the Unified Teaching Service.

The establishment of the Teaching Service Commission was another landmark in the struggle of the teachers' organisation in this country to protect the interests of the teachers. Section 29 of the Unified Teaching Service Act 1975 states, 'any teacher who has been removed from office or is subjected to any other punishment by the exercise of any power conferred on the Director or an appointing authority may dismiss such an appeal or allow it wholly or in part' (Unified Teaching Service Act, 1975).

The National Commission on Education – 1977

One of the most significant and lasting contributions made by the BTU and other teachers was the establishment of the National Commission on Education (NCE). Their input came through the task forces that were created through subject panels. It should be borne in mind that the subject panels had been introduced in the early 1970s to, among other things, make the programmes/curricula relevant to the needs of the country. The colonial administration had leaned heavily on South African syllabuses in a number of subjects and the panels were intended to remedy this trend and make education serve the interests of Batswana. Through their recommendations, the task forces introduced many changes in a number of subjects like history, which was haunted after independence by the lack of teaching materials, geography which lacked specialists, Setswana which needed upgrading in terms of its orthography and improvement of its literature, and mathematics and science which needed far-reaching revisions. It was also going to be necessary to attract teachers for these subjects as they were in short supply. The other subjects that came under scrutiny included, English, developmental studies and French both at the junior and senior levels. Some of the task force's recommendations were adopted and were revised as circumstances changed. Through their contribution in the task forces the BTU showed its commitment to education in this country. Their assistance helped the members of the Commission on Education who were appointed in December 1975, by a directive of His Excellency the late President of Botswana, Sir Seretse Khama in January 1976. The committee was under the Chairmanship of Professor Torsten Husen, the Director of the Institute for International Education, University of Stockholm. The other members of the Commission were Dr Aklilu Habte of Ethiopia, Dr James R. Sheffield of Columbia University, Mr Peter R.C. Williams of the Institute of Education, University of London, and two Batswana educationists, the Honourable B.C. Thema and Professor N.O.H. Setidisho, the former Rector of the University College of Botswana and Swaziland.

The terms of reference as proposed by the Cabinet and refined by the National Committee on Education Policy were as follows. Firstly, identify the major problems affecting education in Botswana and the issues of principal concern to the Government of Botswana. Secondly, to clarify the goals of the education system as perceived by the key parties within and outside government, and thirdly, to review the current education system and propose a programme for its development. Finally it was to present recommendations regarding the implementation of an effective programme to overcome problems and achieve goals.

If anything, the appointment of the NCE showed the Government's concern with the type of education which individuals and associations had condemned as inappropriate and irrelevant to the needs of a developing country. The BPATA and the BTU later had criticised the type of education which was offered at the height of colonial administration and after Botswana had attained independence from Britain. The outgoing President, George Kgoroba, had condemned the pursuit of the outworn colonial education in his address at the Annual Conference of the BTU at Lobatse in 1974: 'It has become very urgent, therefore, that we must review our education system' (BTU Annual Conference, 1974). On that occasion, the teachers were exhorted to commit themselves to mould the future citizens of this country with sound values, attitudes and skills. They were to concern themselves with professional problems of curriculum development and its implementation. It is of interest to note that it was at the BTU conference held at Lobatse Secondary School that the outgoing president made a special plea for the 'appointment of a national education commission to review the whole system led by a Motswana...' (BTU Annual Conference, 1974).

The proposals made by the Commission – A New Strategy for Educational Development in Botswana, were important. The importance of the Commission lay in that they used the very tools and philosophy which the Government and the people had generated. The Commission interpreted these and put them in a clearer perspective.

First of all, they worked on what they called the underlying principles. The new strategy according to the Commission was to be guided by Botswana's national principles of democracy, development, self-reliance and unity. The Commission stressed the need to modify the content and improve the quality of education at all levels to ensure that it provided both the fundamental competencies that would enable young Batswana to contribute to the development of an attitude and understanding that would foster democracy, development, self-reliance and unity – *Kagisano*. Secondly, they advocated the need to consider the education of all the people, as implied by the principles of democracy. The removal of sharp differences in geographical or financial accessibility to different sections of the population. Thirdly, it was imperative to conserve financial resources and to promote economic growth while cultivating the nation's human resources. The principle of development called for an education that is economic and productive. Fourthly, the individual learners and the communities were to be encouraged to help in the provision of education since this is in line with the principle of self-reliance. Finally, the Commission urged that in the name of unity, it was essential for the education system to be a continuum, and therefore reduce or eliminate the differences and distinctions between the different levels of education, between in-school and out of school learning, between government schools and independent schools.

Primary School Enrolments, Standard 1 and Total 1967–76

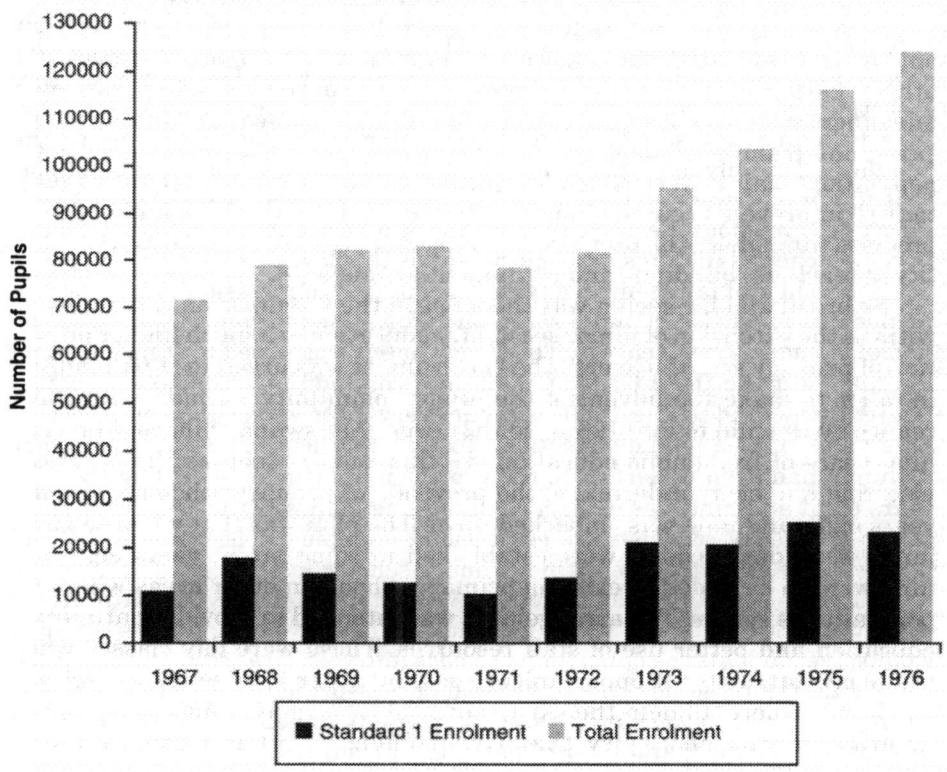

Source: **National Development Plan, 1976–81.**

The Commission also recommended that government work towards the removal of age and financial barriers to learning. Equally, financial barriers to school attendance were to be removed and primary school fees were to be abolished in 1980. This strategy paid dividends, for as had happened earlier when fees were reduced, primary school enrolments soared to alarming heights. 'There was an upsurge in the Standard 1 entry in 1973 following the reduction in schools fees from P6.00 to P3.00 per annum, and enrolments have continued at a higher level than predicted...' (NDP, 1976–81). There were 25 414 pupils enrolled in 1973 compared to 10 992 in 1967.

Secondary school fees for full time schooling was to remain as long as access was rationed, but a generous system of bursaries extending to the full cost of attending school was to be offered.

The development of primary education according to the Commission was to be given priority, since it was the only education that most children would receive and above all it was the basis for further learning. The Commissioners on this point came closer to Patrick van Rensburg and Julius Nyerere's views that primary education should be revitalised as it is invariably the only form of education the majority of children in developing countries ever attain. Perhaps another good example was that of countries like Singapore and others which have enjoyed the highest levels of growth. It was felt necessary that primary schools should be extended to those sections of the population, mainly in rural areas, who did not have it. It was equally important to improve the curriculum and devise a means of assessing children's progress throughout the primary schooling and increase the quality and quantity of teachers, buildings and equipment at this level.

So broad and far-seeing was the scope of the Commission that today we witness the extension of junior secondary education to a much higher proportion of primary school leavers. The Government was urged to start planning in order to make the advent of the junior community secondary schools a reality by the mid to late 1980s, so that every Motswana child could receive nine years of free public education. To this end, as soon as the necessary planning had been undertaken, the provision of primary schooling through years eight and nine was embarked upon. The plan was that when separate junior secondary schools were established in some areas, years eight and nine were to be added to existing primary schools in other areas where the population is sparse. The arrangement was intended to provide continuity of education and better use of staff resources. These were day classes which would give students the opportunity to pass into year 10 at secondary schools.

Furthermore, to help the expansion of post-primary educational opportunities, it was necessary that Government develop a programme of professional support and later of partial financial help to community sponsored junior secondary schools operating on a self-help basis.

The Commission, in some of its recommendations was determined not to ignore those who had been handicapped from attending formal schools by suggesting a part-time education system which needed the generous support of employers who would release their employees for educational purposes. The large part of the demand for continuation courses would be for general education including, mathematics and English at the junior and senior certificate levels, out of school education, and the combination of learning and work to eliminate the major discontinuities in the present education system.

The foregoing background has been given in order to show that some issues raised had been considered at various teachers' fora. The only difference may have been that the teachers were less articulate, and had no ready audience as the distinguished scholars who formed the Commission. At some point, the Commissioners in spite of their eminence realised that, however comprehensive their findings, they needed the input of the teachers engaged in the day-to-day classroom situation.

The Task Forces and Their Contribution

This brings us to the part played by the Primary and Secondary Curriculum Task Forces in helping the NCE, with the assistance of the National Subject Panels, their findings and the recommendations made. The Subject Panels consisted of the finest selection of teachers with experience that this country could muster. They were a knowledgeable lot, for they readily noted merit when evidence was given, and were equally critical of the weak aspects of our education system. The lasting contributions made by the Subject Panels were the far-reaching recommendations they made and which on adoption have brought about commendable changes.

Before a Task Force embarked on its assignment, it adopted a certain position arising from its terms of reference. The clause which dealt with the provision of a practical orientation of the curriculum would serve as the preamble to the report. The preamble indicated the 'need to develop among the pupils a receptive attitude to their work – an attitude which would make possible the goals outlined by the Government in the current Development Plan' (Report of the NCE, 1977).

Again, looking ahead and taking into account the economic climate of the country and the livelihood of its people, thought was given to the establishment of a more practical orientation of primary education. It was considered that that was one of the ways in which lasting basic literacy could be achieved. Children were to be encouraged to spend more time sitting down to write things or draw things or make things. In that way, writing skills and manual skills could be improved and advanced. It was also emphasised that the quality of education would be reflected in the performance of its teachers. For success, therefore, it was important for teachers to be sensitive to the pupil's individual capabilities and encourage them to be achievers rather than retard their progress. To this end, classrooms in turn should be places where children were to be encouraged to achieve. From the solution of problems realistically set, followed by the assessment of information, the students could arrive at rational conclusions. The search and acquisition, discussion and assessment of information and its usefulness was the responsibility of the child. Such an approach to schooling, the task forces believed, could be combined with traditional skills in crafts and debates. The training of teachers was to reflect that approach to the maturing young minds so that divergent thinking could replace the useless repetition of formulae and the remembering of unconnected pieces of irrelevant information which fill the mind rather than train the intelligence. Teachers must insist on accurate, carefully written records and work attempted, so that the children think for themselves.

Of great importance was the maintenance of sound educational materials and facilities such as stationery, apparatus, furniture and so on to which S. Matlhabaphiri had alluded to before. (Matlhabaphiri was a Mokwena from Molepolole, who had great influence and enjoyed a tremendous following.) At that time, he became a strong advocate on educational matters and was most critical of general practices. He hated the sight of shabby schools and the careless treatment of teachers. By being so vocal and uncompromising, he earned the displeasure of the establishment of the time, particularly the DC in Molepolole. Inability to provide these supportive items would be reflected in the quality of the product – a less productive and frustrated individual. Finally, as the country developed, in a position adopted by Patrick van Rensburg and later the Science Panel, it was seen as important to make the curriculum of the schools reflect this aspect of education by including technology and science. The response to this area of study found expression at the Professional Educationists' Seminar – on the 3C's, Communication Consultation and Cooperation held in 1987. 'The Department has conducted in-service courses for all of the junior secondary technical teachers in Botswana and will continue to expand its work in this area' (Professional Educationists Seminar, 3C's, 1987). This point was emphasised by Dr P.M. Jones at the same seminar when he stated that the Department of Technical Education saw it as essential for the technical education programme to be a continuous ladder of opportunity, where even those who leave formal education at the primary level have a route of continuous study to the degree level. (Dr P.M. Jones was the Chief Technical Education Officer who came to Botswana through the Overseas Development Administration (Technical Assistance)).

The findings of the Task Forces, which were helped by practising teachers, reflected their familiarity with Botswana's educational ills. The first of these dealt with the excessive amount of material in the primary syllabus. Nonetheless, this was to be expected if one considered this interest to develop primary education from the years of neglect during the colonial administration. Every conceivable ideal seemed to find a place in the curriculum. Then two alternatives had to be resolved. The first question was if the quality of the teachers was adequate, apparatus and pupil teacher ratio were satisfactory, would the syllabus, after pruning, be adequate? The second question was if the other factors that make up the curriculum were satisfactory, would there be a need to draw a new syllabus?

The subject-by-subject review of the curriculum revealed that the Unit system was constricting. It tended to reduce the number of possible approaches to the teaching of a topic because it specifies the number of lessons available and gives insufficient scope to good teachers who wish to improvise. Above all, the 'Unit' method places more emphasis on teaching than on the learning process in that the teacher tends to do all the work and this leaves no time for full participation by the pupils.

To obviate the Unit approach, the objectives of attainment to age were set, and the sequence of topics of teaching to these objectives were to be determined by teacher consultation on a school basis. It was of utmost importance that teachers be supplied with handbooks outlining various approaches and on the use of apparatuses. With regard to defined objectives, headteachers would exert an in-service training function towards their staff, particularly the untrained.

So great was the desire to set a strong foundation for Botswana's system of education, and to strive for a well balanced curriculum, that the Task Forces first turned to the problem of its organisation. To carry out this mammoth task, a Primary Curriculum Unit was established to review the syllabus and attendant influences. Two factors were to be taken into account in connection with curriculum development. First, that in-service was to be conducted in order to meet the needs of curriculum development and help in its evolution. The idea of the In-service Unit was received warmly by the Government and in the 1980s a fully-fledged In-service Unit was established under the leadership of Bram Swallow of the Overseas Development Administration (ODA). With the advent of Teacher Education and Development, in-service has become a strong component of the training of teachers not only in Botswana, but in some other countries as well. 'A second thrust of in-service training will be the institutionalisation of courses that will enable the successful completer to achieve some form of recognition in the form of a certificate, diploma or award' (Teacher Education and Development Papers, 1990). The seriousness of the Government of Botswana in this respect is exemplified by the upgrading of untrained teachers, through the proposed diploma programme at the Tlokweng Teacher Training College. It is for this reason, that NDP 7 continues to focus on the training of trainers. Secondly, to ensure that the syllabus was flexible enough, alternative approaches to ascertain that the syllabus in particular areas should have direct relevance to the life lived in that area. It had to allow for alternative approaches so that the learning demands made by the syllabus on children in rural areas should be the same as the learning demands made by the syllabus on children living in towns. Finally, the Task Forces made a progressive recommendation outside the terms of reference. In this respect school broadcasting was mentioned and a panel of five people who were familiar with the aims and problems of teachers and children was created.

The link between the Task Forces and the Ministry of Education needs mentioning at this point. The Task Forces were established by the Ministry of Education and were to a large extent formed around subject panels. The subject panels were the brainchild of the BTU which saw them as the cornerstone of educational development through a constant re-examination of curricula. Equally, not all the teachers who served on the Task Forces saw eye to eye with the BTU. It is perhaps in this light that the main contribution of the BTU should be seen as assisting the Commission to achieve its goal.

It was logical that the Secondary School Curriculum Task Force would be in place, since the Botswana Government from the outset had targeted this cycle for rapid development in order 'to create in the shortest possible time, with financial means as may be available, a stock of trained local manpower capable of serving the country's economy' (NDP, 1968–73). This Task Force was again slightly different from the Primary School Task Force, in that its members were assisted by different National Subject Panels who were responsible for the constant review and improvement of the syllabuses. The Secondary Task Force was to review the Junior and Senior Secondary School Curriculum. It dealt with the a comprehensive assessment of the Junior Certificate (JC), and Secondary School Curriculum as it existed, both its strengths and weaknesses, the JC and Cambridge Overseas School Certificate (COSC) examinations, their purpose and the nature of examinations, their influence on the teaching and learning process, examination administration and suggestions for improvement. Furthermore, it was to consider the organisation and conduct of secondary level curriculum development including teachers in curriculum development, and lastly, a subject-by-subject analysis of teaching methods and learning materials.

In general, the Task Forces, commenting on the whole system of education in Botswana, touched on the most sensitive chord when it stated that it was influenced by the fact that, it tended to be geared to the ultimate goal of a university education. However, it is clearly known that in actual fact, only about one per cent of any group of pupils who enter primary school finally enter the university. Another weakness was that practical education was not offered to any considerable extent in Botswana secondary schools, another example of years of neglect by the colonial administration. In fact, it was Swaneng Hill School that introduced practical subjects. In this connection, the Secondary Task Force stated: 'even then they appear to be more tolerated than accepted as a necessary part of the curriculum' (Report of the NCE, 1977). The only comfort was that Government policy encouraged the inclusion of practical subjects like design and technology, technical drawing and woodwork, in the curriculum.

Furthermore, and not surprisingly, all the panels brought out the fact that the JC syllabuses did not link with those of the COSC in all subjects. There was a prevalent view that, some subjects in the JC course were not a preparation for the Cambridge School Certificate, and that too much material was left to be covered in the two years following Junior Certificate. This state of affairs was bound to occur since the two certificates were not run by the same authority. The Junior Certificate curriculum was determined locally, whereas the COSC curriculum was in the hands of the Cambridge Syndicate. At times the criticism was that the curriculum was unsuitable because it had been adapted directly from another education system. Of interest, the staff in charge of the Pre-Entry Science Course (PESC), when interviewed by the Evaluation Team set by the University of Botswana to examine the role of that programme, expressed the view that 'perhaps the current Cambridge Overseas School Certificate (COSC) examination was not geared towards university entry and would benefit from localisation' (PESC Evaluation Report, 1992). In addition to this, some panels raised the often mentioned problem that our curriculum was biased in favour of the academic programme which marked a departure from the proclaimed Government policy to promote and encourage the teaching of practical subjects. The conclusion derived from the fact that 'only one practical subject should be studied by a pupil' (Report of the NCE, 1977).

On the curriculum again, what drew a fair share of criticism was that there was no curriculum development unit within the Ministry of Education. As a result of this, the work of curriculum development was undertaken by the subject panels which were responsible for the constant review and improvement of the syllabuses. They also made recommendations regarding the choice of textbooks and examination questions. To this end, the panels had played an active part in improving the quality and relevance of the syllabuses and preparing of supportive materials. This was evidenced by the emergence of new syllabuses in English, geography, mathematics, integrated science, agriculture and bible knowledge. In the light of these developments, discussions were also going on in respect of woodwork, technical drawing and development studies which are now a part of our curriculum.

To assist the panels in their efforts, the Examinations Council was at first flexible so as to encourage the input by the teachers towards curriculum development. This gave them an assurance that it would not stand in the way of curriculum development. That attitude resulted in a proliferation of syllabuses in different subjects in an attempt to satisfy the national needs and aspirations. That policy made the Council ask for the establishment of the Curriculum Coordinating Committee to study closely the existing syllabuses in order to consolidate the syllabuses that had extensive overlap. Even now the Curriculum Coordinating Committee continues to do a fine job scrutinising syllabuses that require implementation. In support of the call for curricular change, the University of Botswana, Lesotho and Swaziland (UBLS) Schools Examinations Council stated that syllabuses and examinations tended to become entrenched hurdles of informal academic systems. Then,

'if the Examinations Council is to be an agent of change responsive to the needs of its candidates, there is need for an officer of the Council to be concerned with the follow up studies on the relevance of syllabuses and examinations to subsequent life experiences, including those of the candidates who leave formal education after an examination' (Report of the NCE, 1977).

The findings and the recommendations made by the Subject Panels on a subject-by-subject basis will now be examined. It must be remembered again that it was during Selwe's presidency that the subject panels gained stature. It must from the outset, be pointed out that there is no intention to cover all the subjects at secondary school level, for that would be a mammoth task. We shall therefore deal with only the following subjects: English, Setswana, French, social sciences, history, geography, development studies, science, agriculture and mathematics. The importance of this section lies in the participation of teachers in educational reforms in Botswana and it should be borne in mind that the establishment of subject panels came as a result of the efforts of the BTU in order to help teachers, particularly the untrained teachers who lacked a sound academic background. Indeed, it was through the Ministry of Education that the robust Task Forces came to the fore during the time of the NCE. The point to be made clearly is that the latter day subject panels were built around the initial subject panels with a few additions.

English

The English Panel found the materials at the Junior Certificate (JC) level were adequately supplied. Texts for guided writing practice were also widely used; a situation which commended itself admirably. A progressive recommendation made by the Panel was that teachers should work with the senior students in creating their own materials. Nonetheless, the major weakness indicated by the Panel was that the gap between the JC reading skills and those needed for Cambridge was too wide. Presumably the concern arose from the fact that the JC set books were treated as extensive readers and the Cambridge literature books are intensive readers. With regard to the Cambridge Examinations in language and literature, there was general approval of the reformed Cambridge language paper and though the standard was not high it was acceptable. It provided a suitable training in the linguistic skills needed for study in other subjects. With regard to the literature paper, the suggestion was the inclusion of African writers. In addition to that, the Panel welcomed the call for a more localised literature syllabus. A valuable contribution made by the panel was the place of English in the school curriculum. It stressed that all teachers should consider that the teaching of English should help them, particularly in subjects where expression is crucial. This was a call to treat English as a service subject.

Obviously, the Panel was looking ahead, and for further consolidation and improvement of the curriculum in the schools, it recommended far-reaching changes. For instance, the training of teachers at the University of Botswana and Swaziland (UBLS) called for an increase in the time devoted to teaching practice and the tutorial supervision supplied with it. It is important to note that, when this study was mounted, a great number of improvements had been effected to upgrade approaches to teaching practice and supervision. At the same time, it should be mentioned that perfection in teaching is like a mirage. Another change that received attention as a result of the panel's recommendation was that, as soon as feasible, UBS should replace the Concurrent Certificate in Education by a post-graduate one. The change was effected in 1984. Since that time, the debate has raged endlessly with regard to the wisdom of the change. There is a school of thought that maintains that the Concurrent Certificate in Education was ideal as it immersed the trainees in all the training strategies while the post-graduate course familiarises the trainee with the tactics of the trade. The other school believes that the latter is ideal for purposes of making the trainee concentrate on the requirements of the profession, while the Concurrent Certificate tended to compete with degree courses, and faculties compete for the same students. Other recommendations related to the appointment of an education officer for Primary English and that school librarianship courses be offered at UBS for teacher trainees. The University of Botswana has since established a Department of Library and Information Studies, which offers courses at both the diploma and degree levels. The Ministry of Education was to consider the establishment of a library assistant post parallel to a laboratory assistant. Finally, the Ministry was advised to create a School Library Coordinator post and thereafter work towards the establishment of full time librarian post in all secondary schools. These recommendations pointed to the anticipated expansion of secondary schools and teacher training institutions.

SETSWANA

If anything, the Setswana Panel consolidated the image and the status of Setswana. The coming of the NCE was hailed as the most important event, not only to help Batswana to seek self-identity which is embedded in their culture, but to raise Setswana to its rightful place as the national language. People can have a true sense of pride and belonging when they communicate. In the case of Setswana, it was imperative to inject a sense of pride and consciousness of love for their language. There were few generations, since independence in 1966 and the coming of English Medium Schools, which did not have Setswana as a subject from the primary school to university level. On reflection, this was a great mistake which should never be repeated, for it not only turned out children from our education institutions who had missed the finer points of their culture, but had helped to undervalue Setswana, the mother tongue of many children in this country. Above all, it was imperative to improve Setswana since it is spoken by the majority of people in this land.

Some of the problems that beset Setswana and made some goals unattainable, was the disharmony between the syllabuses at different levels of education from primary to degree level. There was, therefore, a lack of a smooth transition from one level to another, a weakness that is common in other subjects as well. This reflected the lack of coordination among committees or panels that were charged with the responsibility of syllabuses and curricula.

It was, therefore, appropriate that the primary school syllabus should prepare the pupils for life outside the school in a predominantly rural and illiterate society. Furthermore, the Setswana syllabus was expected to equip those who later decided to further their education, so that by the time they reach the senior certificate they should be able to decide whether they would pursue Setswana at the post-secondary level.

In order to streamline the Setswana syllabus across the system, the Panel suggested that the Ministry of Education provide close collaboration between committees and panels responsible for the syllabus review for primary schools, secondary education, teacher training and university level. Such a strategy would enable these bodies to discuss ways and means of providing teaching materials for teachers. We are nonetheless aware that from that time – 1977 and later – efforts were made to improve Setswana. It is equally true that the panel to this day experiences snags. For instance, in 1990 Setswana results were extremely poor, even among good students.

FRENCH

French was one subject that became popular prior to Botswana's attainment of independence in 1966. The rationale for the introduction of the language, quite reasonably was that many countries in Africa speak French, it is also an in international language, and the move was intended to ease communication among African states. At times, so popular was French that it was possible for a Motswana child who attended an English Medium School to complete his university education without having studied Setswana at any level. Though few pupils were involved, the practice was not acceptable as it ignored Setswana as the national language.

However, French had its own share of problems. For instance, for most children it was not offered at primary school so that they met it for the first time at the Junior Certificate level. The arrangement was unsatisfactory if Batswana children were to benefit through the study of the language. Apart from that, though the syllabus was suitable for the JC examinations, the books recommended were not suitable because the content was considered too foreign for the students. The books were European-based in content and vocabulary. The content tended to be far removed from the daily experience of the student. The examination questions on the Metro (a French series reading materials) were unsuitable for Batswana students. The problem was further complicated by the difficulty of getting appropriate books, films and the almost non-existent specialist French teacher.

If French was to be handled effectively, the definition of objectives for the teaching of French had to be stated. On the theoretical level, the objectives were to include the use of African context and to extend the learning of French through direct contact with the French civilisation – such as French clubs, French ways and so on. It was equally proper to recommend that the examinations were to be a test of knowledge of French according to the objectives of the syllabus.

Social Sciences

Under the social sciences, history, geography and developmental studies are included. From the outset, the social scientists adopted a philosophic approach, for to them at the centre of all education is man and man fulfils himself in society. Education, therefore, as a social process must concern itself with the type of person that an education system produces.

For instance, a serious and active reorganisation of the Junior Certificate (JC) and the Cambridge Overseas School Certificate (COSC) became necessary as there was an apparent lack of close relationship between the two syllabuses. As a result, the entire JC structure had been relegated to an inferior category and rendered irrelevant. The irreconcilable JC and COSC syllabuses tended to produce a student who was not conversant with the purpose of history (Report of the NCE, 1977). The problem was brought about by the lack of continuity and sufficient time to cultivate keen interest among pupils. It was, therefore, imperative to restructure the entire secondary school system and have a five year Cambridge course. One way of doing that was to integrate JC with COSC. It was also important to lay a solid foundation at the primary school level, and establish a tradition and some type of continuity.

History

In one important respect the debate has raged on that the two year Cambridge course was seen as the reason that made the examination dominate teaching and which hampered effective learning. The pupils were to be encouraged to participate in the process of attaining knowledge, rather than merely committing knowledge to memory. To achieve the relevance of history, it was important to ensure that examinations assessed the pupil's insight into the subject. To this end, the panel emphasised that in view of changes that regularly accompanied the ongoing process of curriculum development, closer contact be regularised between the Ministry of Education and the Cambridge Examinations Council. Perhaps one of the most illuminating recommendations made by the History Panel was to caution against the tendency of comparatively over-emphasising technical education that might 'give rise to a generation of technocrats operating in a cultural vacuum' (Report of the NCE, 1977). The tendency was apparent in the allocation of the least number of hours to history on the timetable. What was needed was a judicious blending of technical and culturally-based subjects.

The tendency to regard history as belonging to the periphery of the curriculum was viewed in a dim light by the panel. History deserved to be one of the core subjects 'since there is no school subject that rivals history in its treatment of society as a whole, revealing the processes and problems of development and change' (Report of the NCE, 1977). To effect some of these changes and provide a firm direction, it was deemed appropriate to appoint an officer in the Ministry of Education to be responsible for the development of the history curriculum from primary to secondary school level.

Geography

The Geography Panel started on a note similar to the History Panel, in that it was assumed that a basic grasp of geographical principles, and the acquiring of skills was more important than the acquisition of a considerable body of factual knowledge for its own sake, or for the examinations. Therefore, selection and study in some depth was preferred to a wide ranging superficial treatment. The influence of the examination on the teaching and learning process reflected pupil participation, and provided the teacher with some indication as to how deeply or widely a topic should be taught.

With regard to the relationship between the JC and COSC, the opposite sentiment was expressed and this was not unexpected, although the JC syllabus was designed to be a unit in itself, and to have a terminal value, the requirements of the COSC were kept in mind when it was drafted. As a result, the JC course dovetailed into the COSC and the aims of the JC Curriculum were considered to be in line with those of the COSC course. In one sense, the panel's report gave the impression that the teachers of geography have always been involved in the development of the geography curriculum. In fact, the teacher participation in the revision of the subject for Botswana was instrumental in prompting the Examinations Council to set up alternative national syllabuses for those subjects that wanted it.

Development Studies

Through the initiative of Patrick van Rensburg and a handful of teachers at Swaneng Hill School, a new subject which was introduced before the attainment of independence by Botswana in 1966, was Development Studies. Basically, it was intended to focus the attention of the young on the problems of hunger and poverty, ignorance and drudgery, disease and other handicaps. It was meant to sensitise the students to political, social, moral and economic problems and imbue them with concern for the less privileged. Despite these grand objectives, Development Studies was viewed with suspicion from some quarters. It was all the old story of being locked up in our narrow outlook and prejudices. The criticism levelled against it was that it lacked direction, dealt with concepts that were advanced for the JC pupils and consequently irrelevant to Botswana's needs.

Nevertheless, the Panel expressed the view that the new syllabus equipped pupils especially with an emphasis on Botswana with the elementary facts and knowledge of social, economic, financial and political institutions of the country. To drive the point home, the Panel recommended that the Ministry of Education should approach the University with a request that Development Studies be offered as one of the major subjects. That was one of the most progressive recommendations ever to come from the Panel. It is now a matter of history that Development Studies was taught at the University of Botswana, but within a couple of years it was dropped as a subject. Despite the usefulness of the subject, it remained a sensitive area of study and what perhaps exacerbated the situation was that it was taught almost exclusively by expatriates, some of whom were inexperienced and with little understanding and commitment to Botswana. The most logical thing, if the subject received support, was to prepare local teachers to teach it. The disappearance of Development Studies at University level was a sad moment, for it denied our young people of an exposure to another form of knowledge.

SCIENCE

The Science Panel was systematic in their approach to their assignment. They were of the view that before considering secondary school science, some knowledge of science education at primary school level was needed. They recommended that the starting point of the course should be the observation and description of the local environment. The fact that the course was not written for classroom teaching was gratifying and the fact that apparatuses required were relatively simple and cheap. As a result they were obtainable locally and moreover made special reference to Botswana. The teaching of the course was so arranged that biology lessons were taught at the time when plants and other items were available.

Despite these favourable comments, certain aspects of the syllabus made it unsuitable for Botswana. For instance, the course was written in English, but the first few years of primary education are taught in Setswana. Therefore, it would have been useful to have a vernacular local environment science study course for the first few years of primary education. It was also likely that many teachers found the teachers' guides difficult to follow and it was most unlikely that the primary teaching force had the background knowledge or training to teach the course. As a consequence many teachers were probably frightened by the course and ignored it as it only involved two periods per week. The Science Panel pointed out that the official science syllabus had many good points but it was unsuitable for primary schools in Botswana and therefore needed some refinement.

It is also fair, while reflecting on science teaching in Botswana, to remember that the revision of curricula has played an important role. From the early 1960s there had been a conscious effort to improve the teaching of science at the primary level. Such efforts received the support of the British Technical Assistance arm of the Overseas Development Agency. The natural consequence of that was the constant monitoring of the science course at secondary level, and by 1974 it had been fully established. The essence of the syllabus was to form the basis of a course which would meet the needs of pupils proceeding to the study of physical sciences and/or biology for Cambridge as well as those who leave after JC. The new JC course had some merit, in that it gave more direction to teachers in their approach to topics and to what depth they were expected to go. More importantly, it gave a better foundation to COSC science studies and called for the involvement of teachers of science in curriculum development.

A common concern expressed then by the science teachers was that too large a gap existed between the work done in the primary school and the work done at the secondary level. The criticism was that the JC course assumed more background knowledge than that which was found in Form 1 pupils. The JC course did not, according to some teachers, give a complete science education to Form 3 leavers. There was also the assumption that the JC course was not intended for children but for all the upper 20 per cent, who by their ability, were in secondary schools.

Nevertheless, there was general satisfaction with the JC science syllabus ranging from teaching methods to the format of examinations. As pointed out earlier, the quest for appropriate management of the curriculum in primary and junior level of secondary education had showed itself earlier in the 1960s and 1970s and this was in keeping with that strategy. For instance, workshops which concentrated on teaching methods through in-service courses gave confidence to many teachers. Many teachers followed the practical discovery approach which reflected the philosophy behind the course. Hence some teachers later expressed the view that the Integrated Science course gave a sound foundation to students and was more relevant to Botswana.

The Science Panel did raise an important issue along with other panels at seminars or workshops, that examinations should be set in such a way that they discouraged rote learning since comprehension and understanding were of greater importance. Following this, some teachers felt that the JC examination should be completely set, marked and controlled within Botswana. The Ministry of Education paid heed to the proposition, since the JC curriculum was controlled internally before the introduction of the 9 years of education for every Motswana child.

With regard to the COSC science syllabus, there was general satisfaction and acceptance. For instance, physical science was comparable to other syllabuses found elsewhere and the biology syllabus provided examples suitable to Botswana. To sustain the trend, there were calls from many teachers to mount a series of in-service courses directed at improving COSC level science teaching.

What was equally gratifying was the recognition that the COSC science courses offered an international standard to which Botswana could relate. Yet at times the course tended to be academic and distant from practical realities. With improvements in science facilities and a better qualified and more stable science staff, results in COSC science would improve. In fact, this point was confirmed fifteen years later in 1993 'Over the last 10 years significant changes have occurred in the secondary schools. This involves improvements both in the quantity and quality of the Cambridge Overseas School Certificate (COSC) output' (PESC Evaluation Report, 1992). The general improvement of curriculum development was the result of a combination of factors ranging from the input of education officers within the Ministry of Education, the school inspections and the running of in-service courses.

Agriculture

Generally, when it comes to agriculture, everyone talks in glowing terms of it as an essential ingredient of secondary education in Botswana, but in practice there is no evidence to this effect. There is a view that it is not designed to provide vocational training. These shortcomings had to be addressed as there was need to help the students appreciate, conserve and develop the environment for the good of the country. To this end, teaching was to emphasise practical work in order to help the students to find out for themselves. As in other subjects, teaching was hampered in agriculture by the lack of Batswana teachers in secondary schools in spite of the desire to diversify the curriculum. The other source of discomfort was the lack of connection between the JC and the COSC syllabuses. There was at the same time the need to discourage areas of overlap between the content of Agricultural Science and that of other of subjects including integrated science, geography and development studies. It was therefore imperative for the panels of the said subjects to reduce the overlaps as they constituted a waste of time.

Mathematics

Mathematics, in common with the other subjects in the curriculum at JC level, serves a dual role. First, as a terminal qualification for Form 3 leavers and secondly as preparation for COSC. As a terminal examination some aspects of JC mathematics syllabus fell within the realm of 'pure' mathematics, with little obvious relevance to life outside educational institutions. Other parts were found to contain a generous measure of content devoted to learners' social and commercial needs. As a preparation for the COSC the JC mathematics syllabus did not constitute an adequate preparation for COSC. For instance, certain topics did not link properly and in general too much material was left out to be covered in the two years following JC. In order to remedy the situation a scheme was drawn up whereby the current syllabus would be improved while retaining if not strengthening those aspects of the syllabus that were of value to Form 3 leavers. While the COSC mathematics syllabus was considered satisfactory, the inadequacies of the present JC syllabus made it difficult for many students. The success rate over the years which was a cause of concern had not been satisfactory. The only comfort was that the course compared favourably with its counterparts in West and East Africa.

The Quality of Teachers at Secondary School Level

Perhaps the work of the Task Force and the subject panels at the secondary education level would have been incomplete without some mention of the quality of the teaching force at that level. The common factor raised by the different subject panels was the high turnover of teachers in Botswana secondary schools. This point was understandable since there was a preponderance of expatriate teachers engaged for specific periods. The English Panel, for instance was unhappy about the lack of a strong core of local teachers which necessitated dependence on non-permanent expatriate staff. That was considered detrimental to the pupils' performance for contracts sometimes expired just before examinations, a critical time indeed. This also resulted in the permanent ineffectiveness of in-service courses which were partly directed at expatriate teachers who sooner or later had to leave. The science course was given as a good example where '36 teachers attended a workshop in 1974, of those only 6 were available to attend a follow-up course the following year' (Report of NCE, 1977). Whilst only 25% of the secondary school teaching force was local, a close study showed that in some areas like practical subjects there were no local teachers. The Panel summed it up well when it pointed out that 'the teaching force is too fluid, mobile and transient – the presence of a stable staff in schools for long periods is completely lacking at this time' (Report of the NCE, 1977). The points raised simply pointed to the fact that teaching is and continues to be regarded as a profession of low status in Botswana and some Batswana enter teaching as a second or a third choice or because nothing else is available. The truth is that as long as that attitude remains, people of the required quality will not be attracted into teaching.

On the question of teachers, the Mathematics Panel while it realised that mathematics is a subject that requires continuity of teaching more than any other subject, only 25% of teachers were employed on a permanent basis. They felt that inexperienced teachers, especially those who came from a background whose education system is different from that in Botswana, should be placed in a supportive situation. It was at the same time not unexpected that about half of the country's mathematics teachers were in the country on a voluntary basis and more than half of those had less than two years experience, and yet many of those teachers considered themselves as the leading mathematics teachers in their school. It was, therefore, important that leading teachers with good qualifications and wide experience should be distributed throughout the system for maximum effect. The imbalance was illustrated by showing that of the six COSC teachers with over ten years experience, four were located in one school. To make the picture more gloomy, it was revealed that there were only eleven Batswana teaching mathematics in the whole country. The picture today may not have changed very much if one considers the fact that since 1977 efforts were made to swell the ranks of mathematics teachers through the Diploma in Secondary Education and the Post Graduate Diploma in Education programmes at the University of Botswana. The number of secondary schools has grown dramatically in Botswana. The Panel then, and even today, is concerned with the lack of an effective effort to encourage young nationals to take up mathematics teaching as a profession. The prevailing situation made the volunteer organisations unhappy with the rate of progress for if they were to withdraw support the country would lose about half its secondary teaching force. An effective formula for attracting and keeping nationals in the teaching of mathematics had to be found as a matter of urgency. One of the ways that comes to mind readily has been to offer a variety of incentives.

Equally important was the consideration of mathematics as a compulsory subject resulting in the enrolment of candidates with a low aptitude for mathematics studying it at the senior secondary level. To obviate a situation (where in 1975 four hundred students failed mathematics) it should be a requirement that a student must have obtained a grade C or better in JC mathematics before he is allowed to take mathematics at COSC level. That would render the teaching of COSC mathematics less frustrating and wasteful. Since some of the problems of mathematical education in secondary schools derives from the primary schools, a dialogue with the primary schools was suggested. After seventeen years of the existence of the University of Botswana Pre-Entry Science Course, its evaluation in 1992 echoed the same sentiments.

The Science Panel, on the quality of the science teaching force, put it well by stating that no matter what syllabus was followed or how well equipped laboratories were, 'the quality of secondary science education depends upon the ability, stability, professional expertise and education of the teaching force' (Report of the NCE, 1977). Some of the shortcomings which faced science education ranged from the fluid and transient nature of the teaching force which resulted in the lack of a stable staff in the schools for long periods. The situation was exacerbated by the short contract periods for which volunteer teachers were recruited. It seemed that one way to address the problem was to offer longer contract periods for expatriate teachers such as a minimum three year contract. The other factor which affected the sound teaching of science was the lack of teachers with professional experience and that was particularly true at the Cambridge level. As in other disciplines, there were too few Batswana in the secondary teaching force. For instance, in 1975 in the fifteen Government schools and grant-aided schools only 94 out of 397 teachers were Batswana (23.7%). The teachers put a finger on the trouble spot when they stated that some of the problems resulted from the fact that 'teaching is regarded as a profession of low status in Botswana and some Batswana enter teaching as a second or third choice or because nothing else is available' (Report of the NCE, 1977). Truly, as long as that attitude remained, it would be hard to attract people of the required quality into teaching. To remedy the situation the conditions of service for the teachers had to improve in order to make teaching similar to other careers available in Government and the private sector for people with similar qualifications. Further, to help young Batswana to settle into science teaching, they could be given a lighter teaching load during the first year of service. To encourage them, they would be linked with a more senior colleague during the first year and thereby receive 'on-the job training'.

The Stop-Order Payment of Subscriptions to BTU

It was also during these momentous years that the BTU scored its greatest and most momentous victory, which was, to gain the unqualified support of the Ministry of Education to concede to their request for teachers who were members of the BTU to pay their levies by the stop-order arrangement. No one should deceive themselves that these BTU successes were easily secured – every inch of the struggle had to be fought ferociously. Hard bargaining had to be entered into on the part of the teachers, sometimes having to resort to eyeball to eyeball tactics.

The acceptance and the implementation of the payment of subscription fees by stop-order must be seen as the breakthrough of all time for the BTU in the early 1980s. Many will recall that this issue had been raised with the Ministry of Education in the 1960s in vain. The Union sought assistance because they were dogged by poor financial resources and as long as they did not have the necessary funds no serious work could be done. The BTU could hardly carry out resolutions which lay squarely on their doorstep. So, for the first time after a long spell, the item requesting assistance from the Ministry for the collection of subscription fees by a stop order system was included in the agenda of the first meeting of the Unified Teaching Service Consultative Committee held on 19 August 1976. The willingness to do so was a great departure from the hard line approach that the Ministry had adopted earlier. At the same time, of course, the teachers were aware that the Ministry was opposed to such an arrangement as they wanted to keep the Union weak. But by the middle of the 1970s there was a change towards the organisation, because as some people speculated, the leadership of the Union tended to receive instruction from the Ministry of Education. In return for this 'good behaviour' on the part of the Union, the Ministry had to reciprocate.

At that meeting, the teachers were faced with another hurdle to clear, for the Ministry of Finance and Development Planning and the Office of the Accountant General had been reluctant to implement the request since that would involve extra personnel. The Committee was, however, requested to assist the Union in the collection of fees. At the same time, one must appreciate that the reluctance to comply with the teachers request earlier lay in that they were employed by different agencies. But since they were now employed by one authority, the Ministry of Education, it was far easier to persuade the Government to assist the BTU.

In principle, the request was acceptable to the Ministry of Education but before the Ministry of Finance and Development Planning could be asked to implement the arrangement, the BTU would have to persuade its members to agree to the deductions and that the deductions would be made only once a year to minimise labour costs. Furthermore, the BTU had to remember that the scheme would apply only to those members of the BTU who were employed by the Unified Teaching Service (UTS) and were paid by the Accountant General. It was extremely progressive for the Ministry of Education to express the view that both the Botswana Government and the Ministry wished 'to encourage the development of a healthy and effective Teachers' Union'. The statement laid the foundation for the future successes of the BTU, and it was reminiscent of President Khama's address to the Union at the Lobatse Conference mentioned earlier in Chapter 3.

It is important to note that while controversy raged between the Ministries of Education and Finance and Development Planning, the BTU President, Selwe spoke up very strongly for the organisation: 'we still believe that we cannot become a strong Union unless we are strong financially and members of our association have always expressed a willingness to pay their dues by the stop order system.' The BTU was even prepared to join hands with the Botswana Civil Servants Association (BCSA) if only to achieve their goal. Perhaps, very strangely, the Office of the Accountant General was unbending in its resolve, but their argument was unreasonable since their concern was the additional workload for an understaffed section working to a strict timetable. There was yet another problem faced by the Office of the Accountant General, for when the Director of the Unified Teaching Service (UTS) joined the fray, he pointed out that the UTS Consultative Committee had made representations that teachers in common with other public officers, should be allowed to elect to have their salaries paid into their bank accounts. Through contingent arguments in support of the BTU by the Permanent Secretary in the Ministry of Education, the proposal was accepted that members of the BTU pay their subscriptions by stop order. That was a tremendous breakthrough and it helped the Union to put their house in order by bringing most of the teachers into the fold. The achievement enabled the organisation to swell its coffers. That was evidenced by the visits of the BTU Executive Committee to places like Kang, Ghanzi, Shakawe, Maun and many others. The breakthrough gave the teachers' organisation the leverage to manage their ever growing responsibilities. Central to these was the need to diversify its fund-raising programmes beyond music and athletic competitions which for many years had been the hub of their activities.

More importantly, the success of the BTU in this respect helped the organisation to become financially viable and this was evidenced by the establishment of the BTU Centre in Mogoditshane. The Centre was necessary for three reasons. First, to enable better organisation and administration of the Union through an office, secondly, to enable the Union to secure property, and thirdly to generate income to support her programmes.

The success secured by the teachers urged them to strive for the betterment of their conditions of service. For instance, one of these was that the Government pay their salaries directly to the bank. The request was in response to the UTS Consultative Committee which was to hold a meeting on 30 July 1980. While the UTS had no objection to the arrangement it was at the same time aware of logistical problems such as the acquisition of the new type of casualty return and a coding system for qualifications so that information was properly organised for the computer to handle.

When the UTS Consultative Committee met on 6 November 1981 it agreed in principle to pay teachers through the bank, in the same way as civil servants. However, it was pointed out that it would not be possible to pay all teachers through the bank and that indeed there were places where there were no banking facilities. The long and protracted negotiations by the UTS and the Office of the Accountant General was laid to rest when the Director of UTS reported at the meeting of the Consultative Committee held in February 1982, that the Accountant General had agreed to extend the arrangement as a pilot scheme to teachers in secondary schools. The same facility could not be extended to the primary school teachers because Government could endure heavy losses as a result of delays by the Council Education Secretaries in processing casualty returns of teachers who might continue to be paid long after they had left the service.

The news of the acceptance of the BTUs request of the payment of teachers' salaries through the bank was received warmly by the representatives of the organisation. However, pressure would be kept on the Government to extend the bank payment to the primary school teachers as well.

The success of the BTU in its quest for payment through the bank was in itself a significant move. Yet its success in persuading the Government, through the Ministry of Education, to accede to their appeal for financial assistance was even greater. This was a resounding success when one considers that the Government was unable to pay teachers a living wage. To ask for financial assistance by an association to run its affairs and for the Government to concede was just unthinkable. Yet we should not take away from the President, Drake Selwe, his diplomatic skill for negotiation. The matter had been raised in resolutions submitted to the Consultative Committee by the BTU in 1979: 'The Ministry organise and sponsor BTU seminars'. (Government paper No. 1 of 1977, 46 (c) and (e) provides for assistance for the BTU conferences). So great was the change of heart on the part of the Ministry of Education that in fact it was prepared to sponsor the BTU in professional matters. The only problem facing the Government was, that no such provision was made in the estimates for the current year 1979. Since the idea of sponsorship was acceptable, the BTU was expected to submit its request for the next financial year (1980–81). It must also be ventured that the noticeable thawing in the commitment and cooperation of the Permanent Secretary, Keetla Masogo, was magnificent. We saw how, earlier, when the BTU and the Ministry of Local Government were on a collision path, Masogo defused the problem through his resolute stand. He was not prepared to have the BTU derailed on its chosen course of advancing education in Botswana.

When the untiring Drake Selwe presented the Ministry with the request for financial assistance there was great uneasiness, as the amount quoted was considered excessive. Whatever may be said about the BTU's submission, it had the full support of the National Commission of 1977. The amount requested by the BTU's President was as follows:

1. Regional and International Conferences – P5000.00
2. Local seminars and workshops – P1000.00

The request was minimal if the Union was to sell itself abroad and attend conferences of the World Confederation of Organisations of the Teaching Profession (WCOTP) and the International Federation of Free Trade Unions (IFFTU). It was essential if the Union was to fulfil its role as a monitor of the development of education,. It had to attract teachers from other countries to share experiences with its membership at local workshops. In spite of the BTU's humble request the Government could not meet the bill but offered P2000.00. The teachers were obviously unhappy with the Government's decision, but pleased with the fact that the Ministry had stood firmly behind them in recognition of the work they were doing and its support of their professional activities. Equally, another achievement of the Union during the period under discussion dealt with gender awareness and the empowerment of women resulting in the formation of the BTU Women's League in the 1980s. The purpose was to enable women to develop their potential as leaders and planners. The League brought the Union into contact with Norwegian teachers, a link that proved useful to the Union as a whole. Workshops, seminars and other forms of gatherings to discuss women's interests became possible as a result of that international cooperation. Also associated with this movement was membership education, which started with the idea of empowerment of women in 1978 in pursuance of the terms of the World Decade for Women. The initial sponsors were the Norwegian Union of Teachers. This was later extended to cover males. The strategy which was adopted later was 'The Study Circle Method' which is a kind of peer teaching. As a result of the Study Circle approach more teachers were reached and taught about the BTU and their privileges and rights as teachers. The positive aspect of membership education through the Study Circle approach produced teachers who already had training for leadership. Some of these teachers rose to the ranks of inspectors and heads of schools.

Equally important and rewarding for female teachers was the granting of full pay during maternity leave. That was a resounding success for the BTU and a complete break with the Dark Ages era as we saw earlier. The success was a joint effort with other organisations such as the Botswana Civil Servants Association (BCSA) and the Botswana Unified Local Government Service Association (BULGSA). The main reasoning on the part of the Union, was that women need finance more in that condition than at any other time. Since the emphasis nowadays is child care, the money is more for the child's upkeep than the mother's needs. The recommendation was approved by B.K. Temane's Report on the Salaries Review of 1992.

Another great achievement was the granting to teachers by Government, of employment on permanent and pensionable terms. In fact, the stand was taken by the Bechuanaland Protectorate African Teachers' Association (BPATA) as early as 1954 requesting that such status be extended to them. It should be borne in mind that when that status was granted in 1980 by W.R. Meswele's Committee the struggle had been raging for a long time. There was indeed another vicious skirmish in 1976 for government to implement the scheme when UTS, later Teaching Service Management, was established.

The WCOTP Link and Its Significance

In the foregoing pages, some of the successes of the BTU locally have been mentioned. The following pages will show how the Association with the WCOTP (now called Education International) enhanced the knowledge of our rights and responsibilities and alerted us to the concerns of the international bodies, like the United Nations Educational, Scientific and Cultural Organisation (UNESCO) and the International Labour Organisation (ILO), for the teaching profession. Earlier, we saw how the BTU was accepted as a member of the WCOTP at the London Conference in 1972. The subsequent years were to witness the cementing of that link between the BTU and the world organisation through invitations to its conferences in different countries throughout the world, such as Brazil in 1980 and Monteaux in 1982. The BTU is now a member of the two international organisations, Education International and the International Federation of Free Trade Unions (IFFTU) which when merged became Education International (EI). These linkages have helped the Union to broaden its horizons.

The most remarkable development during the 1980s in Botswana was the visible presence of the WCOTP and its affiliates such as the Danish Union of Teachers working with teachers through seminars and workshops. The thrust of such visits was concerned with issues relating to the teaching profession. The first series of workshops concentrated on those areas that were then difficult to reach including Kasane, Maun and Francistown, in 1982. So determined was the BTU that, for the first time in 1983, they took the workshop to the Kgalagadi District to demonstrate to the teachers there their interest in their welfare and professional development. The Danish Union of Teachers' visit in 1986 concentrated on such topics as teachers' organisation and development, education and development, the status of teachers, teachers' leadership roles, and many others including the elimination of all forms of discrimination against women – a commendable and progressive stand indeed. In addition, seminars were mounted to expose the teachers to the handling of subjects like mathematics and science which as we know were a cause of concern among the teachers. The interaction between the BTU and the members of the WCOTP was most valuable as it not only exposed teachers to current thinking elsewhere, but sensitised them on issues of gender. Later seminars and workshops held at some remote areas under the direction of the BTU/DLF/WCOTP helped to familiarise teachers with consultation procedures with other international organisations and how to conduct their business with local authorities. Perhaps the significance of the link lay in the fact that the teachers were prepared to take the BTU to those remote places where their members were – far from Gaborone and other big centres.

The seminar held at Matsha Community College in Kang went further than the previous ones as it dealt with the status of teachers. It was based on a UNESCO document adopted by the special inter-governmental conference on the status of teachers in 1966. It was a most refreshing encounter for local teachers with progressive thinking, divorced from the attitude that seeks to treat teachers as objects and not humans with expectations, aspirations and a future. The other document of interest that received attention was entitled 'The Teacher in the Intermediate School', the brainchild of the 1977 National Commission which was set 'to conduct a broad ranging review of Botswana's education system, its goals and major problems and to submit recommendations for improvements in education' (NCE, 1977).

In the education structure of 6+3+3 proposed by *Education for Kagisano* the intermediate school constituted the three years immediately following the six years of primary education. The intermediate school was intended to answer the need for increased opportunity for primary leaving pupils. There was a need for more children to enter the junior secondary cycle. With the increase in enrolments after Botswana became independent in 1966, there were not enough places at the secondary level to absorb the primary school leavers. The Government, therefore, decided on a policy of increased and eventually open, access to secondary schooling.

The heart of the arrangement of the new type of school lay in its relations with local government and central Government in general, and between the school and the local community in particular. The local communities were expected to form boards of governors to run the school in order to create sound working relations between the school and the community that the school served. The central Government was expected to provide stationary and furniture. The parents were to provide teachers' accommodation and the District and Town Councils were helped to build better teachers' quarters. In short the whole strategy aimed to involve the parents in the education of their children, however minimally, rather than leaving everything in the hands of Government. In any event the Motswana parent had for a long time been involved in the management of the education of his child from the early tribal school committees that were largely run on tribal lines. Earlier, these school committees shouldered a great deal of responsibility through raising funds to build schools and pay teachers. But as we know so well, they were handicapped by the lack of funds.

To staff these new schools, the Commission logically recommended that they be staffed by a separate category of junior secondary teachers who were trained to offer a wide range of teaching subjects. The recommendation led to the birth of the Molepolole College of Education in 1984 and later the Tonota College of Education in 1991. They offered a variety of subjects that had hitherto not been offered by the teacher training programme of the University of Botswana such as music, physical education, home economics and technical studies. Except for music, these subjects were introduced at the University of Botswana at the diploma and bachelor's level during the 1994–95 academic year.

The seminar at Kang, in addition to informing local teachers on the programme of the intermediate school, also enlightened them on the crucial programme of national literacy. Through the recommendations of the NCE, the education strategy in both NDP 5 and NDP 6 was based on the assumption that formal and non-formal education could be correlated and integrated, particularly in a country like Botswana that is faced with a variety of educational needs and formal education is inadequate. The Government was urged to give high priority to developing opportunities for people to learn out of school to compliment study in school.

To this end the national objective was to enable 250 000 illiterate men and women and youths to become literate in Setswana and numerate over the five years 1980–85. The teaching was to be undertaken in the context of development issues of relevance to the participants and concerns for the respective districts and the nation. The context was to be built around problems identified in District Plans and based on social, cultural and economic issues, taking into account geographical and environmental differences. The aim was that it would result in the acquisition both of literacy and other skills for better living.

Of general interest was the session on the UNESCO/ILO recommendations concerning the status of teachers. As if to initiate the participants on such events that influence the welfare of teachers throughout the world, they were briefed thoroughly. The UNESCO/ILO recommendation had been prompted by the growing concern over the status of teachers and the improvement of the professional, social and economic conditions of the teaching profession. The BTU suffered in the past because of the neglect of these crucial areas. To them it was the eye opener of all time. Naturally, such shortcomings were taken seriously by both UNESCO and ILO. For instance, in 1947 reference was made to the Teachers' Charter which was reflected in the programme of UNESCO. In 1952, the ILO Advisory Committee on Salaried Employees and Professional Workers drew attention to problems affecting teachers. Again, between 1951 and 1963, UNESCO and the International Bureau of Education made a series of comparative studies on various aspects of the status of primary and secondary teachers. As a result of these studies, recommendations to the Ministries of Education were adopted on these questions by the International Conference on Public Instruction which meets annually in Geneva.

The significance and impact of such information on our teachers cannot be overemphasised. They heard for themselves that the concerns raised by their organisation some fifty years ago, when the BPATA/BTU was founded, were shared by the international community of professionals. The heart of the recommendation was the recognition of growth in the importance of the industry of human affairs, and the importance, in consequence, of the occupation of teaching. The preamble draft that was submitted and adopted by the special Inter-Governmental Conference on the Status of Teachers held in Paris in 1966, refers to education as 'a fundamental human right'. The conference expressed its recognition of the essential role of teachers in educational advancement and the importance of their contribution to the development of mankind and modern society. It was, therefore, of paramount importance that teachers enjoyed the status commensurate with their role.

The question that constantly arose was the extent to which the recommendation can be enforced. The answer is that adoption of the recommendation means no more than that a certain number of member governments of UNESCO have considered that it would be a good thing if matters were to be arranged in a particular way. Its only force is a moral one. In spite of that, there is a regular procedure for checking the extent to which governments are doing what they undertook to do. To this end, a committee of experts, some of whom are appointed by UNESCO and others by the ILO meets at regular intervals every four years to look at the recommendations and the extent to which they have been implemented.

Be that as it may, the recommendation is violated in many countries, but there is nothing that the committee can do about specific violations of the recommendation other than report them. If a Government has ratified a convention and violates it, the international regulatory bodies can advertise that fact and ask for corrective action. Even that does not always work and cannot be enforced. Nonetheless, the seminars and workshops organised by the BTU helped to inform the teachers of the commitment of their government with regard to the recommendation.

All that the BTU can do is to act as a watchdog of the interests of the teachers and to secure satisfaction for the teachers in their working situations. The satisfaction for teachers was summed up by the Secretary General of the WCOTP, Norman Goble, when he said that satisfaction for a teacher derives from the sense of being seen to be doing a valuable job successfully with access to the training and resources that will ensure competence and self-confidence, in circumstances that minimise stress. That promise consists of decent pay and a secure career that provides respect, manageable challenge and opportunity for personal and professional growth. The greatest reward is being able to say 'I am a teacher' (WCOTP, 1983).

So much for the WCOTP and its contribution to the BTU with its message of hope for the teaching profession. It is, therefore, fitting at this stage to mention on a sad note the death of John M. Thompson in 1981 who was the Secretary General of the WCOTP for eleven years. Writing an introduction to the annual report of the WCOTP activities presented on behalf of the Executive Acting Secretary General, Mac-Alain Berberat, described him as a 'person who never measured the time nor the effort he spent working on all continents of the world in the service of education and teachers' (WCOTP, 1981). The President of WCOTP paying tribute to Thompson had this to say:

> 'He changed the face of the teaching profession throughout the world. He infected into education at all levels the serious voice of the organised profession and made a considerable contribution to the enhancement of its status. His life was characterised by his devoted work for education and the promotion of international understanding, human rights and progress through the instrument of teaching' (WCOTP, 1981).

Other topics of interest discussed at the BTU/DLF/WCOTP workshops included the contribution of teachers through the BTU to Educational Development in Botswana. Discussions also centred on teachers' rights and obligations. In fact, many queries were raised concerning the failure of the Government to pay local allowances in the same manner for all Government departments. For instance, questions were asked why teachers did not receive subsistence allowances when on duty, and why employees were not transferred with their posts of responsibility. Such discussions generated a great deal of debate as these affected the teachers most. When it came to the responsibilities of teachers, constant reference was made to the effect that professional issues relating to teacher performance should be defined and maintained with the participation of teachers organisations. If the teachers' organisations were to succeed in their mission they had to cooperate fully with the authorities in the interest of progress, the education service and society generally. It was imperative that the teachers' organisation establish a code of ethics or conduct to ensure the maintenance of the prestige of the profession and the exercise of professional duties in accordance with agreed principles.

The Emergence of Other Teachers' Organisations in Botswana

The Botswana Federation of Secondary Teachers, BOFESETE, was perhaps the greatest news within the ranks of teachers in this country in the 1980s. The story of teachers' organisations in Botswana would be incomplete without mention of BOFESETE and other newly founded splinter teachers' associations. In fact, it would have been a miracle for the BTU to have existed for such a long time without being challenged. The truth is that it had done a marvellous job in the past fifty years and indeed circumstances had changed since its inauguration in 1937. It is again clear that there were now new issues which the BTU could not address to the satisfaction of its new constituents, particularly secondary school teachers, Teacher Training College lecturers, and other categories of teachers. Nothing could have been more dramatic than the birth of BOFESETE which must have raised the hopes of many who saw the BTU as an underachiever. Strangely, while many people anticipated the emergence of other teachers' associations, others were completely complacent since the BTU had never been challenged in the past. Why this complacency? The answer is that everyone was used to one teachers' organisation from the 1930s to the early 1980s, and on the face of it spoke with one voice for all the teachers, irrespective of their level of operation. Looking back, it is possible that the BTU had lost direction and was not representative of all the teachers in this country. It is possible again that in the eyes of many young and ambitious teachers, the Union was irrelevant.

As will be recalled, the BPATA, later BTU, from its inception was the brainchild of the primary school teachers through the initiative of Levi Moumakwa, A.M. Tsoebebe, A.C. Sekunyane and others with the assistance of the first Director of Education, H.J.E. Dumbrell. Because secondary education was introduced into Botswana in the mid-forties with a handful of local teachers later joined by the expatriate teachers who did not wish to be involved in the politics of the teachers' organisation, their participation was indeed minimal and cautious. Even when Batswana began to interest themselves in the Union, their power base was among the primary school teachers. The leadership in the Union appreciated the power of the primary school teachers and used it to the maximum. The achievements that the Union secured were through the unmistakable sacrifice of the primary school teachers with a sprinkle of secondary school teachers who usually spearheaded attacks at various stages. It is, therefore, not unusual that the BTU's programme tended to concentrate largely on issues that were primary school oriented.

We thus need to examine some of the factors that led to the birth of other teachers' organisations. First, from the mid-1970s, with the growth of secondary education, many young Batswana graduates turned to teaching as a career. The change called for the leadership to provide a broad based intellectual programme to meet the interests of all the teachers. When that need was not met, there was a feeling in some quarters that the BTU had reached the end of its tether and was out of touch with reality. Its major programmes, particularly music and sport, had dominated the scene for too long to the exclusion of other meaningful activities. The formation of the independent BOFESETE in 1987 was due to frustration with the BTU. One of the strongest criticisms was that the BTU had lost its soul and had virtually become the arm or the administrative adjunct of the Ministry of Education. Of interest was that the secondary school teachers in order to form their association, met at Mochudi at the Sedibelo Motel in 1986, almost 50 years later, and in the same village where the BPATA/BTU was launched. The secondary school teachers wanted an organisation that would represent their interests and address their issues. Another source of irritation for the secondary school teachers was the control of the BTU by the heads of schools who tended to fraternise with the Ministry of Education. It was therefore, doubtful if such officials could represent the Union since they were involved in the formulation of laws and regulations affecting the teachers. It was for this reason that BOFESETE in one clause of their constitution forbids heads of schools and their deputies from becoming members of its executive. They felt the BTU officials tended to be insensitive to the issues that affected teachers since they were part of the structures of the Ministry of Education. In short, it was doubtful if such officials could represent the Union effectively since they were involved in the formulation of laws and regulations affecting the teachers.

The birth of BOFESETE for some reason or another was ill-timed in that the BTU in spite of its shortcomings had established itself firmly and had been accepted fully within the Government circles. It had come to be accepted as the mouthpiece of all the teachers. There was an appreciation of the role of the BTU as a major partner with Government in nation building. The Ministry of Education, therefore, was at first not keen to recognise the new body and constantly referred to it as a 'splinter group' whose intentions were unclear and possibly mischievous and politically motivated. Obviously, in an environment where only one teachers' organisation had been in existence for over 50 years it was hard to accept a new body like BOFESETE, which was considered a mere duplication. It is equally not surprising that the Ministry refused BOFESETE administrative recognition. Such a stern and unyielding stance on the part of the Ministry must have frightened many a potential member of BOFESETE, particularly the expatriate staff. Foreign teachers, as indicated above, did not wish to be embroiled in local politics as they had been advised against it.

Secondly, failure to grant BOFESETE administrative recognition meant also the denial of payment of the membership subscription through the check-off system. The check-off arrangement which was granted the BTU earlier had given them a leverage in the management of their financial and management concerns. The fact that the BTU was able to build a teachers' centre at Mogoditshane near Gaborone was because of the assistance received from the Ministry of Education. BOFESETE was unable to function effectively without financial support. Also, however well considered, BOFESETE's stand against the heads of schools was disastrous. It turned them against BOFESETE and as a result it was viewed in a dim light by some members.

Thirdly, the other factor which militated against the success of the BOFESETE was the vastness of the country which made communication extremely difficult for organisational purposes. The recruitment of members was arduous as the teachers were 'not necessarily free – since they attended workshops and other extra-curricular activities...'. BOFESETE was also affected by a general apathy on the part of the teachers. Again, if BOFESETE had no appropriate offices for their secretariat to keep their records, their efforts would bear no result.

A Federation faced with so many problems could hardly achieve anything. At this stage it is hard to know whether they ever had any impact on education and society which were their focal points. It is interesting to note the Ministry's hostility. Without any doubt BOFESETE, compared to the BTU, was more militant in its demands. In this respect Ngidi (1993) cites interesting examples. He quotes the boycott by secondary school teachers and the delays in 1986 and 1987 of the marking of Junior Certificate examination scripts. BOFESETE was vehemently criticised for this act and were not to be forgiven for it. Perhaps to render BOFESETE ineffective the members of the first executive were promoted within the Ministry of Education. The combination of apathy on the part of the membership and the fact that the 'not-so-brave' remained to steer BOFESETE from the troubled waters could not save it. It has sometimes been argued that there was no legitimacy for the separate existence of another teachers' association apart from the BTU. Compared to the BTU, BOFESETE was no different considering the objectives reflected in their constitutions. It is thought that this was one of the reasons why it failed to attract the secondary teachers. While it was healthy to allow fresh ideas into the teachers arena, it was believed that teachers at this stage needed only one umbrella body like the BTU, with subsidiary structures all under the control of the Union.

The breakaway of the secondary school teachers was followed by that of the primary school teachers who went on a week long strike in 1989. They were most unhappy with the outcome of the job evaluation exercise. Their action reflected their extreme lack of confidence in the BTU for they did not solicit the assistance of the leadership. They acted jointly under what they referred to as Job Evaluation Unsatisfied Teachers (JEUT). The strike took the Ministry of Education by surprise for such a long stoppage of work had not been experienced in the past. No amount of persuasion or threats were able to sway the teachers from their chosen path. They later formed the Botswana Primary School Teachers' Association (BOPRITA). The unprecedented action taken by the primary school teachers shook the BTU to its foundations, for these teachers were then and continued to be the mainstay of that organisation. The truth was simply that all was not well within the BTU. These events called for thorough introspection on the part of the Union to clean house.

However offended the primary school teachers were they should have resolved their differences within the BTU. The Union was their legitimate professional home and they were not likely to survive on their own and were bound to suffer the same fate as BOFESETE. Denied administrative recognition even if they were registered with the Registrar of Societies, they could not operate effectively. Ideally, Botswana needed a strong and effective teachers' organisation to continue to address the issues that accompany the rapid expansion of the education system.

The above does not complete the list of teachers' associations in this country. The fourth organisation of teachers is the Association of Botswana Tertiary Lecturers (ABOTEL) registered with the Registrar of Societies in 1990. The membership of this Association is drawn from the lecturers in the four Teacher Training Colleges, the Botswana Institute of Administration and Commerce (BIAC), the Institute of Health Sciences (IHS), Colleges of Education, National Vocational Training Centres, the Polytechnic and the Botswana College of Agriculture. This is a hodge-podge organisation of teachers and one trusts that through their efforts they will add a new dimension to our thinking about education and revitalise the solid work that has been done by the BTU. To this list of associations may be added the Headmasters' Conference, which is concerned with the interests of heads of schools, which is well established with a hundred percent membership and has regional and national committees. It also has financial backing from Government and on that alone it should make a reasonable impact on educational issues.

One may wonder if there is justification for the different teachers' associations in Botswana. One tends to think that one association would suffice for a small population such as ours. But it is equally true that different cadres of teachers have different interests and aspirations. Nonetheless these interests should not be the cause of division, for the present upsurge and restlessness is symptomatic of the teaching profession's desire to restore the declining perception of the status of teachers. In the past three decades in Botswana one has seen the lowering of the status of teachers. A paper presented by Professor Weeks and Dr Mautle at the Southern African Comparative and History of Education Society in South Africa in 1992 on teacher incentives underlies the loss of prestige. 'The Ministry of Education, for a number of years, has been concerned about receiving advice from outside the system on how to deal with teacher incentives' (Mautle and Weeks, 1992). Obviously the direct involvement of the Ministry of Education indicates that the decline of the status and prestige of the teaching profession in Botswana is not a perception but a reality.

Also let us remember that the emergence of a few teachers' organisations was a natural development. However effective the BTU was, it could not possibly satisfy all the categories of teachers in its fold. Elsewhere it has been found that teachers organisations break up into different and sometimes smaller units. In South Africa where education was based on racial lines, there were different associations. The Africans themselves formed different associations like the Transvaal African Teachers' Association, the Cape African Teachers' Association and the Cape African Teachers' Union. The same can be said of countries like Zimbabwe, Australia, Zambia and the United Kingdom.

In Nigeria and in some other countries teachers group themselves according to grades and subjects taught indicating that teachers, while they belong to the same profession, have not undergone the same training. Ngidi (1993) in his project on the BTU – *Problems and Prospects* pointed out that one needs a certificate to teach at primary, a diploma or more to teach at a secondary school, and a masters degree to teach at a college of education. It is clear then that the interests of such teachers may not necessarily coincide but at the same time need not be incompatible. To some, the Union has sunk into a quagmire of idleness and opportunism. It has not only lost its direction but its very soul.

Nonetheless BOFESETE and the splinter groups have been blamed for being devisive, when the best they could have done was to help and cure the Union of its maladies. Yet there are those who felt from the beginning that the greatest thing was not that BOFESETE came, but that it is a reality and in that sense has been given the opportunity to prove itself. It should, despite the problems it faces, prove its worth in that it exists for no other cause other than the advancement of education in this country. BOFESETE should be given all the support to realise their dream. But above all they should know that they are able to see so far because they are standing squarely on the shoulders of pioneers.

BTU is 50 Years Old

Fifty years is a long time in the life of an individual, but it is equally a short time in the life of an organisation. The 50th anniversary celebrations took place in December 1987 in Gaborone. Gaborone Secondary School was the centre of activities alternating with Maitisong Hall at Maru-a-Pula School and the BTU Teachers Centre at Mogoditshane, five kilometres outside Gaborone. The celebrations were an occasion for pride, happiness and a sense of achievement – truly a moment to be savoured.

Beyond that, the occasion gave the teachers and the community the opportunity to evaluate the significance of the role the BTU had played and what remained to be done. These were brought out eloquently by the Honourable Minister of Education, Kebatlamang Morake. He commended the teachers for the solid work done. He saw the anniversary as a time, 'fitting for you [teachers] to review the history of the BTU, its objectives, and the contribution it continues to make in educational development' (Morake, 1987). That was a clear challenge to the organisation not only to re-evaluate its goals but to look ahead with determination. Obviously more was expected of the organisation since it had been included in committees within the Ministry of Education such as the powerful Ministerial Consultative Committee to charter new directions, including curricula development, conditions of service, and the maintenance of professional standards.

The minister paid a glowing tribute to the work of the Union in that while the Ministry was largely responsible for education reforms,

> 'the actual implementation of those innovations rests squarely on teachers. In view of this indispendable dual partnership, it is necessary to have a solid and conscientious body of teachers that will help in monitoring the process of our educational programmes and offer professional advice accordingly, based on practical or empirical evidence' (Morake, 1987).

This was an important moment, for it was a year prior to the changes in education in this country, consisting of the introduction of the nine-year curriculum (an attempt to give every Motswana child nine years of education), the drastic revision of the curriculum, and the unprecedented expansion of secondary education. These changes, particularly the increase in the members of secondary schools, were bound to complicate the administrative functions of the Ministry and the teachers in the field.

The realisation of the Ministry's efforts, it became clear, lay in the hands of teachers who were expected to give their time and effort generously. These words of encouragement were echoed by the new President of the BTU, Lloyd Mothusi. A young, shy and unassuming Morolong he burst into the picture with his characteristic simple style of leadership. His address was confined to matters of policy within the Union. The conference was reminded of the achievements the Union had secured. In this respect one could quote the improvement of the conditions of service and above all the full recognition and acceptance of the Association by the Government. For instance, the BTU is represented in a number of committees within the Ministry of Education and some good examples are the National Council for Teacher Education, Joint Committee on Primary Education, Junior Certificate Examinations Council, the University of Botswana Advisory Council, and so on. Such representation of the Union has, without doubt, been a breakthrough throughout the many years of bargaining and negotiation. Mothusi revealed the earnest struggle when he confirmed that, 'every privilege we now enjoy has been earned through our untiring efforts...' (Mothusi, 1987).

On the international scene, the BTU has done well through its association with teachers organisations in the region and overseas associations like the British National Union of Teachers (NUT), and the Canadian Teachers Federation (CTF). The association with such organisations has been important since it helped in the reform of the curriculum efforts of the Union, particularly in the areas of mathematics and science. Equally important was the building of the BTU Teachers' Centre at Mogoditshane which was meant to organise the work of the Union under a stable secretariat. Its importance lay in the fact that it served as the home of the teaching profession, to help solve their problems and plan their strategies.

Of importance was the keynote address that took the delegates on a 'sentimental journey' of successes and disappointments in the Union during the 50 years of its existence. It was therefore fitting for the conference to be vigilant at all times as professionals and help to lay a solid foundation for a sound system of education for Botswana. The crowning hour of the celebrations was the bestowing of the 'Associate Membership' of the Union on the following stalwarts: M.L.A. Kgasa, (later Dr Kgasa), K.G. Kgoroba, R.D. Molefe, M.S. Kgopo, D.E. Maine, Mrs M. Modukanele, T.W. Motlhagodi, F. Phirie, M.J. Pilane, and Rev. J.I.B. Sekgwa.

L. Mothusi

Whither Goeth the Union?

It is encouraging to note that the desirable sound relationship that has been nurtured between the Ministry of Education and the BTU has blossomed with the years. The healthy relations have been a result of give and take from both sides. This healthy climate must be nursed and allowed to grow, for the success of our education system rests on the cooperation of the two institutions. It is gratifying to note that both the Ministry of Education and the BTU have realised that there are more things that unite them than divide them.

The BTU has grown in stature and can claim to speak for the majority of teachers in this country. Internationally, as shown above, it is a respected organisation and this is supported by the interest shown by the teachers' organisations from other countries like Canada, Denmark and countries in Africa. It has put Botswana on the map of the world on educational matters. The Union must not stagnate but become a body of committed professionals whose outlook is not hampered by their narrow parochialism.

In spite of its successes, the BTU is hampered by organisational and professional problems. For instance, the monopoly it has enjoyed in the past as the only teachers organisation has been stopped by the emergence of splinter groups in the profession. The decline of membership has had financial implications as the Union is unable to meet its administrative obligations. With regard to professional problems, Ngidi holds that teachers form the largest portion of the staffing component of the education system and yet appear at the base of the hierarchy in a highly centralised education system. 'They mediate the curriculum to the students as powerless functionaries even in the most remote parts of the country' (Bayona, 1990). Perhaps one of the reasons that compelled BOFESETE to break-away from the BTU was the lack of a code of professional ethics. This has resulted in teaching attracting into its fold job seekers who are not at all committed. Furthermore, the teaching profession has continued to suffer in the public eye because of low pay and the irresponsible behaviour of some teachers. Some of these problems have been tackled by Mautle and Weeks (1992) in their paper on 'Teacher Incentives'.

Author's Epilogue

Notwithstanding these problems, the Union as a living organisation, must begin to diversify its activities and open its doors for membership to all those who can contribute meaningfully to the education of our children. Perhaps for too long the Union concentrated on music and sports to support its activities, but it is now time to form some other committees that may concentrate on other cultural activities including drama and art at a higher level. It may even establish an association with the Botswana Society which has a rich programme from which so much can be learned. Above all, such a relationship would bring in a breath of fresh ideas. The Union should endeavour to enrich its programme by organising festivals which should include music, drama and art. To encourage local composers of music they should be given the opportunity to present their masterpieces on such occasions. These should be festivals in the true sense of the term and not competitions. Such composers and contributors should be rewarded handsomely for their efforts. On such occasions, recognition should be given to those who have contributed to the development of education to this country.

In addition to that, the BTU needs to establish a viable book centre within the teachers' centres which one hopes will grow in different parts of the country. Though the Union at this time is not financially strong, funds must be found in order to engage the services of permanent and part-time staff to direct the affairs of the organisation from day to day. Such staff should help to compile the records of the BPATA/BTU from the earliest times to the present. They must work closely with the local National Archives where there are many records of interest to the BTU. Such information can be reproduced and kept at the BTU Teachers' Centre for the readership. In addition to the availability of literature to suit all tastes, BTU should support the Ministry of Education in its endeavour to build Education Centres in large settlements throughout the country. Such centres of learning should not only help practising teachers to reform the curricula and sharpen their skills but should help encourage those who wish to further their studies.

For the future development and growth of the BTU we must maintain the links with international organisations like the WCOTP and others in order to be part and parcel of the current educational and scientific advancement. In fact we should think seriously of establishing teacher exchange programmes to visit other countries for short periods to learn of their programmes and allow them to acquaint themselves with our educational problems. For it is in learning of other peoples education systems that we shall better know our own.

Finally the BTU must establish a sound philosophy that stems from our own convictions. This philosophy must be dialogical approach in dealing with the general membership of the Union and the community. Dialogue will teach us to be respectful towards other people and their views. To succeed, we need to know ourselves and have faith in our fellow men. To be dialogical, we need to have faith and trust in other people. Much of the strife, conflict and slander that prevails in places of work and high councils is caused by our personal inadequacies, lack of trust and faith. The BTU and the Ministry of Education must keep the dialogue alive for we know the power inherent in it.

As teachers, we must inculcate sound values in those we teach. We must educate to create new values, not only to implant existing values. The values we talk about are those that are concerned with individual freedom and understanding the significance of human life and the dignity of mankind. We must concern ourselves with human beings in their concrete existence, with human beings as thinking, feeling and acting individuals. We must be concerned with the quality of life that people live. The most fundamental principle in this philosophy is that every person is a free and self-determining individual. This would be living fully up to the motto on our crest – WE EDUCATE!

PULA! – BAYETHE!!

References

Akinpelu, JA (1981). *Introduction to Philosophy of Education*. London: Macmillan.

Bayona, ELM (1990). 'School-based Curriculum Development: Implications for Educational Planning in Developing Countries'. *Journal of Curriculum Perspectives 14(4) pp34–42*.

Blake and Haliburton, (1972). *From Stone Axe to Space Age*. Cape Town: Longman.

Crowder, M (ed.) (1984). *Education for Development in Botswana*, London: Macmillan.

De Villiers et al., (1932). *Junior Certificate History*, Cape Town: Maskew Miller.

Freire, P (1972) . *The Pedagogy of the Oppressed*, Middlesex: C. Nicholls and Company, Penguin.

Horrell, M (1964). *A Decade of Bantu Education*, Johannesburg, South Africa: Institute of Race Relations.

Hutton, RS (1965). *Botswana Commission on Salaries and Conditions of Service Report*, Gaborone.

Koma, K (1982). *Education in Africa: The Naked Truth*. Gaborone: (personal publication).

Loram, CT (1917). *The Education of the South African Native*, London: Longman, Green and Co.

Mautle, G and Weeks, G (1992). *Teacher Incentives*, Gaborone (seminar).

New Encyclopaedia Britanica (1991). Chicago: Pan American.

Ngidi, S (1993). *Botswana Teachers' Union Problems and Prospects*, (unpublished article).

Nyerere, JK (1968). *Ujamaa*, Oxford: Oxford University Press.

Okoh, E (1970). *Botswana Commission on Salaries and Conditions of Service*, Gaborone: Government of Botswana.

Omer-Cooper, JD (1966). *The Zulu Aftermath*, London: Longman.

Parsons, N and Crowder, M (eds.) (1988). *Sir Charles Rey, Monarch of All I Survey*, New York: Lilian Barker Press Inc.

PESC Evaluation Report, (1992). Gaborone: University of Botswana.

Peteni, RL (1979). *Towards Tomorrow: The Story of the African Teachers' Association of South Africa*, WCOTP.

Ramage, R (1964). *Commission on Salaries an Conditions of Service. Report on the Structure of the Public Services in Basotholand, Bechuanaland and Swaziland*, Imperial Reserve. Mafikeng.

Rusbridger, GH and Weber, (1959). *B.P. Commission*.

Skinner, TM (1964). *Botswana Commission on Salaries and Conditions of Service*, Gaborone.

Smith, PG (1965). *Philosophy of Education,* London: Harper and Row.

Surridge, R (1958). *B.P. Commission on Salaries and Conditions of Service,* Mafikeng.

Thema, BC (1947). *The Development of Native Education in the BP,* Unpublished MEd Thesis.

University of Botswana, Lesotho and Swaziland, (1970). Students' Petition to Sir Seretse Khama.

University of Botswana, Lesotho and Swaziland, (1970). Students' Petition to Minister of Education, BC Thema.

University of Botswana, (1992). *PESC Evaluation Report.*

van Rensburg, P (1974). *Report from Swaneng Hill – Education and Employment in an African Country,* Stockholm: Ainquist and Wiksell.

Vanqa, T (1979). *A Model Curriculum for Botswana,* Unpublished MEd Thesis.

Wilson, M and Thompson, L (eds.) (1970). *The Oxford History of South Africa.* Oxford: Clarendon Press.

World Confederation of the Organisation of the Teaching Profession Conference (WCOTP), (1972).

Report (1981).

Report (1982).

Report (1983).

Botswana Archives Sources (File References)

BNB 803

DC, GABORONE, (1963)

DC, KANYE (1963)

DC, Kanye, (1947)

DC, Mochudi, (1942)

DC, MOCHUDI, (1942)

DC, Mochudi, (1948)

DC, Mochudi, (1950)

DC, Mochudi, (1951)

DC, MOL.1/8

DC, Molepolole, (1947)

DC, Molepolole, (1948)

DCK

DCK 6

DCK 10/4

DCK 10/4 (1963)

District Commissioner: Kgatleng (Mochudi) (1950).

E/10

E362/1

EDI24/10

EDI24/10, (1966)

EDI24/9

Education Officer's Report: Mochudi, (1950).

Grant, S (1967). Communication to Director of Education.

Grant, S (1970). Communication to President Khama.

Khama, Sir S (1971). Address to Botswana Democratic Party Conference, Francistown, Botswana.

S252/2/1

S252/2/2

S252/3

S252/3/1

S284/2/1

S384/1/4

S384/1/11

S386/1/2

Botswana Teachers' Union Documents

BTU Conference, (1965). Communication to the Minister of Labour and Social Services.

BTU Conference, (1965). Minutes of Conference.

BTU Conference, (1968). Kgosi Linchwe's Address.

BTU Conference, (1969). President Khama's Address.

BTU Conference, (1971). Minutes of Music Committee.

BTU Conference, (1971). Presidential Address.

BTU Conference, (1972). Minutes of Conference.

BTU Conference, (1973). Presidential Address.

BTU Conference, (1974). Presidential Address (Lobatse)

BTU Executive Meeting with President Khama (1970).

Botswana Teachers Union: Morake Keynote Address (1987).

Botswana Unified Teaching Service Act (1975).

Botswana Unified Teaching Service Regulation (1976) No. 26.

Botswana Teacher Education and Development Papers (1990).

Khama, Sir S (1969). Address to the Botswana Teachers' Union. Lobatse.

Kutlwano (1964). Vol. III No 2 Gaborone: Government of Botswana.

Kutlwano (1968). Vol. VII No 4. Gaborone: Government of Botswana.

Kutlwano (1969). Vol. VIII No 1. Gaborone: Government of Botswana.

Morake, KP (1987). Address, BTU Conference, Gaborone.

Mothusi, LG (1987). Address, BTU Conference, Gaborone.

The Teacher, (1969).

The Teacher, (1974).

The Teacher, (1969).

The Teacher, (1970).

The Teacher, (1971).

Government of Botswana Publications

Daily News (1964). BNB 6903 No 876 8/12/64.

Daily News (1971). BNB 6786 No 104 3/6/71.

Daily News (1977). *van Rensburg Pervertor of Youth*, 25 November 1977, No 223.

Daily News (1983). 1 June 1983, No 102.

Department of Education Annual Report, (1945).

Education Statistics (1967–68).

Examiners Reports (1946). On the Standard 6 Examination Results for the African School Leaving Certificate, Mochudi.

Headmaster Returns (1976).

Interim Report on the In-service Project Working in Primary Education (1973–75).

Laws of Botswana (1974). Education, Cap. 58:01

Laws of Botswana (1966). Education . Cap. 58:01.

National Commission on Education (1977). *Education for Kagisano*.

National Development Plan (1968–73).

National Development Plan (1970–75).

National Development Plan (1976–81)

National Development Plan (1979–85).

New Directions in Inspection and Advising (1981).

Professional Educationists Serminar, 3C's (1987).

Report of the Education Department (1942).

Report of the Education Department (1947).

Report of the Education Department (1949).

Report of the Education Department (1965 and 1966).

Standard 7 Results, (1973).

Teacher Education and Development papers (1990).

Transitional Plan for Social and Economic Development (1966).

Unified Teaching Service Act of 1975 No. 26.

Unified Teaching Service Regulations (1976) No. 26, Gaborone.

Appendix

Minutes

DELEGATES AT THE FIRST GENERAL CONFERENCE OF THE BECHUANALAND PROTECTORATE AFRICAN TEACHERS' ASSOCIATION HELD AT SEROWE FROM THE 19TH TO THE 21ST JUNE, 1939.

Mr M. Mpotokwane (President)	Tonota
Mr A.M. Tsoebebe (Retiring organising secretary)	Serowe
Mr D. Mpotokwane	K.M.S Serowe
Mr A.C. Sekunyana	K.M.S. Serowe
Miss B. Lethule	Lechen
Miss I. Kefhitilwe	Mahalapye
Miss B. Sephekolo	Shashane
Miss K. Gochane	K.M.S. Serowe
Miss Mkholokotho	Central Serowe
Mr E.K. Moeti	K.M.S. Serowe
Miss S. Thibatsela	Central Serowe
Miss K. Dithole	Serowe
Mr B. Seleso	Mmadinare
Miss T. Montsho	Serowe
Miss K.M. Tshogah	Serowe
Mrs V.L. Namane	Gaberones
Miss N. Pheelwane	K.M.S. Serowe
Mr M. Mmereki	Sefhare
Miss S.E. Seretse	Serowe
Miss K. Mothobi	Serowe
Mr T. Sebina	Tonota
Mr J.Th. Phooko	Tonota
Mr B. Rakesoketswe	Tonota
Mr A.K. Mokhange	Masunga
Mr D.M. Lesetedi	Mswazi
Mr M.S. Maunge	Masunga
Mr M.M. Sekgoma	K.M.S. Serowe
Mr Ed.M. Rakgole	Central Serowe
Mr L.L. Pheko	Central Serowe
Mr M.M. Ndzinge	Sebina
Mr C. Zaza	Central Serowe
Mr J. Morapedi	Sebina

Mr J.M. Leshona	Masokola Serowe
Mr S.J. Mokhesi	B.N.S. Mochudi
Mr E.W. Letsapa	Gaberones
Mr L. Modise	Maunatlala
Mr B. Mokitime	Ramoutsa
Mr F.H. Tau	Mochudi
Mr M. Maswikiti	Nshakazhogwe
Mr N. Sikwa	Mmutlane
Mr P.M. Lesetedi	Mswazi
Miss H.L. Mokobi	Lechen
Mr N.J. Malikongwa	Rasebolai B.B.1
Mr L. Molawa	Tonota
Mr P. Waheng	Tonota
Mr T. Moalusi	Sebina
Mr M. Mojura	Marobela
Mr M. Chakalisa	Mhashwa
Mr S. Sobawali	Mabuwe
Mr K.K. Baruti	Masokola Serowe
Mr O. Maree	Tlhabala
Mr M.M. Padi	K.M.S. Serowe
Mr Frank K. Sebopen	Serowe
Mr T.T. Kgosi	Serowe
Mr B.K. Mookodi	Serowe
Mr S. Seabelo	Serowe
Mr M.M. Molasa	Moebana
Miss A. Monamo	Serowe
Miss K. Gaolaolwe	Serowe
Mr Tshiamo Tamocha	Mahalapye
Mr Mooketsi Basupi	Mmadinare
Mr Levi M. Holonga	Bobonon
Mr M. Mpatane	Mathangwane
Mr Levi C. Moumakwa	Box 106 Mafikeng
Miss H.B. Moshoela	Central Serowe
Miss L. Matlho	Shoshong
Mr O. Ntule	Serowe

www.ingramcontent.com/pod-product-compliance
Lightning Source LLC
Chambersburg PA
CBHW070603300426
44113CB00010B/1379